STRATEGIC ASIA 2017–18

STRATEGIC ASIA 2017–18

POWER, IDEAS, AND MILITARY STRATEGY
in the Asia-Pacific

Edited by

Ashley J. Tellis, Alison Szalwinski, and Michael Wills

With contributions from

John H. Gill, Christopher W. Hughes, Mark N. Katz,
Chung Min Lee, Thomas G. Mahnken, Oriana Skylar Mastro,
Ann Marie Murphy, and Ashley J. Tellis

 THE NATIONAL BUREAU *of* **ASIAN RESEARCH**
Seattle and Washington, D.C.

THE NATIONAL BUREAU *of* ASIAN RESEARCH

Published in the United States of America by
The National Bureau of Asian Research, Seattle, WA, and Washington, D.C.
www.nbr.org

ISBN (print): 978-1-939131-52-2
ISBN (electronic): 978-1-939131-53-9

Cover images

Front: 150608-N-EH855-654 Waters near Guam ⊚ U.S. Navy photo by Mass Communication Specialist 3rd Class Bryan Mai/Released.

Back (left to right): Successful Mission ⊕ The U.S. Army; Engine Start ⊕ U.S. Air Force photo/ Lt. Col. Robert Couse-Baker; 160328-N-JH293-027 ⊕ U.S. Navy photo by Mass Communication Specialist 2nd Class Chris Williamson/Released; 100727-N-6720T-080 ⊕ U.S. Navy photo by Mass Communication Specialist 3rd Class Adam K. Thomas/Released.

Design and publishing services by The National Bureau of Asian Research.

Cover design by Stefanie Choi.

Publisher's Cataloging-In-Publication Data
(Prepared by The Donohue Group, Inc.)

Names: Tellis, Ashley J., editor. | Szalwinski, Alison, editor. | Wills, Michael, 1970- editor. | Gill, John H., contributor. | National Bureau of Asian Research (U.S.), publisher, sponsoring body.

Title: Power, ideas, and military strategy in the Asia-Pacific / edited by Ashley J. Tellis, Alison Szalwinski, and Michael Wills ; with contributions from John H. Gill [and 7 others].

Other Titles: Strategic Asia ; 2017-18.

Description: Seattle ; Washington, D.C. : The National Bureau of Asian Research, [2017] | Includes bibliographical references and index.

Identifiers: ISBN 978-1-939131-52-2 (print) | ISBN 978-1-939131-53-9 (electronic)

Subjects: LCSH: Asia--Strategic aspects--History. | Asia--Military policy--History. | United States--Strategic aspects--History. | United States--Military policy--History.

Classification: LCC UA830 .P68 2017 (print) | LCC UA830 (ebook) | DDC 355.033015--dc23

Printed in the United States.

The paper used in this publication meets the minimum requirement of the American National Standard for Information Sciences—Permanence of Paper for Printed Library Materials, ANSI Z39.48-1992.

Contents

Preface

Richard J. Ellings

Over the last sixteen years, the United States has been entrenched in wars in Central Asia and the Middle East against violent extremists who do not fight on behalf of an internationally recognized state. These nonstate opponents have ushered in a sea change in warfighting, away from industrial war and toward what British general Rupert Smith masterfully characterized as "war amongst the people."[1] The United States and its allies now use force to alter their enemies' intentions, win over the will of the populations among whom they fight, and pursue the elusive conditions for lasting political settlements. The learning curve of these military ventures has been steep and costly, yet thus far no U.S. president has been willing to abandon the fight. Nine months into the Trump administration, U.S. forces continue to operate in Afghanistan, Iraq, and Syria. It appears that a capacity to wage "war amongst the people" will remain a feature of U.S. military strategy for years to come.

While these trends in warfighting were arguably more foreseeable than military strategists have acknowledged, they have also necessitated a revolution in strategy that would have challenged even the most prescient planners. The same level of prescience was not needed to anticipate and respond to trends in the post–Cold War balance of power. Indeed, this author and others over the years forecast what was coming. In 1992,

---

[1] Rupert Smith, *The Utility of Force: The Art of War in the Modern World* (New York: Alfred A. Knopf, 2007), part 3. For Smith, the essential difference between classic "industrial war" and contemporary "war amongst the people" is that in the latter military force is not used for the purpose of destroying the opponent but for altering the opponent's intentions. Smith delineates six characteristics of "war amongst the people": (1) the ends of war are malleable and not simply a matter of killing the enemy, (2) the sides fighting tend to be nonstate groupings (e.g., international coalitions or violent extremists), (3) war takes place where people live, and combatants compete for the people's political will, (4) war seeks to establish conditions suited to more ultimate objectives, which may take years or decades to achieve, (5) war is fought so as not to lose the force, rather than to achieve the aim at any cost, and (6) the weapons of industrial war have to be adapted to new uses.

for example, I invoked the term "skewed multipolarity" to describe the changing international distribution of power, with the United States and Western Europe still dominant, but Japan reaching its peak economically and China preparing to compete.[2] My coauthor and I noted a range of plausible futures: "Between 2000 and 2010," we wrote, "we may see a confident China turn its attention to regional affairs, feeling no special need to work closely with the United States. If China founders, on the other hand, its weakness would also have major consequences for regional harmony."[3] To prepare for these various possible scenarios, we called for an "engaged balancer" strategy in the Asia-Pacific, one that "integrates the United States defense posture into a broader national strategy" that "requires firm action on both the foreign and domestic fronts to strengthen the American economy, make the alliance with Japan more equitable, and share responsibility for peace in the Asia-Pacific region."[4]

It has been a quarter century, and where do we now stand? The phenomenon of "skewed multipolarity" persists, but with China now the world's second-largest economy, displacing a Japan that is still struggling to resume economic growth. Meanwhile, the United States continues to cope with the political effects of a devastating financial crisis and other economic challenges, and its eagerness to engage abroad has given way to a more circumspect approach to the outside world. Rather than putting ourselves in a position of strength, both at home and abroad, we have allowed major elements of our national power and cultural cachet to erode. In some respects, of course, U.S. leadership has been a victim of its own success. As other countries benefit from participation in global trade and U.S.-led security regimes in their regions, they emerge more powerful than before and more capable of utilizing their power for self-selected ends. But this does not excuse our lack of preparedness, given that these scenarios were imaginable even 25 years ago. If we are to find our way back to credible international leadership, we will need a sound national strategy that embraces both the military and economic dimensions of power and engages in both the national and international arenas in which it is exercised. This will require a thorough assessment of the national power, strategic cultures, and chosen strategies of our government and other governments in the Asia-Pacific, where change has been by far the most dramatic of any region in the world. This volume seeks to do just that with respect to military strategy. In *Strategic Asia 2015–16*, we probed the foundations of national

---

[2] Richard J. Ellings and Edward A. Olsen, "A New Pacific Profile," *Foreign Policy*, Winter 1992–93, 116.

[3] Ibid., 124–25.

[4] Ibid., 135.

power in key Asia-Pacific states, while *Strategic Asia 2016–17* examined their strategic cultures. The third volume in this thematic miniseries addresses how these two elements of power and culture come together to shape the military strategies that a state sees as available to it and analyzes the one it has chosen to adopt.

The People's Republic of China (PRC) is central to our discussion both for its size and for the difficulty scholars and policymakers have had in interpreting its strategic intentions. The United States championed China's economic transformation, and China has benefited immensely from participation in the international regimes of trade and development. Hundreds of millions of people have been lifted out of extreme poverty, and the PRC has gone on to establish international financial institutions and projects like the Asian Infrastructure Investment Bank and the Belt and Road Initiative. At the same time, however, China has yet to show that it will fully comply with the rules of fair trade or protect intellectual property rights. And the United States has too often been asleep at the wheel when it comes to confronting these violations. Meanwhile, concomitant with its economic growth, China has developed its military power, with extraordinary progress made in space, air, sea, land, and cyber capabilities. These developments might not be alarming in and of themselves. In the maritime domain, however, China has taken actions that make its neighbors, and those concerned for international law, nervous. In the East China Sea, it has conducted unsafe intercepts of jets in international airspace, declared an air defense identification zone over the contested Senkaku/Diaoyu Islands, and continued to run coast guard and fishing vessels near the islands. In the South China Sea, China is acting on its claim of sovereignty through massive reclamation projects turning islets into military bases, dwarfing the actions of all other claimants combined. Its installations on these islets, not to mention its rejection of the ruling of the Permanent Court of Arbitration in The Hague, call into question the PRC's motives and professed respect for international law and the peaceful resolution of territorial disputes. China has also pressured the Association of Southeast Asian Nations (ASEAN) to omit mention of these activities in the organization's official statements.

The United States and other observers have again been too slow to react. They find themselves torn between an optimism about China joining the global system and a wariness that, particularly in light of recent behavior, China may try to revise the rules of that system to the detriment of most members. As I have argued before, peacefully integrating China remains the international system's greatest challenge and its greatest opportunity.[5] The PRC is a grand nation with tremendous good to offer the world, but its opaque authoritarian system, preoccupation with regime interests, increasingly nationalist policies, and clout on the world stage foster uncertainty about the actions it is willing to take or the norms it plans to champion. We therefore need a careful assessment of the PRC's national strategy, both real and potential, based on primary sources and the best social science scholarship, with an eye to history as well.

China's Military Strategy of 2015, the first official defense white paper ever issued by the PRC on the subject, calls for a "holistic view of national security" designed to manage and secure the country's increasingly global interests, and speaks of "implement[ing] the military strategic guideline of active defense in the new situation."[6] On the one hand, it is natural for a country whose power has grown so dramatically to redefine its interests and security needs in more global terms. Doing so does not make China a revisionist or even a reformist state. The principle of "active defense" cited in the white paper has also long been a central concept in the primary sources on Chinese military strategy, though scholars are still working to understand how much this concept has been revised in contemporary strategic thinking and practice.[7] On the other hand, observers have also long noted a Chinese strategic culture of "worshipping at the high church of realpolitik," particularly with respect to the use of force.[8] Recent internally distributed Chinese military documents on the South China Sea suggest an expansionist and realist strategy that bodes poorly for the prospect of a peaceful,

---

[5] Richard J. Ellings, "Preface," in *Strategic Asia 2015–16: Foundations of National Power in the Asia-Pacific*, ed. Ashley J. Tellis, Alison Szalwinski, and Michael Wills (Seattle: National Bureau of Asian Research [NBR], 2015), vii–xii, ix–x.

[6] Information Office of the State Council (PRC), *China's Military Strategy* (Beijing, 2015), http://english.chinamil.com.cn/news-channels/2015-05/26/content_6507716.htm.

[7] *The Science of Military Strategy*, authored by strategists at the Academy of Military Science, remains the key source, though it is not official policy. Shou Xiaosong, ed., *Zhanlüe xue* [The Science of Military Strategy] (Beijing: PLA Press, 2013). In a comparison of the 2001 and 2013 editions, M. Taylor Fravel argues that Chinese military strategy remains grounded in the traditional concept of "active defense," but with adaptations to global technological advancement, the military posture of adversaries, and China's expanding interests overseas. See M. Taylor Fravel, "China's Changing Approach to Military Strategy: The Science of Military Strategy from 2001 and 2013," in *China's Evolving Military Strategy*, ed. Joe McReynolds (Washington, D.C.: Jamestown Foundation, 2016), chap. 2.

[8] Alastair Iain Johnston, *Cultural Realism: Strategic Culture and Grand Strategy in Chinese History* (Princeton: Princeton University Press, 1998); Thomas J. Christensen, "China, the U.S.-Japan Alliance, and the Security Dilemma in East Asia," *International Security* 23, no. 4 (1999): 49–80; and Christopher A. Ford, "Realpolitik with Chinese Characteristics: Chinese Strategic Culture and the Modern Communist Party-State," in *Strategic Asia 2016–17: Understanding Strategic Cultures in the Asia-Pacific*, ed. Ashley J. Tellis, Alison Szalwinski, and Michael Wills (Seattle: NBR, 2016), 29–60.

law-based resolution of the disputes.[9] And close studies of Chinese primary sources on the Belt and Road Initiative likewise suggest a Sino-centric vision for Eurasia, facilitated by Chinese-led investment and regional economic integration.[10] Meanwhile, the Chinese Communist Party continues to stymie the rule of law at home, crack down on intellectual freedom, promote Xi Jinping as "core leader" in a strongman fashion not seen since at least Deng Xiaoping, and pursue the "China dream" of re-establishing China's historic "central" place in international affairs.

Two additional states, Russia and North Korea, pose immediate threats to Asia-Pacific and global security, and both are connected to China through complex historical and contemporary ties. Chinese and Russian interests have been largely complementary since the Cold War, with China focused on Asia and Russia on Europe. This has allowed each one to benefit without directly compromising the other. In recent years, Russian economic power has faltered, and its prospects are not bright under the policies of Vladimir Putin, making Russia all the more economically dependent on China.[11] Add to this mix the tendency of authoritarian populist leaders to engage in risky ventures abroad to show their strength and you have a recipe for ongoing Russian-generated instability in the region. By annexing Crimea and waging a medium-intensity war in eastern Ukraine, Putin has already demonstrated that he is willing to use military power for "traditional" aggression. His domestic popularity rose from 61% before invading Ukraine to 86% after the annexation of Crimea, and it remains above 80% as of this writing.[12] His regime has also interfered in a U.S. presidential election and in European elections, and the ramifications of the former are still wreaking havoc here in the United States. Putin has legitimized his tightening grip on power through anti-Western rhetoric and identity and religious politics that play to Russian nationalism.

Leaders in China, rather than criticizing such rhetoric or actions publicly, have spoken in admiring terms of Russia and the Sino-Russian relationship. The two nations are cooperating strategically in significant ways, including by providing various forms of support to North Korea and conducting joint military exercises. This summer they issued a joint

---

[9] Ryan Martinson and Katsuya Yamamoto, "Three PLAN Officers May Have Just Revealed What China Wants in the South China Sea," *National Interest*, July 9, 2017, http://nationalinterest.org/feature/three-plan-officers-may-have-just-revealed-what-china-wants-21458.

[10] Nadège Rolland, *China's Eurasian Century? Political and Strategic Implications of the Belt and Road Initiative* (Seattle: NBR, 2017).

[11] Michael S. Chase, Evan S. Medeiros, J. Stapleton Roy, Eugene B. Rumer, Robert Sutter, and Richard Weitz, "Russia-China Relations: Assessing Common Ground and Strategic Fault Lines," NBR, Special Report, no. 66, July 2017.

[12] "Indicators," Levada-Center, https://www.levada.ru/en.

statement opposing the deployment of Terminal High Altitude Area Defense (THAAD) in South Korea and endorsing China's call for a "freeze-for-freeze" of North Korean missile and nuclear tests and large-scale joint exercises between the United States and the Republic of Korea (ROK).[13] Chinese and Russian policies are becoming more closely coordinated as the situation on the Korean Peninsula intensifies.

North Korea, for its part, has accelerated its pursuit of a nuclear deterrent and, in my view, of the ultimate objective of unifying the Korean Peninsula under the Kim Jong-un regime. Kim has already tested more weapons and missiles than his father and grandfather combined, including conducting a sixth nuclear test in September 2017. It is now nearly a foregone conclusion that in the very near future, if not already, North Korea will be able to strike Los Angeles, San Francisco, or Seattle with a nuclear-tipped intercontinental ballistic missile. The United States has no good options for dealing with this situation through a preemptive strike. Its only hope for reversing the nuclear program would be through strong support from China, the North's sole formal ally.

Why has Beijing refrained from pressuring Pyongyang more? One argument is that China does not want North Korea to collapse, as this could lead to refugee flows across the border and a weakening of China's northeast economy. Indeed, many would flee the North and significant economic impacts would be felt early on, but I do not believe it would be beyond the PRC's capacity to manage or contain these effects. Another theory holds that the PRC would prefer unification under South Korea rather than the North. Here one can point to the fact that Xi Jinping has yet to meet with Kim Jung-un, unlike Xi's predecessors who all visited Pyongyang before Seoul. But if this were the case, why has China been so resistant to THAAD, and more importantly, why has it continued to abet the North's nuclear development? A third, and in my view more plausible, explanation is that China is seeking to end the U.S.-ROK alliance by supporting North Korea to challenge the credibility of the United States' promise to defend the South should it be attacked. If successful in these efforts—if North Korea makes the United States blink—what options are left for the South? If China cared more about regional security than about the U.S. presence, it would have pursued a more vigorous policy of reining in the Kim family over the years. Instead, it has assisted North Korea in testing the United States and attempting to show that Washington cannot be trusted to defend its allies. Should the U.S.-ROK alliance collapse as a consequence of the United States

[13] "Joint Statement by the Russian and Chinese Foreign Ministries on the Korean Peninsula's Problems," Ministry of Foreign Affairs (Russia), July 4, 2017, http://www.mid.ru/en/maps/kp/-/asset_publisher/VJy7Ig5QaAII/content/id/2807662.

flunking one of these tests, Japan would also likely abandon its reliance on U.S. security assurances—and might even go nuclear—while probably seeking an accommodation with China. Frighteningly, the North might have a limited window to attack the South before the latter could develop its own nuclear deterrent. The Kim regime might calculate that military victory is possible through a conventional assault on Seoul coupled with a nuclear attack on Busan.

It could get worse. With a shattering post–World War II system in Northeast Asia and a U.S. retreat, Russia and China could in turn decide to divvy up theaters in tandem regional power grabs. The United States' chief coalitional threat is having to face off with those two nations at the same time. Through the Cold War, the United States sustained forces with the capacity to fight major wars in two theaters simultaneously. However, under the headiness of the post–Cold War period and the tribulations of the wars in Afghanistan and Iraq, this two-theater doctrine gradually eroded.[14] Today, the United States is mentally and materially unprepared for a two-theater war, and its unpreparedness is not lost on the two ambitious powers that most wish to lay claim to greatness. With Russia coveting hegemony in Europe and China in Asia, simultaneous ultimatums or military action by both would disperse U.S. forces and test the United States' will, with a decent chance of bringing an end to Pax Americana.

None of these scenarios need come to pass. Precluding them, however, will require the United States to make long-term investments in offensive as well defensive systems for Northeast Asia (and Europe), probably larger numbers of forward-deployed forces, greater mobilization efforts, and fuller cooperation and communication with our allies. It will mean developing and deploying advanced weapons systems capable of strengthening U.S. deterrence. Only if China sees that its strategic position is worsening might it recalculate its support of North Korea's nuclear program. As I have argued for some time now, the closest analogy that we have is the U.S-led response to the Soviet deployment of SS-20 intermediate-range ballistic missiles in Europe. Only when outgunned through the subsequent deployment in Western Europe of superior U.S. weapons—ground-launched cruise missiles and Pershing II ballistic missiles—did Gorbachev and the Soviet Union agree to the "zero-zero option," resulting in sharp reductions in

---

[14] The Pentagon's 2012 Defense Strategic Guidance speaks of reducing the size of the force, while its 2014 *Quadrennial Defense Review*, in a departure from preceding editions, notes that "a smaller force strains our ability to simultaneously respond to more than one major contingency at a time." U.S. Department of Defense, "Sustaining U.S. Global Leadership: Priorities for 21st Century Defense," January 2012, 7, http://archive.defense.gov/news/Defense_Strategic_Guidance.pdf; and U.S. Department of Defense, *Quadrennial Defense Review 2014* (Washington, D.C.: March 2014), 22, http://archive.defense.gov/pubs/2014_Quadrennial_Defense_Review.pdf.

intermediate-range nuclear forces in Europe. A comparable response in Northeast Asia is required today. In addition, Washington needs to figure out ways to change Russian interests and calculations in both Europe and Asia, so that Russia's stakes are greater with the United States and its allies than with China.

Like it or not, great-power competition is back, and with it the potential for great-power conflict has reached heights not seen since the peak of the Cold War. We cannot turn back the clock to the 1990s and 2000s, but we can energize and bring to bear the resources of U.S. power and the best of U.S. strategic culture. Great-power relations and coalition behavior are the salient drivers of international relations again, and we have proved in the past that we can prevail in such circumstances.

Acknowledgments

Special thanks are owed to Ashley Tellis, who has directed the Strategic Asia Program for fourteen years. His guidance has been essential to the planning and intellectual coherence of each annual volume during that time, and in particular to the ambitious three-year series on power, culture, and military strategy that we are concluding here. Ashley's co-editors, Alison Szalwinski and Michael Wills, also deserve immense thanks. They have worked tirelessly with the contributing authors to produce a book of the highest caliber.

The wider NBR staff also contributed in critical respects to this year's volume. NBR's publications team, led by Joshua Ziemkowski with the assistance of Jessica Keough, Tim White, Matthew Newton, and Daniel Rechtschaffen, provided meticulous copyediting and proofreading in their ever-professional and graceful fashion. The researchers and interns in NBR's Political and Security Affairs group—Jessica Drun, Bonnie Nordstrom, Brian O'Keefe, Amber Qin, and Nicole Smolinske—supplied valuable research, logistical, and editing support to the volume's authors. Finally, Roy Kamphausen, Tiffany Ma, and Dan Aum helped oversee the research process, integrate it with other NBR research initiatives, and coordinate outreach to the policy community.

Of course, a volume such as this would not be possible were it not for the hard work of scholars committed to understanding how military strategy takes shape through a complex interplay of power and culture. This year's authors have addressed their countries of focus with great care, seeking to understand the strategies these states adopt as well as the key challenges they perceive. That is an unusual form of scholarship—an effort of both area expertise and empathy—and one necessary for facilitating not only precise understanding of political phenomena but also wise policymaking and, ultimately, a more peaceful world. I am deeply grateful to these authors, as well as to the anonymous peer reviewers who helped shape their ideas.

Finally, the Strategic Asia Program itself could not exist without the long-running generosity of its core sponsor, the Lynde and Harry Bradley Foundation. The foundation has supported the program from its inception and very first volume sixteen years ago. With each passing year, the Asia-Pacific has grown only more challenging and more important, and I cannot adequately express my immense appreciation for the foundation's role in bringing continued attention to this crucial region. It is my hope that this year's volume on military strategy will promote richer scholarship and more productive policy toward the Asia-Pacific.

Richard J. Ellings
President
The National Bureau of Asian Research

STRATEGIC ASIA 2017–18

EXECUTIVE SUMMARY

This chapter analyzes the variables that shape a country's grand and national military strategies and discusses their implications for U.S. policy in Asia.

MAIN ARGUMENT

All nations possess grand strategies and affiliated, but subordinate, military strategies. The former refer to the totality of resources and how they are utilized to achieve policy goals. The latter pertain to the economic resources and manpower needed to sustain the armed forces and achieve military objectives. Four variables prove to be significant determinants of grand and national military strategies. The first is a state's strategic geographic and political environment, including the internal and external circumstances that shape its identification of adversaries and allocation of power between the tasks of external security and internal order. The second variable is national resources, which include both a country's physical assets and its intangible capacities to produce these goods. Third, grand and national military strategies are influenced by the ambitions and effectiveness of the political leadership. Finally, a country's strategic culture affects how its leadership interprets the security environment, prioritizes military instruments and strategies, and defines the norms that shape the pursuit of power in international politics.

POLICY IMPLICATIONS

- Because most U.S. partners in Asia are handicapped in different ways where their grand and national military strategies are concerned, preserving the liberal international order that protects U.S. interests will depend on the rejuvenation of U.S. power.

- U.S. alliances and partnerships are vital tools for preserving U.S. hegemony and cost less over the long term than the alternatives of economic autarky and strategic solipsism.

- Recognizing and coping with the threats posed by China is critical if the traditional U.S. military strategy of power projection supporting U.S. primacy is to be sustained.

Power and Ideas in the Making of Strategy

Ashley J. Tellis

Although the notion of grand strategy is familiar to both academics and policymakers, it can often be elusive. Edward Mead Earle first elaborated the concept in *Makers of Modern Strategy: Military Thought from Machiavelli to Hitler*, a classic work published at the height of World War II, wherein he described grand strategy as "the art of controlling and utilizing the resources of a nation—or a coalition of nations—including its armed forces, to the end that its vital interests shall be effectively promoted and secured against enemies, actual, potential, or merely presumed."[1]

If grand strategy thus refers to "the capacity of [a] nation's leaders to bring together all of the elements, both military and nonmilitary, for the preservation and enhancement of the nation's long-term (that is, in wartime *and* peacetime) best interests,"[2] it is evidently "an inherent element of statecraft at all times."[3] It may even be identical to statecraft, insofar as it is oriented toward enlarging and utilizing national power to procure the highest ends that a country seeks as a matter of self-interest. Grand strategy, accordingly, is fundamentally reflected in policy. Any examination of what a nation's grand strategy actually is requires a close examination of that nation's priorities, the manner in which it balances ends and means, and how it incorporates various resources to secure its principal strategic aims.

Ashley J. Tellis holds the Tata Chair for Strategic Affairs and is a Senior Fellow at the Carnegie Endowment for International Peace. He is also Research Director of the Strategic Asia Program at the National Bureau of Asian Research. He can be reached at <atellis@ceip.org>.

[1] Edward Mead Earle, ed., *Makers of Modern Strategy: Military Thought from Machiavelli to Hitler* (Princeton: Princeton University Press, 1943), viii.

[2] Paul Kennedy, "Grand Strategy in War and Peace: Toward a Broader Definition," in *Grand Strategies in War and Peace*, ed. Paul Kennedy (New Haven: Yale University Press, 1991), 5. Emphasis in the original.

[3] Earle, *Makers of Modern Strategy*, viii.

The role of "fighting power" as "one of the instruments of grand strategy," then, acquires importance mainly at a more derivative level of planning, one that is concerned with "national military strategy," as it is usually labeled in the United States.[4] This intellectual abstraction encompasses understanding the strategic environment surrounding a country as well as the threats, opportunities, and constraints confronting its armed services; delineating the operational objectives that the services are expected to satisfy; specifying the ways in which these aims will be accomplished; and explicating the means by which they are to be realized at some given level of risk. National military strategy in this sense obviously derives from grand strategy: whereas the latter refers to the totality of resources and how they are utilized by a country to achieve "the goal defined by fundamental policy," the former pertains only to "the economic resources and manpower [necessary] to sustain the fighting services," along with an explication of how these are intended to achieve the military objectives derived from larger political interests.[5]

Neither a country's grand strategy nor its subordinate national military strategy may necessarily find expression in any written document. The United States is in fact a conspicuous outlier in this regard because it is perhaps the only modern great power that has, at least in the postwar era, articulated both its national aims and the usage of its coercive instruments in publicly available texts—the former though its *National Security Strategy* documents and the latter through the *National Defense Strategy* and the *National Military Strategy* series. No other country historically has followed a similar practice, and even the terminology employed in the naming of these documents is uniquely American.

However, it would be hard to conclude that merely because such documents are absent, other great powers do not possess either grand strategies or national military strategies of their own. On the contrary, their purposeful behavior in international politics suggests that they do consciously pursue specific strategies, even if these are not formally articulated in particular documents. The larger methodological point, therefore, is that all nations, and especially the great powers, possess grand strategies and affiliated military strategies. These may exist at a subconscious level or, when conscious, may be found only in scattered form, such as in speeches by elected functionaries or senior government officials, parliamentary proceedings and debates, ministerial reports, and other official documents such as white papers.

---

[4] B.H. Liddell Hart, *Strategy*, 2nd ed. (New York: New American Library, 1967), 322.

[5] Ibid.

The diffusion of these materials implies that the task of elucidating both grand strategy and military strategy often requires discernment rather than simple description. This is true even if singular documents exist because there is no assurance that any country's policies in practice actually comport with its publicly disseminated texts. Analyzing grand strategy as well as national military strategy, therefore, requires reviewing formal documents (when these exist), but more importantly looking beyond them. It entails consciously integrating knowledge about a country's geographic and political environments, national aims and resources, historical inheritance and self-understanding, and institutional and technological capacities through whatever sources convey them in order to produce a defensible interpretation that, when bisected with the understanding of other nations' objectives, interests, and calculations, enables some judgment of the strategic consequences.

Through these investigations, which constitute the thrust of much national security research, it is possible to describe the broad contours of a country's grand strategy and military strategy. How these strategies come to be produced within a given political system is more challenging to discern. Most of the efforts thus far have focused on understanding how particular strategy documents are crafted at the bureaucratic level, examining from which offices they originate, how the process of collating ideas proceeds, and where crucial decisions about a country's ultimate direction are made.[6] This volume of *Strategic Asia* has a different intellectual focus: it concentrates on analyzing the national military strategies of the key Asian states within the context of their overall grand strategies and understanding how these strategies have developed as a result of the interactions between their material power and strategic cultures.

The Making of National Strategies

This volume represents a capstone that builds upon the work undertaken in the Strategic Asia Program during the previous two years. The first phase of this three-year effort, *Strategic Asia 2015–16: Foundations of National Power in the Asia-Pacific*, examined the capacity of various Asian states to produce material power through a study of both their resource bases and their state and societal performance insofar as these bear on the generation of military capabilities. The second phase, *Strategic Asia 2016–17: Understanding Strategic Cultures in the Asia-Pacific*, focused on explaining the ideational frames of

---

[6] For a useful example, see Alan G. Stolberg, *How Nation-States Craft National Security Strategy Documents* (Carlisle: Strategic Studies Institute, 2012).

reference that shape how countries understand their political environment and the value, purpose, use, and limitations of coercive power in competitive politics. As such, this volume served as a companion to the previous year's study, with its focus on the material foundations of national power.

The current volume identifies what the major states in the Asia-Pacific region view as their most important security problems and, against this backdrop, examines how their material capabilities and intangible worldviews combine to shape the specific strategies that these states have adopted in dealing with their most important challenges. The thrust of each chapter, consequently, is at once both analytical and interpretative. To explain how a country's grand strategy and national military strategy serve as solutions, the most important contemporary problems facing the country are first identified. Thereafter, the various plausible strategies available are delineated through a rational reconstruction of the range of alternatives. This framing is intended to examine how certain strategies become dominant as a consequence of the intersection of a nation's material power and subjective understanding of its strategic circumstances. The country's external environment, capacity for generating hard power, historical memory, strategic ambitions, and domestic institutions (especially political leadership) all play a critical role in explaining why some strategies come to be preferred over others. These insights are finally employed to assess the durability of the dominant strategy (that is, its susceptibility to change), its adequacy for satisfying the country's principal geopolitical aims (given the wider regional changes), and the impact of the strategy on regional or global stability (in the context relevant for each country and especially for the United States).

When the chapters that follow are examined synoptically, the interaction of four variables proves to be particularly significant in shaping grand and national military strategies. The first obviously is the strategic environment. The spatial-political context within which a country is located is critical because it defines the predicaments, and by implication the tasks, that grand strategy and national military strategy must satisfy. "Environment" in this context refers not merely to a country's geographic location, which often identifies its adversaries and allies, but also to its internal circumstances, because these affect how a nation's power has to be allocated between the tasks of external security and internal order. This is particularly true in the Asia-Pacific region where many countries are still young as modern states and the task of producing order has both internal and external dimensions.

The second variable that becomes immediately relevant is national resources, which include both a country's physical assets and its intangible capacities—entrepreneurship, innovation, and technology—to produce these goods. Because most national resources must be produced by artifice, meaning that they are not available in ready-made form in nature, the character of the economic system and the quality of economic performance function as critical constraints that define the level and kind of resources to which a political leadership has access. The quality of military technology available to a state is particularly relevant here because it shapes the military strategies that can be developed to secure various political aims.

The ambitions and effectiveness of the political leadership constitute the third variable that determines the character of a country's grand strategy and military strategy. Political leadership effectively personifies the state, both to its own population and to other countries on the outside, and therefore—irrespective of the character of the political regime—serves as a functional proxy for the preferences of the country as a whole. The role of the executive is therefore important at multiple levels: it serves as the mediating instrument between state and society, directing how resources are to be extracted from the latter and how they should be applied toward securing various strategic ends; it directs the governing bureaucracies in formulating national policies, both domestic and foreign; and it affects international outcomes as a consequence of the goals, ambitions, and methods of leaders operating on their nation's behalf. To the degree that leaders consciously pursue the objective of expanding national power in the international arena, and are highly instrumentally rational toward that end, their grand strategies and military strategies would reflect their ambitions accordingly, being limited only by their levels of risk aversion.

Finally, strategic culture—the worldviews of a country's elites and especially decision-makers—makes a significant difference for the character of a nation's grand strategy and its military strategy. Ideas matter. They affect how a country's leadership interprets its national security environment and how it prioritizes the importance of military instruments in mitigating external and internal threats; they influence the emphasis placed on offensive versus defensive strategies in achieving military ends; and they articulate the values held by the polity, thereby reproducing the norms of behavior that define what a state considers to be acceptable or unacceptable in the pursuit of power in international politics. Strategic culture thus proves to be critical not simply in illuminating what causal effects states seek through the exercise of their power but equally in giving meaning to the variety of observed behaviors, which even when they appear similar could be driven by different strategic intentions.

Examining National Military Strategies in Asia

The chapters in this volume show how these four key variables and others interact to produce a wide variety of strategies depending on the unique strategic predicaments of the countries involved.

Oriana Skylar Mastro's study of China describes its current national military strategy as one of regional power projection, with the region defined expansively as radiating beyond East Asia and the South and East China Seas to Central Asia and South Asia, which include both the Indian Ocean and the Persian Gulf. This gradual broadening of China's military interests could in time be manifested in military strategies aimed at regional hegemony or even a global presence, depending on how China's economic performance is sustained. What is clear, however, is that the grand strategy bolstering these military derivatives is ambitious and is driven entirely by Beijing's desire to become a conventional great power in international politics. What is fascinating about Mastro's analysis is that the four components that shape the making of national military strategy are present in China's case in virtually equal measure. China finds itself in a challenging security environment surrounded by both major external rivals and significant internal security threats, the latter exacerbated by the authoritarian regime. These problems would by themselves justify the production of considerable military power, but the spectacular performance of the Chinese economy during the last 40-odd years has provided the state with the means to build its coercive capabilities with fewer burdens than might have been the case otherwise. Furthermore, China's impressive technological capabilities have enabled the country to pursue increasingly capital-intensive military solutions, whether these be manifested in reducing Chinese military manpower or in developing sophisticated anti-access capabilities intended to check U.S. power projection along the Asian rimlands.

The drive to implement such solutions—which as a consequence threaten to shift local balances of power to China's advantage—has received singular impetus from the current leadership of Xi Jinping. Xi appears to have cast aside Deng Xiaoping's older strategy of "hide and bide" in favor of a bolder goal of "striving for achievement," which is intended to rejuvenate the Chinese people and restore China as a world power of consequence. This ambition finds ready reinforcement from China's strategic culture: given its understanding of the country's history as one of unjust humiliation, the importance of remedying past wrongs in a political environment that is viewed as still pervasively conflictual makes assertive international policies a natural outcome. Furthermore, offensive military solutions are preferred for both technological and ideational reasons, and all elements taken together make the concerted expansion of national power a critical necessity for Beijing's success. China thus represents the best example of how the political environment, material capabilities, the character of leadership, and strategic culture combine in virtually equal measure to create a grand strategy and a national military strategy that matches it.

The chapter on Russia authored by Mark Katz is fascinating because, perhaps only second to China, the character of the political leadership overwhelmingly determines the character of Russia's grand strategy and the military strategy designed to support it. Although the strategic environment, weaknesses in material capabilities, and strategic culture all play a role in shaping Russia's national military strategy—which emphasizes hybrid warfare backstopped by revitalized nuclear capabilities for coercion short of war—neither this military approach nor the larger grand strategy of confronting the West would have taken shape without the singular role of Vladimir Putin. For all practical purposes, therefore, Russia's grand strategy and national military strategy are shaped largely by Putin's preferences, his perception of Russia's interests, and his reading of recent Russian history. Putin's conviction that NATO's expansion following the West's victory in the Cold War and the United States' continuing support for democracy movements worldwide are intended to fundamentally weaken Russia makes the Western powers appear to be a far greater threat to Moscow than even jihadist Islam or China.

This perceived threat fosters a tacit Russia-China alliance against the West, even at the cost of Russia being the junior partner, and a military strategy that focuses both on strengthening Russian control in its near abroad and on weakening Western democracies through "non-kinetic" means. The former objective has driven the modernization of some Russian conventional capabilities, whereas the latter underwrites the expanding use of instruments of political influence, cyberwarfare and other covert warfare capabilities, and the ultimate guarantor, nuclear weapons. Russia's continuing material weaknesses place the heavy-handed military competition of the Cold War beyond Moscow's reach. But its strategic culture, which provides confidence that Russia can weather its present adversity and make a comeback, as it has before, seems to reinforce Putin's conviction that the current grand strategy of confronting the West despite Russian weaknesses is already paying dividends. Whether it remains the best approach for protecting long-term national interests is a different question, but the preeminent role of political leadership in the making of Russia's current strategy ensures that Moscow's pugnacity will persist so long as Putin remains in power.

Christopher Hughes's chapter on Japan illuminates the current effort of Prime Minister Shinzo Abe to steadily expand Japan's military capabilities under the rubric of the U.S.-Japan alliance, to bring Japan's military contributions closer to the ideal of active support for the United States regionally and globally (as well as the United Nations and other regional organizations involved in protecting international security), and to enlarge the scope of Japan's military operations in both their combat orientation and their geographic presence. This evolution of Japanese national military strategy, which is by no means complete, would continue under the aegis of the country's current grand strategy—the Yoshida doctrine of aligning with the United States and relying on its nuclear umbrella—but aims to stretch that inheritance by pushing Japan closer toward the goal of becoming a more "normal" nation.

Clearly the role of political leadership in the person of Abe is critical here, but unlike in the case of Putin, who has shifted Russian strategy primarily through his own will, Abe's efforts at reorienting Japanese military strategy have received a decisive fillip from significant changes in the country's strategic environment—namely, the rising threats posed by China and North Korea and the unsettling ambivalence of the United States in regard to its traditional role as security guarantor in the Asia-Pacific. Japan's material capabilities largely remain unchanged: its economic strength and technological sophistication remain impressive and could easily support a more expansive shift in military strategy. But its strategic culture still exhibits considerable diffidence and could yet prevent Abe's vision from being fully realized. In this instance, then, even a determined political leadership and a propitious external environment may not suffice to engineer the major changes in Japanese strategy that have been debated in recent years.

One country that has had no option but to cope with the dramatic transformations in its external environment is South Korea. Chung Min Lee's chapter on the changes in South Korea's military strategy vividly describes how a nation that until not too long ago had to cope mainly with the threat of an invasion by North Korea now must simultaneously cope with the emergence of a powerful China (that still protects Pyongyang in many ways), North Korean nuclear weapons (which can increasingly threaten South Korea's principal security guarantor, the United States), and the Kim regime's persistent brinkmanship (both diplomatic and military). These challenges only complement Pyongyang's traditional threats of artillery attacks, cyberwarfare, sabotage, and conventional military operations, not to mention the ever-present possibility of a major domestic crisis in North Korea.

Given this worsening environment, Lee argues that preparing for extremely complex combined operations will come to replace South Korea's traditional military strategy of linear defense along the frontier and protection of its rear areas. Seoul's grand strategy, however, remains unchanged: it still seeks peaceful reunification if possible but, given the odds against success, is content to settle for preserving the status quo peacefully. Yet the steady worsening of South Korea's strategic environment puts these objectives at increasing risk. Although the country's material capabilities have not decayed despite the significant long-term risks to its economic growth and technological innovation, these advantages would nonetheless be endangered immediately should conflict break out on the peninsula. The country's deeply conflicted political system and the emphasis on autonomy fostered by its strategic culture have not helped its elites develop a consistent response to the emerging threats, thus leaving the nation buffeted by many forces that are proving hard to control. This fact notwithstanding, the burdens disproportionately levied by the external environment on the processes and outcomes of strategy formation make South Korea quite unique.

Like the studies of China, Japan, and South Korea in this volume, John Gill's chapter on India also represents a case study of a country whose national military strategy is in the throes of significant transition. Whereas the transition in the three East Asian powers is not fundamentally constrained by resources, India, alone among the emerging global powers, seems challenged by the demand for a new national military strategy that can service both its own ambitions and the expectations of its well-wishers at exactly the time when it is still not fully liberated from the shackles of economic constraints. All the same, Gill demonstrates that the traditional Indian grand strategy of nonalignment and the derivative national military strategy of static frontier defense concurrently oriented against Pakistan and China have passed the limits of success. New threats are posed by China's and Pakistan's nuclear arsenals, Pakistan's continuing terrorism against India, and China's growing military presence in Tibet, naval presence in the Indian Ocean, activities in space and cyberspace, and projection of economic power across Asia through the Belt and Road Initiative. New Delhi needs to develop new military strategies to cope with these emerging threats as well as support India's evolving grand strategy of seeking strategic partnerships in order to maximize its national power.

As India struggles with these tasks, Gill highlights multiple changes: deficiencies in material capability are still significant and institutional weaknesses at the political, civil-military, and military levels are rampant, suggesting acute vulnerabilities at multiple levels of leadership. The political shortcomings may in fact be the most troublesome. For all of its grandiose ambitions, India's civilian leadership has never treated national security with the attention it deserves. Internal security continues to drain attention and resources, and external security is managed as if it were merely synonymous with maintaining a large military establishment and ensuring corruption-free defense acquisitions. India's strategic culture only exacerbates these problems through its reactive impulses and preference for incremental change. The net result is that even the pressures from an increasingly hostile environment seem insufficient to force the kind of change necessary to develop national military strategies that are adequate to India's ambitions of becoming a leading power.

Ann Marie Murphy's chapter on Indonesia suggests that its national military strategy is likely to prove even more inadequate to its security challenges than India's. Like India, Indonesia has pursued a grand strategy of nonalignment, opting to sit out superpower competition during the Cold War in favor of dealing with the problems of national integration at home. Indonesia's national military strategy, accordingly, was centered on building its land forces, which were most relevant for managing the internal threats arising from ethnic, religious, class, and regional cleavages in a vast and disparate archipelago. The relative neglect of external security was viable only because U.S. power was present in much of Southeast Asia, thus ensuring that neither the Soviet Union nor China could threaten Indonesia or its smaller regional siblings for much of the Cold War. Indonesia supplemented nonalignment by building up the Association of Southeast Asian Nations (ASEAN), which served as a peace pact among regional elites and prevented mutual interference in internal affairs.

This traditional military strategy centered on internal security is now at risk because of changes in the environment deriving from China's regional assertiveness, but Jakarta seems unable to rise to the challenge appropriately. Although Indonesia is an economic success story by many indicators, significant budgetary constraints prevent it from shifting appropriately to the air- and naval-centric military strategies that are necessary. Hesitations stemming from its strategic culture—its traditional desire to chart an independent course—prevent Indonesia from easily aligning with the United States as well. And its political leadership seems divided about the character of the Chinese threat, while simultaneously being unable to mobilize national power concertedly enough to deal with the problems posed by China. The shift in national military strategy that is desirable for enhancing security thus seems far away, leaving Indonesia's security dependent on China's forbearance or inattention, the modest protections from solidarity with ASEAN, or the U.S. regional military presence. The latter, though likely to continue, may be insufficient if it is not coupled to political and strategic understandings with Washington.

Finally, Thomas Mahnken's chapter highlights the centrality of the United States for Asian security, a strategic fact of life since the end of World War II. Throughout this period, Washington pursued a unique national military strategy centered on defense at a distance: protecting U.S. interests by meeting threats as far away as possible from the continental United States. That goal resulted in major investments in power-projection capabilities intended to underwrite U.S. extended deterrence obligations around the world. These commitments were backstopped ultimately by strategic nuclear forces that were coupled—even if this was not always admitted—to strategies of damage limitation associated with doctrines of deterrence by denial. In tandem, the United States also sought wherever possible to preserve favorable regional balances of power so that its protectees could enjoy local advantages that lowered the burdens levied on U.S. extended deterrence. The U.S. military strategy of power projection, which entailed the use of forward-deployed and forward-operating combat forces to exert political influence at great distances, proved tenable because Washington enjoyed economic and technological superiority throughout the postwar era. This dominance made the U.S. grand strategy of preserving primacy a rational course of action, although it was frequently questioned by domestic critics because of its cost and international consequences.

The dramatic changes in the international environment that have occurred in the 25-plus years since the Cold War ended—the rise of China as a major rival, Russia's emergence as a disgruntled competitor, and the appearance of troublesome regional antagonists such as North Korea and Iran—now raise questions about the viability of this traditional military strategy of power projection. The material capabilities of the United States have by no means diminished during this period, and the country's scientific and technological base still permits it to overcome the operational obstacles extended by these challengers should the United States apply itself to doing so. As Mahnken notes, the real impediments to buttressing the nation's traditional military strategy of power projection actually arise from the character of the current political leadership and the contestations inherent in U.S. strategic culture. The rise of nationalism in U.S. politics and the election of a leader championing the vision of "America first" raise serious questions about whether the United States will stay committed to preserving its global primacy and, more importantly, whether that primacy will be protected through a sturdy network of alliances that require successful U.S. power projection for their continued value and effectiveness.

The Impact of Asian National Military Strategies on U.S. Interests

Taken together, the chapters in this volume and those in its two predecessors expand our understanding of how various Asian nations have developed their grand and national military strategies as a function of different, but comparable, external and internal variables and how the evolution of these strategies will continue to shape the ongoing geopolitical competition in the Asia-Pacific.

Understanding the impact of the various Asian strategies—at both the grand and military levels—on U.S. interests in particular would have been easier if U.S. grand strategy were set on a stable course, as seemed to be the case before Donald Trump's 2016 election as president. If the United States, reflecting the upsurge in nationalist sentiment and Trump's own inclinations to reduce U.S. responsibilities for the maintenance of global order, settles for a genuinely different grand strategy from that pursued throughout the Cold War period—for example, replacing the strategy of preserving primacy with one of settling for a global balance of power that ostensibly leaves the United States alone—how the various Asian military strategies evolve could have less significance for U.S. interests. The operative word here is "less," because it is entirely possible, as U.S. policymakers have understood since World War II, that even developments that do not initially affect U.S. security could eventually come to undermine it if the United States either cannot or will not play a role in shaping the development of other nations' strategies from the outset. An America-first strategy that attempts to maintain U.S. primacy in an insular sense may thus end up being far costlier than a strategy of maintaining primacy through sustaining "confederations" intended to preserve both the power superiority of the West and the benefits of the liberal international order. Although the latter may require the United States to bear the cost of producing some global public goods, the net benefits to Washington in terms of common security would make the inconveniences worthwhile.

If the United States, therefore, hews to the traditional course of preserving its global primacy through maintaining the power-projection capabilities necessary for onshore balancing in critical regions of the world, the challenges posed by China—at the levels of both grand strategy and national military strategy—would rank simply as the biggest threat to U.S. hegemony for many years to come. This challenge acquires additional significance because the expansion in Chinese military capabilities is likely to be sustained for a long time: environmental factors, increasing material capabilities, resolute leadership, and a parabellum strategic culture all combine to make the threats posed by Beijing quite formidable. It is unfortunate, in this context, that U.S. policy has been unable to peel Russia away from its tacit alliance with China. Although Russian material power is weakening, Moscow's capabilities are still significant in certain narrow areas, and when committed in support of China, they make the latter more troublesome than it might otherwise be.

In these circumstances, Japanese power still offers formidable benefits to the United States. Tokyo's material capabilities are substantial and its military power is significant. But Japan's conflicted strategic culture may yet prevent it from developing its combat potential to the degree necessary to effectively supplement U.S. military power along the Asian rimlands. South Korea's national capabilities are similarly hampered by its strategic culture, its diffidence about a full partnership with Japan, and its sympathy for China. Moreover, the immensity of the challenges posed by North Korea ensure that it will be a long time before South Korea will have any surplus of either national or military power that could be allocated to aiding the United States in protecting the liberal order in Asia in the face of Chinese resistance.

India undoubtedly remains an important partner in this regard given its political incentives to oppose China's assertiveness. The country's significant weaknesses in material capability, hesitant strategic culture, and institutional and leadership infirmities imply that U.S. assistance will be necessary for quite some time before India is capable of balancing China independently. Until that point is reached, balancing China in partnership with the United States remains the only viable option for New Delhi—and for Washington, if the value of the affiliation with India is correctly appreciated. Indonesia is even further away than India from the viewpoint of securing cooperation for balancing China, given both its capacity constraints and its political reservations about allying with the United States. But Indonesia, along with Singapore, Vietnam, and the Philippines, are potentially important partners in this effort and hence are worth the investment of U.S. resources in building their national capacities.

Because most U.S. partners in Asia are handicapped in different ways where their grand and national military strategies are concerned, preserving the "balance of power that favors freedom" in the region will depend disproportionately on the rejuvenation of American power.[7] Trump's America-first strategy encapsulates this fundamental insight—which bodes well for success, but only if the administration can craft sensible policies aimed

---

[7] Condoleezza Rice, "Wriston Lecture: A Balance of Power That Favors Freedom" (speech presented at the Manhattan Institute, New York City, October 1, 2002).

at renewing U.S. strength.[8] Toward that end, Washington must recognize that U.S. alliances and partnerships, properly appreciated, are vital tools for preserving American hegemony at the least cost compared to the alternatives of economic autarky and strategic solipsism.[9]

---

[8] For an extended analysis of what such rejuvenation entails, see Ashley J. Tellis, *Balancing without Containment: An American Strategy for Managing China* (Washington, D.C.: Carnegie Endowment for International Peace, 2014).

[9] For an elaboration of this argument, see Ashley J. Tellis, "Seeking Alliances and Partnerships: The Long Road to Confederationism in U.S. Grand Strategy," in *Strategic Asia 2014–15: U.S. Alliances and Partnerships at the Center of Global Power*, ed. Ashley J. Tellis, Abraham M. Denmark, and Greg Chaffin (Seattle: National Bureau of Asian Research, 2014), 3–32.

EXECUTIVE SUMMARY

This chapter explains how a broad base of national power, the prevalence of perceived maritime threats, and national narratives about the "century of humiliation" and Chinese exceptionalism combine to make regional power projection the most attractive national military strategy to Chinese leaders.

MAIN ARGUMENT

China faces a wide range of internal and external challenges, ranging from maintaining domestic stability and sustainable economic growth to asserting its position in the international system and protecting its sovereignty and territorial integrity. China has five potential national military strategies to choose from to mitigate these challenges: internal security, external defense/continental power, regional power projection, regional hegemony, and development of a globally relevant military. Official statements, as well as the nature of training, investment, and structural reform of the People's Liberation Army (PLA), suggest that the current strategy is one of regional power projection. China's national power has not reached the point at which regional hegemony or a global strategy is a realistic option, nor is the country likely to downgrade its ambitions to an internal stability or external defense strategy.

POLICY IMPLICATIONS

- China's military strategy is likely to remain one of regional power projection, though the contours of the region are expanding beyond East Asia and the South and East China Seas to Central Asia and South Asia.

- Given that China's march toward regional power projection is unlikely to decelerate, the U.S. must ensure that its presence and posture in Asia, including in South Asia and Central Asia, keep apace.

- Because significant changes in threat perceptions and ideas will precede a move toward regional hegemony or a global strategy, continued attention to the content of authoritative Chinese sources as well as the exercises, activities, training, and procurement of the PLA should be the priority of the U.S. defense community.

Ideas, Perceptions, and Power: An Examination of China's Military Strategy

Oriana Skylar Mastro

China is a country of contradictions. Capitalist and Communist, it is home to some of the world's richest and poorest populations, with domestic politics characterized by nationalism and dissent.[1] The Chinese leadership wants close positive relations with the United States even as it criticizes and challenges U.S. policy; it strives for a professionalized military while also refusing to allow the People's Liberation Army (PLA) to shed its responsibilities as the armed wing of the Chinese Communist Party (CCP).[2]

Many of these contradictions are the result of attempts to manage and mitigate key strategic problems, both internal and external, as China seeks to achieve great-power status. Domestically, the party's core motivation

Oriana Skylar Mastro is an Assistant Professor of Security Studies in the Edmund A. Walsh School of Foreign Service at Georgetown University. She can be reached through her website at <http://www.orianaskylarmastro.com>.

The author would like to thank Danni Song, Danni Wang, Jimmy Zhang, Annie Kowalewski, and Amber Qin for their expert research assistance.

[1] Ronald Coase and Ning Wang, "How China Became Capitalist," Cato Institute, Cato Policy Report, January/February 2013, https://www.cato.org/policy-report/januaryfebruary-2013/how-china-became-capitalist; and Gabriel Wildau and Tom Mitchell, "China Income Inequality among World's Worst," *Financial Times*, January 14, 2016.

[2] On U.S.-China relations, see "Wang Yi tan Zhongmei guanxi: duguo moheqi, zoushang genghao fazhan daolu" [Wang Yi Talks about China-U.S. Relationships: Get on a Path of Better Development after the Transition Period], Ministry of Foreign Affairs of the People's Republic of China (PRC), February 7, 2017. On the party's demand for loyalty from the PLA, see "Cong 'sanda guilü' kan 'dang dui jundui juedui lingdao'" ["The Party's Absolute Leadership" in "Three Laws"], *Qiu Shi*, October 17, 2016, http://theory.people.com.cn/n1/2016/1017/c40531-28785422.html; and "Xi Jinping shicha haijun jiguan bing fabiao zhongyao jianghua" [Xi Jinping Visits Navy Authority and Gives Important Speech], *China Military*, May 24, 2017, http://www.81.cn/theory/2017-05/24/content_7616607.htm.

continues to be to stave off the threat of revolution, which at times leads to repression and propaganda, but also in more recent years has heightened the government's responsiveness to public opinion.[3] The source of the party's legitimacy has changed over time from ideology (under Mao Zedong) to performance (under Deng Xiaoping, Jiang Zemin, and Hu Jintao) to nationalism (under Xi Jinping).[4] However, the economic reforms that propelled China into the rising power club have created internal disruptions as well. The Chinese people are now demanding not only continued growth but also development that is environmentally sustainable and equitable.[5] Meanwhile, separatist movements persist in Tibet and Xinjiang, and Taiwan continues to enjoy de facto independence and at times threatens *de jure* independence.[6]

In addition to these internal threats, Chinese leaders are facing mounting external pressures as they seek the "rejuvenation" of the nation from the era of colonial subjugation, a key theme of Xi's "China dream."[7] To this end, Xi has launched broad sweeping military reforms to ensure that the PLA "push forward preparations for military struggle through insisting on using the criteria of actual combat…to train them [soldiers] for [real] warfare."[8] China has also pushed for a new formulation for U.S.-China relations—a new type of major-power relations—that stresses conflict avoidance but also mutual accommodation of core interests.[9] At the same time, China has become more assertive in its maritime disputes in the South and East China Seas to, from Beijing's perspective, safeguard Chinese sovereignty and territorial integrity.[10]

How has China's national military strategy developed to address these internal and external challenges? Additionally, what factors have been essential drivers of continuity and change in China's approach? To answer these questions, this chapter builds on the past two *Strategic Asia* volumes, which examined the foundation of national power and the impact

---

[3] Simon Denyer, "In China, Communist Party Takes Unprecedented Step: It Is Listening," *Washington Post*, August 2, 2013.

[4] The author would like to thank Rory Truex for this insight.

[5] Junjie Zhang, "Delivering Environmentally Sustainable Economic Growth: The Case of China," Asia Society, September 2012.

[6] Xue Li, "China's Potential Pitfalls #4: Splittist Forces," *Diplomat*, November 13, 2015.

[7] "Xi Jinping's Vision: Chasing the Chinese Dream," *Economist*, May 4, 2013.

[8] Willy Lam, "Commander-in-Chief Xi Jinping Raises the Bar on PLA 'Combat Readiness,'" Jamestown Foundation, China Brief, January 18, 2013, 3.

[9] Michael S. Chase, "China's Search for a 'New Type of Great Power Relationship,'" Jamestown Foundation, China Brief, September 7, 2012.

[10] Oriana Skylar Mastro, "Why Chinese Assertiveness Is Here to Stay," *Washington Quarterly* 37, no. 4 (2014): 151–70.

of strategic culture, respectively.[11] Specifically, it will assess how ideational factors such as strategic culture and structural factors like national power interact to produce a particular military strategy. By providing a comprehensive and detailed overview of the motivations, and therefore objectives, of China's military strategy, this chapter will contribute to an assessment of the future character of geopolitical competition in the Indo-Pacific region.

To achieve this goal, this chapter first reconstructs the military strategies that Chinese leaders theoretically have at their disposal to deal with this wide range of internal and external challenges and demonstrates that China is currently pursuing a military strategy of power projection. It then follows in the tradition of the previous two *Strategic Asia* volumes to devise the structural and ideational factors that have made regional power projection more attractive than the alternatives. Specifically, I argue that the improving technological base and broad financial resources resulting from China's rising national power permitted such a strategy, while threat perceptions and ideational factors combine to make this strategy preferable to one focused purely on internal security or external defense. However, these same three factors—threat perceptions, national military power, and ideas—currently constrain China from moving beyond regional power projection to pursue regional hegemony or a globally relevant military. The chapter concludes with a discussion of the implications for U.S. policy and the conditions under which China's military strategy may change.

A Rational Reconstruction of Possible National Military Strategies

What are the national military strategies at China's disposal to promote the continued rise and rejuvenation of the Chinese nation? Given that a country's military strategy is designed to promote national interests in the face of external constraints and opportunities, it is logical to think of the possible range of strategies as derived from China's view of itself and its role in the world. Specifically, there are five distinct types: (1) internal security, (2) external defense/continental power, (3) regional power projection, (4) regional hegemony, and (5) development of a globally relevant military. These are ideal types, and in practice some overlap is likely. For example, leaders may choose to focus on internal power consolidation but try to simultaneously

---

[11] Ashley J. Tellis, Alison Szalwinski, and Michael Wills, eds., *Strategic Asia 2015–16: Foundations of National Power in the Asia-Pacific* (Seattle: National Bureau of Asian Research, 2015); and Ashley J. Tellis, Alison Szalwinski, and Michael Wills, eds., *Strategic Asia 2016–17: Understanding Strategic Cultures in the Asia-Pacific* (Seattle: National Bureau of Asian Research, 2016).

protect their country's borders; or they may aim to project power regionally but have limited global capabilities (which is a good description of Xi's current approach). However, in practice one can determine what types of operations the Chinese military is currently optimized to conduct—internal stability, external defense, regional, or global operations—and classify its national strategy accordingly. Furthermore, given limited resources, being capable in one area often comes at the expense of another.

At one extreme, an internal security strategy is one in which the sole concern is maintaining internal stability and party control. For example, in countries plagued by civil war, the government may be bogged down with internal threats and therefore be unable to dedicate sufficient resources to addressing external threats. Mao's military strategy in the first decade of the People's Republic of China (PRC) falls within this category. During this period, Mao was focused on defeating the nationalists, consolidating power, and regaining territories such as Tibet that had been a part of the Qing Dynasty.[12] This strategy is ground-force centric, with military training, rhetoric, and equipment focused on supporting political repression and control. While today's PLA continues to serve as a party army whose main mission is to follow CCP directives and protect the party, internal stability is now a small portion of its operational focus; since 1989, the PLA has only conducted one internal security operation, which occurred in 2008 in Tibet.[13]

Once a government has control over the domestic political situation, the next step is to incorporate external defense into the national security strategy. This is the most basic responsibility of a state: to ensure a monopoly of violence within and protection from violence from the outside. China's military doctrine of "people's war" concerned itself with the threat of invasion from materially superior but numerically inferior invaders—first from the United States during 1949–60 and then from the Soviet Union during 1960–85.[14] China also offered concessions to its neighbors to help resolve seventeen border conflicts so that it could free up resources to deal with

---

[12] William Andrew and Charles Adie, *Chinese Strategic Thinking under Mao Tse-tung* (Melbourne: Australia National University Press, 1972).

[13] Murray Scot Tanner, "How China Manages Internal Security Challenges and Its Impact on PLA Missions," in *Beyond the Strait: PLA Missions Other Than Taiwan*, ed. Roy Kamphausen, David Lai, and Andrew Scobell (Carlisle: Strategic Studies Institute, 2009), 39–73.

[14] As Soviet forces gained unprecedented accuracy, range, and destructiveness of firepower, the doctrine changed to "people's war under modern conditions," which placed greater emphasis on positional warfare, combined arms tactics, and use of regular and mechanized forces to blunt an invasion before it could penetrate. Ellis Joffe, "'People's War under Modern Conditions': A Doctrine for Modern War," *China Quarterly*, no. 112 (1987): 555–71. After the Soviet Union collapsed, and with it the possibility of major nuclear war, China shifted from a personnel-intensive doctrine to a technology-intensive one with the introduction of "local war under modern high-tech conditions."

instability in the frontier areas and guarantee neighboring states support in these efforts.[15]

China could have remained focused on external defense to become a continental power, choosing land-based power projection through conventional missiles and air power, but instead it has chosen over the course of the past two decades to focus on regional power projection, and therefore on the development of its maritime capabilities. In this situation, the military moves from a ground-centric, manpower-heavy force to a professionalized force with a strong and high-tech air force and navy capable of projecting power beyond a country's borders on the ground, in the air, and at sea. The objective is to leverage the military to protect national interests throughout the region, shape the decisions of regional actors, and perhaps play a greater role in the regional security architecture.[16] China is currently adopting this strategy, which will be discussed in more detail in the next section.

Because a regional power-projection strategy does not necessarily come at the expense of other military strategies, it makes sense to devise a distinct fourth category for regional hegemony. A national military strategy of regional hegemony takes power projection one step further to exclude other countries' military activities.[17] In the case of China, this would mean adopting a military strategy that would allow Beijing to push the U.S. military out of East Asia. While China is clearly pursuing regional power projection, it is debatable whether this strategy serves as a precursor to a bid for regional hegemony.[18]

Last, the most expansive national military strategy is one that strives for a global role. With the United States having eight hundred bases in around 70 countries, U.S. national military strategy falls at the extreme of this category.[19] A more limited understanding of a globally relevant military includes extensive military engagement, exercises, or arms sales with countries beyond one's immediate region, but not necessarily a forward presence, unrestricted global reach, and constant pace of global operations. The determining factor for this category is whether the military predominantly concerns itself with

---

[15] M. Taylor Fravel, *Strong Borders, Secure Nation: Cooperation and Conflict in China's Territorial Disputes* (Princeton: Princeton University Press, 2008).

[16] Thomas Kane, "China's 'Power Projection' Capabilities," *Parameters* 44, no. 4 (2014–15): 27–37.

[17] Timothy R. Heath, Kristen Gunness, and Cortez A. Cooper, *The PLA and China's Rejuvenation: National Security and Military Strategies, Deterrence Concepts, and Combat Capabilities* (Santa Monica: RAND Corporation, 2016).

[18] Aaron L. Friedberg, "Hegemony with Chinese Characteristics," *National Interest*, July/August 2011, 19, http://users.clas.ufl.edu/zselden/coursereading2011/friedberg.pdf; and Paul H.B. Goodwin, "China as a Regional Hegemon?" in *The Asia-Pacific: A Region in Transition*, ed. Jim Rolfe (Honolulu: Asia-Pacific Center for Security Studies, 2004).

[19] John Glaser, "Why We Should Close America's Overseas Military Bases," *Time*, October 7, 2016.

conducting operations around the world in pursuit of global aims. At the present time, China is still far from being able to project power globally, but its current military strategy has some global aspects.[20] For example, Hu's "new historic missions" called for greater Chinese involvement in military operations other than war on the global stage. Chinese deployments to the Gulf of Aden since 2008, originally to combat piracy, and troop contributions to UN missions are two notable examples. China's move to construct its first overseas base in Djibouti has caused some observers to wonder if its military strategy under Xi will expand to include global aims, but currently China's primary objectives remain firmly regional.

China's Current Military Strategy: Regional Power Projection

Official statements, as well as the nature of China's military modernization to date, indicate that the central focus of China's military strategy is to project power regionally. In terms of party rhetoric, Xi Jinping's foreign policy of "striving for achievement" (*fenfayouwei*) expands China's interests to the country's greater periphery and calls for proactive efforts to achieve the two centenary goals: domestic prosperity and a strong, peaceful socialist state.[21] Xi aims to make China a great power whose regional role is no longer confined to economic cooperation but which exercises leadership and influence in the realm of security and politics.[22] Along these lines, China's top leader has never used the phrase popularized by Deng Xiaoping "biding your time and hiding your capabilities" (*taoguangyanhui)* in a public speech, while he has referred to the more proactive goal of "striving for achievement" seven times.[23]

---

[20] For limitations, see Oriana Skylar Mastro, "A Global Expeditionary People's Liberation Army: 2025–2030," in *The Chinese People's Liberation Army in 2025*, ed. Roy Kamphausen and David Lai (Carlisle: U.S. Army War College Press, 2015), 207–34.

[21] "Shixian zhonghua minzu weida fuxing shi haineiwai Zhonghua ernü gongtong de meng" [Great Rejuvenation of the Chinese People Is the Dream of Every Chinese around the World], CPC News, June 6, 2014, http://cpc.people.com.cn/xuexi/n/2015/0717/c397563-27322408.html.

[22] Wang Yiwei, "Quanqiu zhili de Zhongguo zixin yu zijue" [China's Confidence and Initiative in Global Governance], *People's Daily*, November 11, 2016, http://theory.people.com.cn/n1/2016/1109/c40531-28847772.html; and Mu Ren and Wang Yuexin, "Xi Jinping waijiao lilun he shijian chuangxin" [Xi Jinping's Diplomatic Theory and Innovative Actions], *Theoretical Research*, no. 6 (2016).

[23] The terms used are *fenfayouwei, fenfaxiangshang,* and *fenfatuqiang.* For some examples, see Xi Jinping, "Xi Jinping chuxi Di Shiwujie Zhong-Yue Qingnian Youhao Huijian huodongshi de jianghua" [Xi Jinping's Speech at the 15th Sino-Vietnam Youth Friendship Meeting], Xinhua, April 8, 2015, http://news.xinhuanet.com/politics/2015-04/08/c_127664786.htm; and Xi Jinping, "Zai jinian Sun Zhongshan xiansheng danchen 150 zhounian dahui shang de jianghua" [Speech at a Commemoration for the 150th Anniversary of the Birth of Sun Yat-sen], Xinhua, November 11, 2016, http://news.xinhuanet.com/politics/2016-11/11/c_1119897047.htm.

A strong military, specifically one prepared to fight and win local wars—in other words, one that can project power regionally—is a critical component of Xi's proclaimed grand strategy of national rejuvenation.[24] China's national defense white paper calls on the PLA to "implement the military strategy of active defense, guard against and resist aggression, contain separatist forces, safeguard border, coastal and territorial air security, and protect national maritime rights and interests and national security interests in outer space and cyber space." China is "developing internal control, peripheral denial, and limited force projection capabilities consistent with these objectives."[25] Accordingly, Chinese naval strategy has undergone three phases since 1949: (1) littoral/near-coast defense (*yan'an fangyu/jin'an fangyu*), (2) offshore defense (*jinhai fangyu*), and (3) a dual approach of offshore defense and open-seas protection (*yuanhai huwei*).[26] An additional indicator of China's regional power-projection focus is the fact that the country's most recent military reforms included a restructuring of the organization to shift power from the army, which had been central in an era of external defense, to the air force and navy, the two services central to regional power projection.[27] These moves, as well as the creation of theater commands to take the place of military regions, all stress mobility, joint operations, and the importance of logistics, the trifecta of power-projection operations.

The types of military capabilities in which China has invested over the past three decades also point to a regional power-projection strategy. During the past 25 years, China's navy has been transformed from a glorified coast guard to a force of 51 frigates, 35 destroyers, and 2 functional aircraft carriers capable of conducing operations in the near seas (Yellow, East China, and South China Seas), with limited capability beyond the second island chain defined by the Kuril Islands, Japan and the Bonin Islands, the Marianas Islands, Palau, and the Indonesian archipelago.[28] China has begun to diversify

[24] Ren Tianyou, "Jianchi junshi fucong zhengzhi, zhanlüe fucong zhenglüe" [Supporting Politics over Military, Political Strategy over Military Strategy], *Zhongguo Junwang*, January 6, 2017, http://www.81.cn/jmywyl/2017-01/06/content_7439669.htm.

[25] Information Office of the State Council (PRC), "The Diversified Employment of China's Armed Forces," April 16, 2013, http://www.scio.gov.cn/zfbps/ndhf/2013/Document/1312843/1312843.htm.

[26] *Zhanluexue* [The Science of Military Strategy] (Beijing: Military Science Press, 2013), 207.

[27] Currently, most of the Chinese defense budget is spent on boosting China's PLA Navy and Air Force capabilities in projecting power. "Document: China's Military Strategy," U.S. Naval Institute, May 26, 2015, https://news.usni.org/2015/05/26/document-chinas-military-strategy.

[28] "China Military Strength: Current Military Capabilities and Available Firepower for 2017 Detailed," Global Firepower, http://www.globalfirepower.com/country-military-strength-detail.asp?country_id=china; Ronald O'Rourke, "China Naval Modernization: Implications for U.S. Navy Capabilities—Background and Issues for Congress," Congressional Research Service, CRS Report for Congress, April 24, 2009; and Michael McDevitt, "China's Far Sea Navy: The Implications of the 'Open Seas Protection' Mission," CNA, April 2016, https://www.cna.org/cna_files/pdf/China-Far-Seas-Navy.pdf.

its focus from ballistic and cruise missile programs, capable of delivering munitions but not controlling airspace, to developing advanced modern fighters like the J-20 and J-31 that can be used to support joint operations.[29] Now China operates routinely in the East and South China Seas at sea and in the air; the Japanese military recorded 571 intercepts in 2015 alone, and China has nearly completed four air bases on the Spratly and Paracel Islands, allowing Chinese military aircraft to operate over the entire South China Sea.[30]

China is equally interested in developing its own C4ISR (command, control, communications, computers, intelligence, surveillance, and reconnaissance) infrastructure to support joint operations in the region. China has indeed made great strides in developing communication and navigation satellites. On the latter, the Beidou Satellite Navigation System, which completed regional coverage in 2012 and is projected to be a complete global network by 2020, has an accuracy on a par with GPS.[31] In August 2016, China launched the world's first quantum satellite, designed to provide "hack-proof communication" in a military sphere increasingly dominated by cyberespionage and space-based warfare. The satellite became operational in early 2017 and will provide secure communications to Chinese units in the South China Sea and Chinese embassies.[32]

Because the progression of China's military strategy has been linear to date—from internally focused to regional to global—we take the current regional power-projection strategy as inevitable. But Xi's China dream could have theoretically been focused on domestic, continental, or more expansive global aims. The next section dissects how China's material power and subjective understanding of its strategic circumstances shaped the country's choice of a regional power-projection strategy.

---

[29] China is also making significant progress in unmanned aerial vehicle (UAV) deployment, conducting the largest swarm of fixed-wing drones ever flown in December 2016. Its recently developed Sharp Sword UAV, the first non-NATO stealth attack drone, will most likely be used in reconnaissance in areas with dense air-defense networks, as well as for tailing foreign warships. David Hambling, "If Drone Swarms Are the Future, China May Be Winning," *Popular Mechanics*, December 23, 2016.

[30] "Japan Scrambled Fighters against China a Record 571 Times in Fiscal 2015," *Japan Times*, April 23, 2016, http://www.japantimes.co.jp/news/2016/04/23/national/japan-scrambled-fighters-china-record-571-times-fiscal-2015/#.WTrf5xPyso8; and "China's Big Three Near Completion," Center for Strategic and International Studies (CSIS), Asia Maritime Transparency Initiative, March 27, 2017, https://amti.csis.org/chinas-big-three-near-completion.

[31] Viola Zhou, "China's Version of GPS 'Is Now Just as Accurate,'" *South China Morning Post*, September 26, 2016, http://www.scmp.com/news/china/diplomacy-defence/article/2022462/chinas-version-gps-now-just-accurate.

[32] Qiu Chenhui, "Liangzi weixing 'mozi hao' hiaofu, kewei Nanhai zhudao deng tigong liangzi tongxin maozhang" [Quantum Satellite Successfully Launches, Capable of Providing Quantum Communications to South China Islands], *Zhongqing Zaixian*, January 2017, http://article.cyol.com/news/content/2017-01/18/content_15337398.htm.

The Impetus of National Power

A rich tradition in political science posits national power as a primary driver of military strategy. For this reason, Nadège Rolland evaluated the status and trajectory of China's national power in her contribution to the 2015–16 *Strategic Asia* volume.[33] Extended, her analysis suggests that natural, economic, and human resources can enable, hinder, or even drive a nation's military strategy. In China's case, the current foundation of national power has driven the country's strategic vision beyond its borders to include a role in the region; however, aspects of that same national power hinder more aggressive moves toward regional hegemony or a truly global national military strategy at this time.

First, China's growing national power allows it to incorporate regional power projection into its national military strategy without having to sacrifice internal security and external defense.[34] Since 2002, China has spent approximately 2% of its GDP on the military each year, which amounted to over $193 billion in 2015.[35] **Figure 1** tracks China's Composite Index of National Capability (CINC) score, or its share of total global material capabilities, which increased from 10.4% to 21.8% during 1949–2012.[36] The graph clearly shows China's foundation of national power expanding significantly over time, allowing, among other things, for an increase in military expenditures during the same time period by $103.9 billion.

China has also tried to more effectively use these resources to enhance national performance by investing in education, training, and innovation and technological development. According to the Organisation for Economic Co-operation and Development (OECD), between 1991 and 2016 Chinese gross domestic spending on R&D increased by $363.4 million.[37] The World Intellectual Property Organization indicates that between 2001 and 2015

---

[33] Nadège Rolland, "China's National Power: A Colossus with Iron or Clay Feet?" in Tellis, Szalwinski, and Wills, *Strategic Asia 2015–16*, 22–54.

[34] Much of the focus on ground control in the founding years of the PRC was because China lacked the material resources to develop its navy. Guo Yuhua, "Xinzhongguo chengli yilai Zhongguo Gongchandang haiyang zhanlüe de lishi kaocha" [An Investigation on the Chinese Communist Party's Naval Strategy since the Founding of the People's Republic of China], *Guangxi Social Sciences*, no. 9 (2014); and He Canhao, "Cong haifang yishi kan Zhongguo jindai shuailuo de yuanyin" [China's Decline without the Sense of Coast Defense during the Modern Period], *Nankai Xuebao*, no. 6 (2004).

[35] "What Does China Really Spend on Its Military?" CSIS, http://chinapower.csis.org/military-spending.

[36] "National Material Capabilities (v5.0)," University of California–Davis, Correlates of War Project, 2017. See also J. David Singer, Stuart Bremer, and John Stuckey, "Capability Distribution, Uncertainty, and Major Power War, 1820–1965," in *Peace, War, and Numbers*, ed. Bruce M. Russett (Beverly Hills: Sage, 1972), 19–48.

[37] "Gross Domestic Spending on R&D," OECD, Main Science and Technology Indicators, 2017, https://data.oecd.org/rd/gross-domestic-spending-on-r-d.htm.

FIGURE 1   China's CINC score, 1949–2012

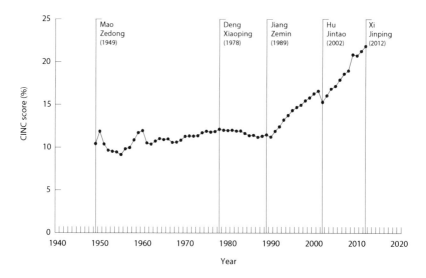

SOURCE: "National Material Capabilities Dataset (v5.0)," University of California–Davis, Correlates of War Project, 2017. See also J. David Singer, Stuart Bremer, and John Stuckey, "Capability Distribution, Uncertainty, and Major Power War, 1820–1965," in *Peace, War, and Numbers*, ed. Bruce M. Russett (Beverly Hills: Sage, 1972), 19–48.

NOTE: The Composite Index of National Capability (CINC) score measures a country's share of total global material capabilities.

Chinese intellectual property (IP) filings for patents rose by 979,174, IP filings for trademarks rose by 1,908,256, and IP filings for industrial design rose by 532,823.[38] The Chinese defense sector also has growing demand for new generations of scientists, engineers, and managers to replace aging personnel and to fill new positions in the high-technology sector. Between 1999 and 2005, the seven universities affiliated with the State Administration for Science, Technology and Industry for National Defense had a 86% increase in the number of students enrolled.[39]

---

[38] "WIPO Statistical Country Profiles—China," World Intellectual Property Organization, WIPO Statistics Database, 2017, http://www.wipo.int/ipstats/en/statistics/country_profile/profile.jsp?code=CN.

[39] Tai Ming Cheung, "The Chinese Defense Economy's Long March from Imitation to Innovation," *Journal of Strategic Studies* 34, no. 3 (2011): 325–54.

Although national power has permitted China to embrace a regional power-projection strategy, it has not reached a level that facilitates a regional hegemony or global strategy, partially because of the need to expend national resources to meet domestic demands. China needs to feed 1.3 billion people, and only 11% of its land is arable. An aging population, mass urbanization, and booming energy consumption will put pressure on economic resources and physical and social infrastructure.[40] Moreover, while China has successfully imitated and reproduced technology, it has been unable to develop the disruptive original technologies that would be needed to challenge the United States or play a dominant role globally. As Rolland points out, there has been "no major Chinese innovation or technological breakthrough" from the global perspective.[41] Lastly, China's economy is slowing down, with 6% growth per year as the new norm.[42] Slower growth could have an impact on national power through two mechanisms—it creates fewer resources to draw on and could lead to more domestic instability, both of which would draw China inward, perhaps back to an external defense or even an internal security strategy.[43] Just this year, the CCP announced that its military budget would increase by only 7% compared with the 2016 budget, the slowest growth since 2010.[44]

Economic motivations could also drive China toward a global military strategy in the future in a less direct fashion. Approximately 20,000 Chinese companies have a presence in more than 180 countries and regions, creating a constant demand for government protection of these assets.[45] Chinese overseas investment is growing as well; at $60 billion, China's annual outward FDI in 2010 was twenty times the 2005 amount.[46] Threats to those assets are occurring more frequently and are increasingly challenging the CCP's strategic and political interests. Statements made by Chinese political and military leaders acknowledge that China's need for stable access to natural resources, in addition to exploding foreign investment, has expanded its

---

[40] "China to Cap 2017 Energy Consumption at 4.4 Bln Tonns Coal Equivalent," Reuters, December 28, 2016, http://www.reuters.com/article/us-china-energy-idUSKBN14H1EG; and "China Population (Live)," Worldometers, http://www.worldometers.info/world-population/china-population.

[41] Rolland, "China's National Power," 35.

[42] For a list of the challenges, see "China—Economic Forecast Summary," OECD, November 2016.

[43] Christian Shepherd and Philip Wen, "China to Strengthen Defenses, No Word on Budget," Reuters, March 4, 2017, http://www.reuters.com/article/us-china-parliament-defence-idUSKBN16C01A.

[44] "China's 2017 Military Budget Rise Slows Again," Al Jazeera, March 4, 2017, http://www.aljazeera.com/news/2017/03/china-2017-military-budget-rise-slows-170304072324642.html.

[45] Keira Lu Huang, "'Not Enough' Consular Officers to Serve Chinese Nationals, Foreign Ministry Says," South China Morning Post, May 19, 2014, http://www.scmp.com/news/china/article/1515554/consular-staff-struggling-cope-rising-number-foreign-trips. This paragraph is from Oriana Skylar Mastro, "China Can't Stay Home," National Interest, November/December 2014, 39.

[46] Daniel H. Rosen and Thilo Hanemann, "The Rise in Chinese Overseas Investment and What It Means for American Businesses," China Business Review 39, no. 3 (2012): 18–22.

interests beyond the region, while the country's capabilities lag behind.[47] China's 2013 defense white paper, noting that "security risks to China's overseas interests are on the increase," included for the first time a section on protecting overseas interests.[48]

In sum, abundant human, physical, and economic resources, coupled with policies that have improved their application to national performance, allowed China to expand its ambitions to regional power projection but have not reached the level necessary for regional hegemony or development of a globally relevant military. The next section will show that while an internal security or external defense strategy was also theoretically possible at this level of national power, changes in national interests and threat perceptions accompanying China's rise demanded a regional power-projection strategy at a minimum. However, any significant deterioration in this national power base could pull China back to a strategy of external defense, though current trends suggest that a push toward a more ambitious regional power-projection strategy or even a global military strategy is more likely given that the Chinese economy will continue to grow.

Perceptions about Threats and Sources of Power

National power not only enables a country's military to operate farther and farther from its own territory but also creates new vulnerabilities that China's military then in turn needs to address. Some, like the regional competition with the United States and reliance on imported national resources, push China to develop at a minimum a regional power-projection capability. Others, like maintaining domestic stability, are a necessary condition for a regional power-projection strategy, given that heightened unrest could encourage retrenchment. While the validity of certain threat perceptions is debatable, it is important to recognize that many in China believe that Beijing's military strategy has been largely a reaction to growing external challenges.[49]

---

[47] Kathrin Hille, "China Commits Combat Troops to Mali," *Financial Times*, June 27, 2014, https://www.ft.com/content/e46f3e42-defe-11e2-881f-00144feab7de.

[48] Information Office of the State Council (PRC), "The Diversified Employment of China's Armed Forces."

[49] Zhang Xiaolin et al., "Haishang anquan weixie jingshi: Jiajin tuijin Zhongguo haifang jianshe" [Threats from the Sea: Accelerating the Building of China's Sea Defense], *Haiyang Daoyu yu Guofang*, no. 9 (2012): 27–29; Zhang Xiaodong, "Jinqi Zhongguo haiyang junshi zhanlüe zhi guancha yu zhangwang—Cong 2015 niandu zuixin fabu de baipishu shuoqi" [Observation and Outlook of Recent China's Sea Power Strategy—Starting from the New Version of Defense White Paper in 2015], *Pacific Journal* 23, no. 10 (2015): 65–74; and Yang Zhen and Zhou Yunheng, "Lun houlengzhan shidai de Zhongguo haiquan yu hangkong mujian" [On the Chinese Sea Power and Aircraft Carriers in the Post–Cold War Era], *Pacific Journal* 22, no. 1 (2014).

Perceived Threats to Sovereignty and National Interests

The source of threats is a key input into national military strategy. China gradually shifted the focus of its military strategy toward projecting power at sea when it realized that most threats emanating from the U.S.-led alliance, and countries such as Russia, Japan, and the Philippines, come from the sea rather than from land.[50] At the 18th Party Congress in November 2012, the CCP adopted a strategy of "building China into a sea power nation" in response to rising challenges related to access to resources, disputes over islands, and the U.S. rebalance to Asia.[51] China's main sources of concern, namely the reunification with Taiwan and the territorial disputes in the East and South China Seas, are exacerbated by pressure from both the United States, which is taking an "active intervening" position, and other regional actors such as Japan and India.[52] It is clear to PLA leaders that, in the event of a crisis, their main challenges would come from "intensive medium- and long-range precision missiles," as well as "sudden attacks from the air, space, and cyber domains initiated by enemies located on the sea."[53] Thus, the previous approach of "offshore waters defense," relying on land-based weapon systems coupled with naval assets, was a stopgap measure (*quanyi zhiji*); regional power projection is necessary to counter "strategic encirclement" and create the layered defense and deterrence necessary to "release the pressure from the near sea."[54] China will be in a "passive" or even "dangerous" position, both strategically and operationally, if it confines its naval power to the near sea.[55] Therefore, regional power projection is a minimum requirement if China is to protect its sovereignty and territorial integrity (as Beijing defines it). Going forward, the PLA Navy is expected to build the capabilities to establish

---

[50] Zhang et al., "Haishang anquan weixie jingshi: Jiajin tuijin Zhongguo haifang jianshe," 27–29.

[51] Wu Xiaoyan, "China's 'Sea Power Nation' Strategy," Institute for Security and Development Policy, Asia Paper, June 2014, http://isdp.eu/content/uploads/publications/2014-wu-chinas-sea-power-nation-strategy.pdf.

[52] Ma Jianying, "Meiguo dui Zhongguo zhoubian haiyang zhengduan de jieru—yanjiu wenxian pingshu yu sikao" [The U.S. Intervention of Chinese Territorial Disputes—Literature Review], *Journal of American Studies*, no. 2 (2014): 70–82; and "Zhongguo haiyang fazhan baogao 2015" [China's Ocean Development Report 2015], 2015, 293.

[53] *Zhanluexue*, 210.

[54] Zheng Yiwei, "Luhai fuhexing de Zhongguo fazhan haiquan de zhanlüe xuanze" [Maritime Power Strategic Options for a both Continental and Maritime Nation], *Forum of World Economics and Politics*, no. 3 (2013); Fang Xiaozhi, "Jiaqiang Zhongguo yuanyang haijun jianshe de biyaoxing yu kexingxing tanxi" [Analysis of the Necessity and Feasibility of Strengthening the Construction of an Ocean-Going Navy], *Journal of China and International Relations* 2, no. 2 (2014): 109; and *Zhanluexue*, 216–18.

[55] "Jiexi Zhongguo haijun sanda fazhan jieduan hangmu heqian dazao 'lanshui haijun'" [Decoding the Three Phases of the PLAN Development], *Renmin Wang*, August 12, 2014, http://military.people.com.cn/n/2014/0812/c1011-25447731.html; and Fang, "Jiaqiang Zhongguo yuanyang haijun jianshe de biyaoxing yu kexingxing tanxi."

command of both the sea and air in wartime, while strengthening its presence in peacetime.[56]

But before China can project power regionally, it needs to be able to counter the U.S. ability to operate freely against Chinese interests. The quick and precise devastation that the U.S. military inflicted in the Gulf War in 1991, coupled with the United States sending two carriers during the 1996 Taiwan Strait crisis, caused Beijing to focus on developing capabilities to fight "high tech wars under informatized conditions."[57] According to the *Chinese Military Encyclopedia*, the first Gulf War showed the importance of dominating the electromagnetic spectrum; aerial attacks as a strategic factor; deception, coordinated operations among different services, and deep attacks in the rapid attainment of campaign objectives; fortifications and minefields; and logistical support to sustain high-tech weapons.[58] China saw especially the value of improved information technology, as precision-guided munitions were generally more accurate and aircraft were used more efficiently. The PLA also assessed that the United States' success in the Gulf War was largely because the Iraqi battlefield was essentially transparent to the coalition forces.[59]

To be able to dissuade the United States from intervening against China in a similar fashion—for example, during a large-scale theater campaign in Taiwan or the South China Sea—China has poured its resources into developing its anti-access/area-denial (A2/AD) capabilities.[60] Anti-access strategies "aim to prevent U.S. forces from operating from fixed land bases in a theater of operations," while area-denial "aims to prevent the freedom of action of maritime forces operating in the theater."[61] This strategy, referred to as *jiji fangyu* (active defense) in Chinese, started as an external defense strategy in the 1980s, but the current focus is on ensuring adequate protection from U.S. counteroffensives and freedom of maneuver for Chinese forces to

---

[56] *NIDS China Security Report 2016: The Expanding Scope of PLA Activities and the PLA Strategy* (Tokyo: National Institute for Defense Studies, 2016), 16, http://www.nids.mod.go.jp/publication/chinareport/pdf/china_report_EN_web_2016_A01.pdf.

[57] Information Office of the State Council (PRC), *China's Military Strategy* (Beijing, 2015), http://www.mod.gov.cn/auth/2015-05/26/content_4586723_2.htm.

[58] PLA Encyclopedia Committee, *Chinese Military Encyclopedia*, vol. 7 (Beijing: Academy of Military Science Publishing House, 1997), 404.

[59] This discussion draws on Andrew Scobell, David Lai, and Roy Kamphausen, eds., *Chinese Lessons from Other Peoples' Wars* (Carlisle: Strategic Studies Institute, 2011), http://ssi.armywarcollege.edu/pdffiles/pub1090.pdf. The volume contains one specific chapter (chap. 2) on the lessons that the PLA drew from the Falklands/Malvinas conflict on anti-access/area-denial. See also Robert Farley, "What Scares China's Military: The 1991 Gulf War," *National Interest*, November 24, 2014, http://nationalinterest.org/feature/what-scares-chinas-military-the-1991-gulf-war-11724.

[60] U.S. Department of Defense, *Annual Report to Congress: Military and Security Developments Involving the People's Republic of China 2017* (Washington, D.C., 2017), https://www.defense.gov/Portals/1/Documents/pubs/2017_China_Military_Power_Report.PDF.

[61] Andrew F. Krepinevich, "Why AirSea Battle?" Center for Strategic and Budgetary Assessments, February 19, 2010, 9–10.

project power regionally. To do so, the PLA needs to be able to hold at risk strategic targets such as critical nodes and high-value assets, which are usually located in the rear of an enemy's force, creating the requirement for regional power-projection capabilities.[62]

As a result, China has invested heavily in modernized technologies capable of attacking long-range adversary forces that may deploy or operate within the air, maritime, space, electromagnetic, and information domains. China is also investing in its long-range precision-strike capabilities and building a "missile defense umbrella" that could strike U.S. bases in Japan and Guam and intercept potential missile attacks on the coast.[63] To better detect incoming missiles, China has invested in the JL-1A and JY-24 indigenous radars and the Shendiao and Yilong unmanned aerial vehicles to provide surveillance support. It has also prioritized developing fifth-generation fighter forces (J-20 and FC-31) and Russian-origin long-range surface-to-air missiles to expand its integrated air-defense system to extend to over 556 kilometers. To be able to project naval power, China is investing in cruise missiles; air-, surface-, and subsurface-launched anti-ship cruise missiles; sub-launched torpedoes; naval mines; and the CSS-5 anti-ship ballistic missiles to hold aircraft carriers at risk 1,500 kilometers off China's coast.

In addition to boosting its capabilities in traditional spheres of war, China also includes information warfare and electromagnetic capabilities as crucial components to its A2/AD strategy. Its view of information warfare includes information campaigns and "information blockades" across space and cyberspace to disrupt adversary networks in the region, such as surveillance, reconnaissance, and warning systems. Key technologies in this sphere include advanced electronic warfare systems, counter-space weapons, cyber operations, and space systems such as the Beidou navigation system.[64]

Energy Security

Outside intervention in regional issues is not the only type of threat driving Chinese decision-making. The safety of economic "lifelines"—trade and energy routes—is also a main security concern for a rising China.[65]

---

[62] *Zhanluexue*, 217–18.

[63] Long-range precision-strike capabilities include conventionally armed short-range ballistic missiles and ground- and air-launched land-attack cruise missiles. A key technology in this regard is China's DF-26 missile, an intermediate-range ballistic missile with an operational range of 3,000–4,000 kilometers, which puts U.S. bases in Japan and Guam within range. U.S. Department of Defense, *Annual Report to Congress*, 49.

[64] Information in this paragraph comes from the U.S. Department of Defense, *Annual Report to Congress*, 49–53.

[65] *Zhanluexue*, 209.

The country became the top energy consumer in the world in 2011. It is ranked first in coal consumption and second in oil consumption and is also the largest importer of petroleum.[66] Beijing feels the acute need to develop military capabilities to protect its supply lines in the Indian Ocean and South China Sea, in particular by ensuring that no country can blockade its access, especially in the Malacca Strait.[67] In addition to developing power-projection capabilities, China has pursued diversification strategies, such as establishing land pipelines, to reduce its dependence on sea lines of communication that are easily within reach of the U.S. military.[68] In the future, China may also prioritize acquiring more ports and bases that can support the PLA Navy's forward power projection, thereby enhancing the Chinese military's role in the Indian Ocean region.[69]

Internal Instability

Last, the greatest potential threat to the CCP is domestic unrest, and therefore internal stability is a necessary condition for a regional power-projection strategy. If unrest were to become unmanageable, the PLA would need to shift its mission set to spend more time, money, and effort at home. Moreover, the use of the military for internal stability often weakens its warfighting capabilities because the equipment and training appropriate for one type of use are rarely ideal for the other.[70] To date China has been able to avoid these trade-offs by implementing a series of reforms to develop non-PLA security forces to ensure domestic stability and protect the PLA's domestic reputation. Known as the People's Armed Police (PAP), domestic security organs are trained in controlling riots, predicting incidents of social instability, providing natural disaster relief, securing the premises for large-scale events, and de-escalating potentially unstable situations, ideally without resorting to violence. The PLA is therefore only called on in these scenarios as a last resort, which has allowed it to modernize its forces

---

[66] China imports 60% of its oil. The majority of this comes from the Middle East, 80% of which passes through the Strait of Malacca. "China," U.S. Energy Information Administration, https://www.eia.gov/beta/international/country.cfm?iso=CHN.

[67] Shi Chunlin and Shi Kaice, "Maliujia haixia anquan wenti yu Zhongguo zhanlüe duice" [The Security of the Malacca Strait and China's Strategic Options], *Xindongfang*, no. 2 (2014): 6–11.

[68] "'Maliujia kunju,' qishi shi yige weimingti?" ["Malacca Dilemma," a Pseudo-Proposition?], Sina, January 14, 2017, http://finance.sina.com.cn/roll/2017-01-14/doc-ifxzqnva3525655.shtml. For a map of the transit routes, see U.S. Department of Defense, *Annual Report to Congress*, 44.

[69] Anthony H. Cordesman and Abdullah Toukan, *The Indian Ocean Region: A Strategic Net Assessment* (Washington, D.C.: CSIS, 2014), 326.

[70] Stanislav Andreski, "On the Peaceful Disposition of Military Dictatorships," *Journal of Strategic Studies* 3, no. 3 (1980): 3–10.

to concentrate on external missions.[71] To a great degree, China's immense economic resources make this dual structure possible. But if internal instability were to reach a critical level, or Chinese economic growth drop significantly, the CCP would need to prioritize internal stability, which would discourage an active regional military strategy.[72]

The Influence of Ideational Factors

The degree to which ideational factors truly influence decision-making, and when they are merely rhetorical devices designed to mask more realpolitik motivations, was a central topic of the 2016–17 *Strategic Asia* volume. This section evaluates how ideational factors shape China's choice of military strategy. Specifically, I argue that ideational factors create the urgency for the rejuvenation of the Chinese nation to return to a balance of power in which foreign powers cannot interfere in its domestic affairs. At the same time, such factors impose caution on any ambitions to reach further for regional hegemony or a globally relevant role for the military.

National Humiliation and the Emphasis on Protecting Sovereignty against "Foreign Aggression"

For most of its history, China was the predominant political, economic, cultural, and military power of East Asia. But for roughly one hundred years following the First Opium War (1839–42) through World War II, Chinese history was characterized by defeat, subjugation, and humiliation at the hands of the West and Japan. Today, the narrative of this "century of humiliation" has become the basis for the CCP's claim to legitimacy as the only Chinese political party that was able to stand up to foreign intervention and aggression.[73] This narrative of the party returning China to its rightful place of regional preeminence appeals to the public's sense of Chinese exceptionalism and civilizational pride.[74]

---

[71] Tanner, "How China Manages Internal Security Challenges," 40–58.

[72] China spends slightly more on domestic security than external defense. See Ben Blanchard and John Ruwitch, "China Hikes Defense Budget, to Spend More on Internal Security," Reuters, March 4, 2013.

[73] Alison A. Kaufman, "The 'Century of Humiliation' and China's National Narratives," testimony before the U.S.-China Economic and Security Review Commission, March 10, 2011, 3, https://www.uscc.gov/sites/default/files/3.10.11Kaufman.pdf.

[74] See, for example, Jin Minqing, "Zhongguo Gongchandang shi Zhonghua minzu weida fuxing de zhongliudizhu" [The Communist Party of China Is the Cornerstone of the Rejuvenation of the Chinese People], *Guangming Daily*, July 6, 2016, http://epaper.gmw.cn/gmrb/html/2016-07/06/nw.D110000gmrb_20160706_1-06.htm; and Li Wenhai, "Shixian Zhonghua minzu weida fuxing de genben baozheng" [Implementing the Fundamental Guarantee of the Great Rejuvenation of the Chinese People], *People's Daily*, 2001, http://www.people.com.cn/BIG5/paper85/4118/482479.html.

The narrative of national humiliation influences Chinese military strategy in two ways. First, inherent in the call for the rejuvenation of China is the desire to rectify losses in territory, control, and international standing and dignity.[75] The first step along these lines was for China to consolidate its borders. Mao thus prioritized ground operations to regain Chinese control over Tibet and Xinjiang. The remaining territories—Taiwan and disputed islands in the East and South China Seas—require the projection of naval power. Moreover, if China hopes to keep its internal affairs free from outside influence, it needs to develop military capabilities to deter foreign countries from intervening, with the most likely culprit being the United States. Hence, as discussed in the earlier section on threats to Chinese interests, the PLA has worked to develop its A2/AD capabilities. Without the ability to secure a maritime buffer zone, China will always be vulnerable to Western aggression. Since China has a long maritime boundary, becoming a sea power is an important and necessary step to achieving the status of a regional and even global power.[76]

Second, the view that China is the rightful leader of East Asia is rooted deeply in this narrative. Even at points when the country was too weak to engage in regional power projection, China tried to be the leader in other ways outside the scope of military strategy. Mao, for example, competed with Khrushchev as the leader of the "correct" form of socialism and portrayed himself as the leader of the developing world. Later, Chinese leaders promoted multipolarity as a way to dilute U.S. influence.[77] This cultural and historical drive to be a leading regional power makes a military strategy focused on internal security or external defense less desirable.

Chinese Exceptionalism and Aversion to Hegemony

Because of its humiliation at the hands of "hegemonic" powers, China needs to believe that it would be a different type of great power from those that came before it. Specifically, China expounds on how it would respect the sovereignty of other countries (hence, the noninterference policy) and not rely on force to accomplish its goals. This last point is likely related to China's cult of defense—the belief that China is an inherently peaceful country that

---

[75] Kaufman, "The 'Century of Humiliation' and China's National Narratives," 4.

[76] For discussions along these themes, see Zhang et al., "Haishang anquan weixie jingshi: Jiajin tuijin Zhongguo haifang jianshe"; Yang and Zhou, "Lun houlengzhan shidai de Zhongguo haiquan yu hangkong mujian"; and Zhang, "Jinqi Zhongguo haiyang junshi zhanlüe zhi guancha yu zhangwang—Cong 2015 niandu zuixin fabu de baipishu shuoqi."

[77] C. Fred Bergsten, Nicholas R. Lardy, Derek J. Mitchell, and Bates Gill, "China and the Developing World," in *China: The Balance Sheet—What the World Needs to Know Now about the Emerging Superpower* (New York: PublicAffairs, 2006).

only uses force to protect itself.[78] Western nations, on the other hand, are "fundamentally rapacious, greedy, and aggressive" that "pillage to expand their territories [and] plunder wealth [to] expand their sphere of influence."[79] China claims to be in a unique position to understand the priorities and needs of developing countries and to create a new international order that does not infringe on countries' ability to govern domestically as they see fit.[80]

The CCP has consequently been ideologically averse to alliances and overseas bases that tend to accompany a more global military strategy.[81] Some Chinese international relations scholars have recently shown greater flexibility by promoting quasi-alliances, issue-specific coalitions, or strategic partnerships that can help China protect its expanding global interests without sacrificing self-reliance.[82] Some have publicly argued that China needs to form alliances to protect itself in a confrontation with the United States, with Russia being a top contender.[83] The aversion to traditional alliances may not prevent China from gaining overseas access, though questions about how this may be done were dismissed by a Chinese defense ministry spokesperson as "thinking too much ahead."[84]

Without a change in ideas about alliances and overseas bases, China will be unable to directly challenge and push the United States out of the

---

[78] Information Office of the State Council (PRC), "Zhongguo de heping fazhan" [China's Peaceful Development], September 6, 2011, http://www.gov.cn/jrzg/2011-09/06/content_1941204.html; and "Xi Jinping shouti 'siguan' chanshi Zhongguo heping fazhan jiyin" [Xi Jinping's First Mention of "Four Views" Explaining China's Genes of Peaceful Development], Xinhua, May 16, 2014, http://news.xinhuanet.com/politics/2014-05/16/c_1110731703.htm.

[79] Peng Guangqian and Yao Youzhi, eds., *The Science of Military Strategy* (Beijing: Military Science Press, 2005), 426.

[80] Yang Jiemian, "Buduan puxie Zhongguo tese daguo waijiao xin pianzhang" [Constantly Revising the New Chapter of China's Unique Superpower Diplomacy], *People's Daily*, April 14, 2016, http://opinion.people.com.cn/n1/2016/0414/c1003-28274335.html. Xi reassures developing countries of China's righteous intention for its assertiveness and promises a positive-sum game to everyone who is willing to follow China's lead. "Wei goujian yatai huoban guanxi zhuru xin dongli" [Adding Momentum to Building Partnership in the Asia-Pacific], *People's Daily*, November 25, 2016, http://paper.people.com.cn/rmrb/html/2016-11/25/nw.D110000renmrb_20161125_1-03.htm.

[81] Huang Yingxu, "Weilai Zhongguo xuyao shenme yang de junshi liliang?" [What Kind of Military Power Does China Need in the Future?] *Xuexi Shibao*, April 29, 2009, http://theory.people.com.cn/GB/136458/9216420.html.

[82] Liu Ronan and Liu Feng, "Contending Ideas on China's Non-alliance Strategy," *Chinese Journal of International Relations*, no. 2 (2017): 151–71.

[83] Yin Junlang, "Zhongguo nianlin guojia anquan kunjing, shi shihou dijie guojia anquan tongmeng le!" [Facing National Security Challenges, China Should Form Security Alliances!], September 2016, http://military.china.com/important/11132797/20160902/23454650_all.html; Fu Ying, "Are China and Russia Partnering to Create an Axis?" *Contemporary International Relations*, no. 4 (2016): 1–10; and Xie Chao, "Will China Form Alliances? Russian Interests and Prospects of a Sino-Russian Alliance," *Journal of Contemporary Asia-Pacific Studies*, no. 4 (2016).

[84] "Zhongguo yao xiang Meiguo yiyang jian haiwai junshi jidi? Guofangbu sizi huiying" [Is China Building Overseas Military Base Like the U.S.? Ministry of National Defense Responds with Four Characters], *Fenghuang Wang*, May 1, 2017, http://phtv.ifeng.com/a/20170501/44581095_0.shtml. For more on overseas access, see U.S. Department of Defense, *Annual Report to Congress*, 5.

Asia-Pacific, nor will its military be able to play a significant global role. But Beijing's ideology could potentially be reshaped to fit pragmatic realities if required. Christopher Ford notes in last year's *Strategic Asia* volume on strategic culture that while it is important for China to view itself as a peace-loving nation, this idea masks a reality in which the CCP has a strong propensity to use force both domestically and internationally to protect elite or national interests.[85] Along these lines, China could pursue formal treaties to institutionalize arrangements to use facilities for military purposes in other countries. To maintain the appearance of consistency, Beijing would retain its rhetoric against alliances and put forth strategic guidance that describes these arrangements as win-win agreements between equal partners seeking to enhance stability and security in the region. In short, while it is possible that ideas will evolve to buttress a more aggressive regional hegemony or global military strategy in the future, for now ideational factors continue to render regional power projection the preferred course of action.

Conclusion: Power, Ideas, and the Future Trajectory of China's Military Strategy

The Trajectory of Chinese Military Strategy

China's view of itself and its role in the world has changed significantly since its founding in 1949. In the Maoist era, the CCP was largely internally focused; Mao endeavored to transform Chinese society and erect institutions that would sustain the process of revolution.[86] Moreover, the CCP needed to transition from a guerrilla force to a governing party and develop a military strategy to end the civil war by defeating the nationalists in Taiwan. After Mao, Deng Xiaoping rose to power in 1977 and embraced greater integration into the global economic system, though still mainly to advance internal aims. After Deng's tenure, with Jiang Zemin at the helm, China more fully embraced global integration, joining most major international institutions in the 1990s.[87] Under Hu Jintao, the era of Chinese assertiveness in the region began, especially with respect to territorial disputes. Moreover, Hu introduced overseas operations into an expanding set of new historical

---

[85] Christopher A. Ford, "Realpolitik with Chinese Characteristics: Chinese Strategic Culture and the Modern Communist Party-State," in Tellis, Szalwinski, and Wills, *Strategic Asia 2016–17*, 29–60.

[86] Henry Kissinger, *On China* (New York: Penguin Books, 2012), 94–95.

[87] Elizabeth C. Economy and Michel Oksenberg, eds., *China Joins the World: Progress and Prospects* (Washington, D.C.: Council on Foreign Relations Press, 1999).

missions for the PLA.[88] Xi Jinping, in contrast to his predecessors, has pushed the boundaries on challenging the United States regionally, expanded the contours of "the region" beyond East Asia, and embraced a greater global role for China.

For most of the PRC's history, its national narrative corresponded well with the strategic options available, given its level of national power and the degree and nature of internal and external threats. The drives to build national power and reclaim a position as a regional leader resistant to external pressure were mutually enforcing; a regional power-projection strategy was the ideal military strategy given Chinese strategic culture and threat perceptions from the onset, but China's level of national power only made it possible in this decade.

Disruption of this trajectory is possible if the values of the critical inputs—national power, ideas, and threat perceptions—change drastically. First, there is a possibility of reversion to an external defense and continental power strategy if significant threats to China's borders arise (e.g., from Russia, India, or Vietnam) or the economy weakens to the point that the CCP has to divert resources from power projection to these missions. Second, if there is significant domestic instability, then China may return to an internal stability strategy with limited aspects of external defense and regional power projection.

But given the trajectory of Chinese national power, it is more likely that China will either consolidate its position as a regional player through regional power projection or move beyond this strategy to secure regional hegemony or a global role for its military. Going forward, ideas may get ahead of power. Chinese leaders may decide that regional hegemony is necessary to truly protect the country's sovereignty, address its historical memory of humiliation, regain its rightful position as a leader in Asia, and ensure regime legitimacy in the eyes of its people. But to secure regional hegemony, China would have to convince Japan, South Korea, the Philippines, and Australia to break their defense ties with Washington. It is difficult to imagine China succeeding in this effort, especially if its hands are tied in terms of influencing the domestic politics, public opinion, and elections in those countries. Additionally, the Chinese military would need to improve to the point of being able to succeed in a direct major and protracted war with the United States and its allies. But if concerns about U.S. intentions toward China's rise intensify and the leadership comes to believe that the United States is highly likely to launch a preventive war or help groups seek independence from

---

[88] Dean Cheng, "How China Views the South China Sea: As Sovereign Territory," Heritage Foundation, November 5, 2015, http://www.heritage.org/asia/commentary/how-china-views-the-south-china-sea-sovereign-territory.

Beijing, or if other countries gain territory at China's expense, then pushing the United States out of the region may become the top priority regardless of the degree of difficulty.[89]

A shift to a global military strategy is also unlikely in the near term. China will continue to rely primarily on political and economic power to protect its global interests. In 2017, Xi gave a number of speeches that suggest a more global outlook, including his remarks at Davos as well as the articulation of the "two guidelines," which are "to guide the international community to shape a more equitable and reasonable new global order" and "to uphold international security." These ideas signal China's potential willingness to undertake "responsibility" in a new, more proactive role that benefits the international system as a whole.[90] In the latest state of the nation speech given by Prime Minister Li Keqiang, the terms *quanqiu* (global) and *quanqiuhua* (globalization) were used thirteen times, compared with five times last year.[91] The military will also likely play a greater role in China's global strategy largely due to threat perceptions—military modernization is increasingly falling behind the expansion of Chinese interests overseas.[92] After 2013, when the Belt and Road Initiative began to pick up momentum, China realized that its military capabilities were largely insufficient for securing the "crucial strategic energy and resource" regions, such as the Middle East and Africa.[93] The PLA Navy, in particular, has been pushing for a blue water navy, one capable of protecting Chinese interests around the globe.[94]

While China's current strategy has global aspects, its approach will fall short of shifting to a global military strategy for several reasons. First, China

---

[89] For more on Chinese perceptions about China's rise and U.S. preventive war, see Oriana Skylar Mastro, "The Vulnerability of Rising Powers: The Logic Behind China's Low Military Transparency," *Asian Security* 12, no. 2 (2016): 63–81.

[90] "Xi Jinping shou ti 'liang ge yindao' you shenyi" [Deep Meanings of Xi Jinping's Initial Remark on the "Two Guidelines"], *Xuexi Zhongguo*, February 21, 2017, http://www.ccln.gov.cn/hotnews/230779. shtml; and Xi Jinping, "Xi Jinping: Zai jinian Liu Huaqing tongzhi danchen 100 zhounian zuotanhui shang de jianghua" [Xi Jinping's Speech at a Meeting Commemorating the 100th anniversary of the Birth of Liu Huaqing], Xinhua, September 28, 2016, http://news.xinhuanet.com/politics/2016- 09/28/c_1119642521.htm.

[91] "Is China Challenging the United States for Global Leadership?" *Economist*, April 1, 2017.

[92] Yin Zhuo, "Wo haijun zuozhan liliang zengqiang yu haiyang iyi xuqiu rengyou chaju" [The PLA Navy's Operational Capabilities Are Falling Behind the Needs to Secure Maritime Interests], CNR, March 3, 2017, http://military.cnr.cn/ycdj/20170303/t20170303_523632795_1.html.

[93] See ibid.

[94] "Zhuanfang haijun silingyuan Wu Shengli—Renmin haijun yu gongheguo gong chengzhang: Fangyan shjie, suixing duoyanghua junshi nengli buduan tisheng" [An Interview on Admiral Wu Shengli—The PLAN to Share Growth and Development with the People's Republic: To Have the Whole World in View and to Contentiously to Improve the Capabilities to Respond to Diversified Military Missions], April 15, 2009, Xinhua, http://news.xinhuanet.com/mil/2009-04/15/content_11185909_5. htm; and "Yin Zhuo Shaojiang: Fazhan haiyang qiangguo xuyao xiangpipei zhifa liliang" [Major General Yinzhuo: A Maritime Power Requires Matching Law Enforcement Capabilities], Xinhua, March 11, 2013, http://news.xinhuanet.com/mil/2013-03/11/c_124444091.htm.

does not have the national power to truly develop a globally relevant military at this stage. Moreover, the national narrative would have to shift to support such operations. Some scholars are already arguing to abandon the current commitment to nonalignment, but they are still a minority.[95] Finally, Beijing would have to come to believe that its greatest challenges lie beyond East Asia—an unlikely scenario with the Taiwan and South and East China Sea disputes outstanding.[96] Given that the power gap between China and the United States is great regionally, and even greater globally, it may be foolhardy at this stage for China to try to compete on the global stage militarily.[97]

The most likely next step for China is to maintain a strategy of regional power projection but expand the contours of the region to focus more on the Indian Ocean and Central Asia, in addition to the current priorities of East Asia (out to the second island chain).[98] Aspects of Chinese policy, such as the Belt and Road Initiative and the establishment of a logistics base in Djibouti, already hint at this eventuality. China's western expansion to create a "community of common destiny" increases its global reach and influence while officially maintaining its aversion to hegemony. Moreover, the Belt and Road Initiative in particular is a low-risk strategy; it is less likely to provoke a strong U.S. government response than expansion into areas of more strategic importance to Washington.[99] Additionally, China is likely to see opportunities to establish logistical bases for its military, and some "co-located" with the commercial ports, which closely aligns with China's future logistical needs.[100] The availability of national resources will determine the extent and pace of China's expansion of the contours of its "regional" power projection; threat perceptions and ideas already essentially support this trajectory.

---

[95] Yan Xuetong, "From Keeping a Low Profile to Striving for Achievement," *Chinese Journal of International Politics* 7, no. 2 (2014): 153–84; and Jin Xu and Zheyuan Du, "The Dominant Thinking Sets in Chinese Foreign Policy Research: A Criticism," *Chinese Journal of International Politics* 8, no. 3 (2015): 251–79.

[96] For more on what the Chinese military would have to do to establish a global expeditionary force, see Mastro, "A Global Expeditionary People's Liberation Army."

[97] Gao Qing, ed., "Zhongguo chuan qiangguo waiyi shijie guanzhu 'dakuaitou' zenme zou" [China Dons a Superpower Robe, the World Watches the "Big Player's" Moves], *Cankao Xiaoxi*, January 12, 2015, http://china.chinadaily.com.cn/2015-01/12/content_19300029.htm.

[98] "Xi Jinping: Rang mingyun gongtongti yishi zai zhoubian guojia luodi shenggen"[Xi Jinping: Let the Idea of Community with Shared Destiny Be Rooted in Neighboring Countries], Xinhua, October 25, 2013, http://news.xinhuanet.com/politics/2013-10/25/c_117878944.htm. One scholarly article posits that the greater periphery extends to Central Asia, the Middle East, the South Pacific, and even Europe. See Wu Zhicheng and Li Jintong, "Jian xing quyu hezuo gongying yu quanqiu xieshang gong zhi de Zhongguo fangan" [China's Strategy for Implementing Regional Win-Win Cooperation and Compromise on Global Governance], *Contemporary World*, no. 5 (2015): 18–22.

[99] Nien-chung Chang Liao, "China's New Foreign Policy under Xi Jinping," *Asian Security* 12, no. 2 (2016): 82–91; and Xi Jinping, "Mai xiang mingyun gongtongti kaichuang yazhou xin weilai" [Moving Toward a Community of Shared Destiny, Creating a New Asian Future], March 28, 2015, http://politics.people.com.cn/n/2015/0329/c1024-26765442.html.

[100] U.S. Department of Defense, *Annual Report to Congress*, 5.

In sum, a significant change in threat perceptions, national power, and ideas would precede any transition to a regional hegemony or global military strategy. While external factors will largely determine whether China pushes beyond its current strategy, internal factors could force a regression. If the country becomes economically or domestically unstable, constraining the resources at the party's disposal to promote its national military strategy, China is likely to revert to an internal stability or external defense strategy. The China dream will then have to become a dream deferred until a more auspicious time.

Implications for the United States

The fact that national power, ideas, and threat perceptions drive Chinese national military strategy and currently coalesce to support a regional power-projection strategy creates a number of implications for the United States. First, China's march toward regional power projection is unlikely to decelerate, and Washington has to ensure that its presence and posture in Asia keep apace even if it means an increase in the frequency and size of U.S. operations from historical levels.

Second, as China's strategic vision now extends to South Asia and Central Asia, the United States needs to reassess its interests in those regions and the best way to protect them in the face of heightened Chinese influence. The answer may be a greater U.S. military role to encourage peaceful and stable Chinese policies or enhanced cooperation with the Chinese military to achieve shared objectives.[101] The United States should increase security cooperation with India—for example, through combined exercises, especially in mountain warfare and antisubmarine warfare, or greater sharing of military intelligence and maritime domain awareness in the Indian Ocean.[102]

Third, U.S. planners and strategists need to monitor Chinese national power, threat perceptions, and national narratives to be able to best predict if a change in national military strategy is on the horizon. In terms of capabilities, if global power projection were to become the primary objective, specific changes to China's current posture would precede this change. China would strengthen and expand its investment beyond current levels in airlift,

---

[101] For a useful typology of when greater Chinese involvement may be beneficial to the United States, see Kristen Gunness and Oriana Skylar Mastro, "A Global People's Liberation Army: Possibilities, Challenges, and Opportunities," *Asia Policy*, no. 22 (2016): 131–55.

[102] Promoting the military capabilities and influence of regional partners such as India may serve to advance U.S. interests regarding China, even if those partners do not consistently align with U.S. policy preferences. See Ashley J. Tellis and C. Raja Mohan, *The Strategic Rationale for Deeper U.S.-Indian Economic Ties: American and Indian Perspectives* (Washington, D.C.: Carnegie Endowment for International Peace, 2015).

sealift, C4ISR, and logistics; build more large transport aircraft and tankers, amphibious combat ships, hospital ships, and landing dock platforms; and acquire a robust, space-based ocean surveillance system.[103] On the other hand, if China restricts its strategic objectives to border protection or internal security, the ground force may once again receive budgetary priority over its more expensive brother services. Moreover, less time would be spent on "realistic" power-projection exercises and more on political indoctrination to ensure PLA loyalty and defensive operations.

Identifying shifts in the nature of China's internal debate is as important as monitoring capabilities. The process of creating norms begins with official statements or publications that posit an idea that diverges from the dominant view at the time in order to gauge international and domestic reactions. Then, intellectuals and scholars are given more freedom to debate (within limits) aspects of these ideas, and through this process new viewpoints are normalized and become less controversial. In the case of overseas bases, this process has already begun to set the stage for an announcement of more PLA "access points" beyond Djibouti in the near future. Thus, continued attention to the content of authoritative Chinese sources, as well as the exercises, activities, training, and procurement of the PLA, should be the priority of the U.S. defense community.

---

[103] For more on prerequisites for a global expeditionary force, see Mastro, "A Global Expeditionary People's Liberation Army."

EXECUTIVE SUMMARY

This chapter discusses Russia's military strategy under Vladimir Putin, its connection to Russian material capabilities and strategic culture, and Putin's reasons for prioritizing the U.S. and the West as the greatest external threat that Moscow faces.

MAIN ARGUMENT

Putin's focus on the U.S. and the West as the principal external threat that Russia faces results from several factors. Although Sunni jihadists and China's rise pose other challenges for Russia, neither is perceived as presenting a threat to Putin's authoritarian rule in the way that the West does. He has built up Russia's nuclear and conventional forces in order to both limit the U.S. ability to act unilaterally and increase Russia's ability to do so. Yet despite this buildup, Putin has not sought to directly engage the U.S. and NATO in conflict. However, the hybrid warfare capacity he has developed (including techniques for interfering in elections) appears designed to weaken the U.S. and the West by means short of war. Putin may well remain in power for many years and seems unlikely to change his mind about seeing the U.S. and the West as Russia's primary threat.

POLICY IMPLICATIONS

- Putin's buildup of a formidable array of military tools as well as the capacity to weaken other states through cyber and other nonconventional means has created difficulties for the West in responding to the challenges that Moscow poses.

- Putin is unlikely to both make geopolitical gains for Russia at the West's expense and persuade the West to accept his actions and go back to doing business as usual with Russia.

- As long as Putin pursues a strategy that primarily targets the U.S. and the West, Washington will have to expend resources toward Russia that could have been used to counter other threats.

Putin and Russia's Strategic Priorities

Mark N. Katz

Over the course of the nineteenth and twentieth centuries, Tsarist and Soviet Russia often had hostile relations, and sometimes open hostilities, with the West, the Muslim world, and China as well as other Asian states. Throughout this period, though, Russia usually saw the West as a greater threat than these other two. This was because economically and technologically more advanced Western states usually posed a greater military challenge than Russia faced either from the Muslim world or from Asia. Indeed, Russia saw the West threatening it even from the Muslim world and Asia due to the strong position that first the British Empire and later the post–World War II United States acquired in these regions. The situation now is very different. Although Sino-Soviet relations became quite hostile during the Cold War era, the Soviet Union was economically stronger than China during that period. Now China is much stronger than Russia economically, and its military might has also grown impressively. In addition, even though states in the Muslim world suffer from many problems, they are much stronger now than in the past. The Muslim world is also home to powerful jihadist movements such as al Qaeda and the Islamic State of Iraq and Syria (ISIS) that threaten Russia as well as the West. By contrast, the United States appears much weaker as a result of its largely fruitless "war on terrorism" and growing internal divisions, and the Western alliance is in disarray.

Yet despite the diminished standing of the United States and the West, Russia still sees them as its greatest adversary. This is because

Mark N. Katz is a Professor of Government and Politics in the Schar School of Policy and Government at George Mason University. He can be reached at <mkatz@gmu.edu>.

The author would like to express his thanks to Elinor Hayes, an undergraduate at George Mason University, for her research assistance on this project.

President Vladimir Putin views the principal security challenge confronting Russia as the possibility of internal opposition growing strong enough to overthrow his regime through a democratic revolution—similar to what occurred in Eastern Europe and the Soviet Union at the end of the Cold War, in certain former Soviet republics via "color revolutions," and in the Middle East during the Arab Spring. The Kremlin prioritizes external challenges on the basis of how much it sees them (correctly or not) as supporting (or even creating) an internal threat to Putin. First and foremost among these challenges are the United States and the West more broadly, which Putin has repeatedly accused of seeking to promote a color revolution inside Russia. Putin sees the expansion of not just NATO but also the European Union as aimed at limiting or even reducing Russian influence in any country that either organization expands to include. Moscow has even described NATO expansion as posing a military threat to Russia.[1] Further, Putin sees U.S. and Western support for democratization—especially via democratic revolutions—as being U.S.-orchestrated efforts to install pro-Western governments. Putin and top Russian officials have even accused Washington of seeking to promote just such a revolution in Russia itself.[2]

The rise of jihadist sentiment (which is anti-Russian as well as anti-Western) among Sunni Muslims is of concern to Moscow not just because of the negative impact on Russia's own large (and predominantly Sunni) Muslim population but also because of the impact on Russian interests in the Middle East and the Muslim world more broadly. What Moscow especially fears is that anti-Russian jihadist forces (and certain governments that Moscow believes support them) outside Russia will come to the aid of anti-Russian Islamist groups inside the country, just as outside groups supported the Chechen rebels in the 1990s and early 2000s. In his initial justification for Russian intervention in Syria in 2015, Putin argued that it was preferable to fight Islamist militants from the former Soviet Union "there" (Syria) rather than "here" (Russia).[3]

With its much larger population, stronger economy, and rapidly modernizing armed forces, China could be seen as a classic geopolitical threat to Russia. At present, though, Russia and China have close, cooperative

---

[1] David Filipov, "Putin Says Russia Planning 'Countermeasures' to NATO Expansion," *Washington Post*, November 21, 2016, https://www.washingtonpost.com/world/putin-says-russia-planning-countermeasuresto-nato-expansion/2016/11/21/83f5673c-afe1-11e6-ab37-1b3940a0d30a_story.html.

[2] Evan Osnos, David Remnick, and Joshua Yaffa, "Trump, Putin, and the New Cold War," *New Yorker*, March 6, 2017, http://www.newyorker.com/magazine/2017/03/06/trump-putin-and-the-new-cold-war.

[3] Vladimir Putin, "Interview to American TV Channel CBS and PBS," President of Russia website, September 29, 2015, http://en.kremlin.ru/events/president/news/50380.

relations, including in the military realm. Divergent economic trends over the last three decades that have made China stronger than Russia, though, are likely to continue. But because the Putin regime considers the United States and the West to be an existential threat, "a close relationship with China—even as a junior partner—is the only sensible choice" for Moscow.[4] Despite this, there are some indications that Moscow is engaging in a certain amount of hedging behavior against Beijing.

Several factors contribute to Moscow's difficulty in responding to these challenges. One is Russia's inability to develop its economy beyond the petroleum sector, resulting in a high dependence on petroleum exports as the country's main revenue source. Obstacles to developing the non-petroleum sectors of Russia's economy are Putin's strong dependence on a security service elite whose interests would be threatened by a real crackdown on corruption and by his (and their) unwillingness to establish an attractive legal and economic climate that would lead to the increased foreign and domestic investment needed to transform the Russian economy. As a result of its ongoing dependence on petroleum exports, Russia has been particularly hard hit by the prolonged low oil price environment. Yet another factor is the aging and overall decline of the Russian population, which affects the size of the armed forces that Russia can maintain.

National power is based on a country's natural and human resources as well as its economic, technical, and administrative capacities. These material components of national power, especially in comparison to other countries, broadly determine the range of military strategies that a nation can pursue. A nation's strategic culture is an important factor in determining why one particular strategy is pursued while other possibilities are not. The two are related: strategic culture seeks to compensate for a nation's weaknesses through adopting a strategy that relies on its strengths. A nation's strategic culture, though, also reflects its historical experience of past threats and how best to overcome them. Isabelle Facon observed in *Strategic Asia 2016–17* that Russian strategic culture "is deeply rooted in the geographic and spiritual parameters of Russia's historical path."[5] Such concerns may in fact lead to a military strategy that focuses on some states in particular as enemies and not others.

This chapter begins with a discussion of why Moscow prioritizes the actual and potential threats it faces in the way that it now does. The next

---

[4] Eugene B. Rumer, "Russia's China Policy: This Bear Hug Is Real," in "Russia-China Relations: Assessing Common Ground and Strategic Fault Lines," National Bureau of Asian Research (NBR), Special Report, no. 66, July 2017, 21.

[5] Isabelle Facon, "Russian Strategic Culture in the 21st Century: Redefining the West-East Balance," in *Strategic Asia 2016–17: Understanding Strategic Cultures in the Asia-Pacific*, ed. Ashley J. Tellis, Alison Szalwinski, and Michael Wills (Seattle: NBR, 2016), 71.

section focuses on explaining why Putin has identified the United States as the leading threat to Russia, how he sees it as linked to the possibility of an internal color revolution challenging his rule, and what specific means he has adopted to thwart both given the interaction of Russian material capabilities and strategic culture. This is followed by an assessment of the durability of Putin's anti-U.S. strategy as well as a discussion of the circumstances that might lead him or a subsequent Russian leader to alter it. The chapter concludes with an exploration of different policy options that the United States might consider in responding to the challenge posed by Putin.

A Survey of the Range of Plausible Military Strategies Available to Russia

Russia could define as well as respond to the different internal and external challenges that it sees in several plausible ways. The first step in doing so is assessing what the potential threats are, how severe each threat is, and how much Moscow should focus on countering them. If, for example, Moscow regarded Sunni jihadists or China as most threatening, then seeking rapprochement with the West to facilitate cooperation against these common threats would be the logical response. Reforming Russia both economically and politically would also make sense in order to obtain Western assistance for ameliorating the country's internal challenges, particularly its lack of economic development, and hence strengthening its ability to deal with more serious external challenges.

Indeed, many in the West believe that this would be the most logical strategic choice for Russia to make. According to this view, the United States and the West are not only less threatening to Russia than Sunni jihadists or China; they are not a threat at all. Despite the expansion of NATO, the Western alliance does not have any plan to attack Russia.[6] Russian statements, however, indicate that Moscow does regard the United States and the West, particularly NATO, as a threat.[7] Further, since Putin regards Western support for democratization—and perhaps even Western democracy itself—as a threat to his own authoritarian rule, it is clear that he also regards the United States and the West as a threat.

---

[6] See, for example, Adam Twardowski, "Why NATO Isn't a Threat to Russia," *National Interest*, Skeptics, web log, September 22, 2016, http://nationalinterest.org/blog/the-skeptics/why-nato-isnt-threat-russia-17797.

[7] See, for example, Olga Oliker, "Unpacking Russia's New National Security Strategy," Center for Strategic and International Studies (CSIS), Commentary, January 7, 2016, https://www.csis.org/analysis/unpacking-russias-new-national-security-strategy.

Yet even if the United States and the West do pose a threat to Russia, simple prudence would suggest that Moscow ought to regard China—with its large population, growing economy, and modernizing military right on Russia's border (which China has contested in the past)—as at least a potential threat to be guarded against through beefed-up military deployments and alliances with other states fearing China. But Putin has not taken such steps, as was evident by his unwillingness to cooperate meaningfully with Japanese prime minister Shinzo Abe's efforts to improve Russo-Japanese relations in 2016.[8]

Moscow has arguably done more to counter threats emanating from the Sunni Muslim world. Russia has cooperated with others also fearing threats from it, including Shia Iran, Israel, secular Arab regimes (particularly Syria, Egypt, and Algeria), conservative Arab monarchies, Turkey (where the Erdogan government is at least somewhat Islamist), and even the United States. Yet despite Russian calls for cooperation with the West against the common jihadist enemy in Syria, numerous reports indicate that Moscow has not done much to defeat such groups there.[9] Indeed, there have even been reports that at the time of the Sochi Olympics in early 2014, Moscow facilitated the migration of Russia's homegrown jihadists from the North Caucasus to Syria.[10] In early 2017, U.S. officials accused Moscow of cooperating with the Taliban who are fighting against U.S. forces and allies in Afghanistan.[11] What this suggests is that Putin regards Sunni jihadists as a threat inside Russia, but he does not regard those groups active outside Russia as a greater threat than the United States and the West.

The strategy that Putin has pursued instead is one that prioritizes the West as the main threat to Russia, pays some attention to Sunni jihadists (but seems willing to tolerate or even support their actions vis-à-vis the United States on

---

[8] Eugene Rumer has described Abe's efforts as "partly motivated by the rather transparent desire for a rapprochement with Russia at the expense of China." See Rumer, "Russia's China Policy," 21.

[9] Michael Kofman, "The Misadventures of Russia and the United States in Syria: Complete Strategy Implosion Edition," War on the Rocks, October 11, 2016, https://warontherocks.com/2016/10/the-misadventures-of-russia-and-the-united-states-in-syria-complete-strategy-implosion-edition. See also Rowan Scarborough, "U.S. Finds Russia Focusing Fight on Syrian Rebels, Not Islamic State," *Washington Times*, February 3, 2016, http://www.washingtontimes.com/news/2016/feb/3/putins-forces-refuse-attack-islamic-state-syria; and Rahim Rahimov, "Russia's Security Dilemma: To Fight the Islamic State in Syria or Not?" Woodrow Wilson International Center for Scholars, Russia File, March 2, 2017, https://www.wilsoncenter.org/blog-post/russias-security-dilemma-to-fight-the-islamic-state-syria-or-not.

[10] International Crisis Group, "The North Caucasus Insurgency and Syria: An Exported Jihad?" Europe Report, no. 238, March 16, 2016, 16–18.

[11] Phil Stewart and Idrees Ali, "Russia May Be Helping Supply Taliban Insurgents: U.S. General," Reuters, March 23, 2017, http://www.reuters.com/article/us-usa-afghanistan-russia-idUSKBN16U234; and Thomas Gibbons-Neff, "Russia Is Sending Weapons to Taliban, Top U.S. General Confirms," *Washington Post*, April 24, 2017, https://www.washingtonpost.com/news/checkpoint/wp/2017/04/24/russia-is-sending-weapons-to-taliban-top-u-s-general-confirms.

occasion), and cooperates with China despite the potential threat it poses to Moscow. In fact, Putin's prioritization of the United States and the West as Russia's main adversary may actually drive Russian cooperation with China. As Eugene Rumer has observed, "considering Russia's long-term trajectory as a declining power, there was, and continues to be, no alternative to a strong relationship with China."[12]

Further, with Russia facing both internal and external challenges, what neither Putin nor any Russian leader wants is for two or more of its actual or potential adversaries to ally with each other. This was the disastrous situation that Moscow faced in the Cold War; first, when the United States and China set aside their differences, united by common opposition to the Soviet Union; and then when Sunni Muslim governments (with U.S. support) backed the *mujahideen* forces resisting the Soviet occupation of Afghanistan. From 1979 until the end of the Cold War, Moscow faced a de facto alliance of its three main external opponents. While Putin has not had to face an alliance of these three, or even any two of them, this may be more the result of ongoing differences between the United States and China, the United States and Sunni jihadists, and China and Sunni jihadists than anything Moscow has done to keep them apart. Preventing an alliance between the West, Sunni Muslims, and China from arising again is undoubtedly a priority for Putin.

But why the Kremlin's focus on the internal threat and on the United States and the West as Russia's principal external challenges has led to the particular military strategy that Putin has adopted requires explanation.

Explaining Putin's Strategy

Putin's Perceptions of the United States and the West

The focus of Putin and many other Russians on the United States and the West as Russia's primary adversary appears to be based on several strands of thinking prevalent among Russian security and foreign policy elites and Russian society generally. One is deep resentment that the Cold War ended with the loss of Soviet influence in Eastern Europe and elsewhere, the collapse of the Soviet Union itself, and a series of U.S. foreign policy actions thereafter viewed by Moscow as taking advantage of Russia's "temporary weakness" (as many Russians insist on describing it). These include the expansion of NATO; U.S. and European military action against Russia's Serbian allies in Bosnia-Herzegovina and Kosovo; recognition of Kosovo's declaration of independence from Serbia without Belgrade's

---

[12] Rumer, "Russia's China Policy," 21.

consent; U.S. efforts to limit Russia's relations with Iran; Washington's withdrawal from the 1972 Anti-Ballistic Missile Treaty soon after Putin had expressed support for the United States after September 11; the U.S.-led intervention in Iraq without UN Security Council (and hence Russian) approval; U.S. support for color revolutions in former Soviet republics, particularly Georgia (2003) and Ukraine (2004); U.S. support for the Arab Spring opposition to governments allied to Russia in both Libya and Syria; U.S. support for what Moscow regarded as another color revolution in Ukraine in 2014; and the imposition of economic sanctions in reaction to Russia's annexation of Crimea and support for secessionists in eastern Ukraine.[13] The United States, of course, is not alone in incurring Russian resentment; especially since Ukraine's Maidan Revolution of 2014, Russians have also seen the EU as being hostile toward Moscow.[14]

Underlying this resentment is a Russian notion, which Putin shares, of how international relations—especially relations between great powers—should work. Moscow sees the great powers as the primary actors in international relations and believes that they can make agreements among themselves demarcating "spheres of influence" for each that the others respect.[15] Examples of this kind of great-power agreement include the 1939 Nazi-Soviet pact (which Putin himself has praised) and the 1945 Yalta agreement concerning the international order after World War II.[16] Many Russians came to believe that the end of the Cold War would lead to an international order co-managed by Washington and Moscow.[17] In 2008, then president Dmitri Medvedev asserted Russia's "privileged interests" in countries where Russia has "traditionally had friendly cordial relations."[18] The United States' rejection of this approach has been seen in Moscow as reflective not of concern about whether the countries that Russia claims lie within its sphere of influence want this but of a desire both to deprive

[13] Angela E. Stent, *The Limits of Partnership: U.S.-Russian Relations in the 21st Century* (Princeton: Princeton University Press, 2014).

[14] Natalia Chaban, Ole Elgström, and Olga Gulyaeva, "Russian Images of the European Union: Before and after Maidan," *Foreign Policy Analysis* 13, no. 2 (2017): 480–99.

[15] Fiona Hill, "This Is What Putin Really Wants," *National Interest*, February 24, 2015, http://nationalinterest.org/feature/what-putin-really-wants-12311.

[16] Michael Birnbaum, "A Day after Marking Nazi Defeat, Putin Praises a Soviet-era Pact with Hitler," *Washington Post*, May 11, 2015, https://www.washingtonpost.com/news/worldviews/wp/2015/05/11/a-day-after-marking-nazi-defeat-putin-praises-a-soviet-era-pact-with-hitler.

[17] Dmitry Suslov, "The Russian Perception of the Post–Cold War Era and Relations with the West" (Harriman Institute lecture, Columbia University, New York, November 9, 2016), https://www.sant.ox.ac.uk/sites/default/files/university-consortium/files/suslov_harriman_lecture_on_post-cold_war_era.pdf.

[18] "Medvedev on Russia's Interests," *Economist*, September 1, 2008.

Russia of any sphere of influence and to increase U.S. influence over former Soviet republics.[19]

In addition to this pessimistic view of U.S. intentions, a highly optimistic view about Russia's ability to "rise like the phoenix" after suffering setbacks or even defeats is pervasive within Russia. Russian history itself is seen as validating this belief. Russia, after all, was able to reassert itself as a great power after suffering numerous catastrophes, including centuries of Mongol rule, the seventeenth-century "time of troubles" between the downfall of one tsarist dynasty and the rise of another, Napoleon's invasion, the collapse of the Russian empire in World War I, the Nazi invasion in World War II, and the collapse of the Soviet Union bringing the troubles of the 1990s under the weak leadership of Boris Yeltsin. An integral part of this view is the belief that because Russia overcame previous setbacks to become stronger than before, it can and will do so again. Russia's re-emergence as a great power under Putin is seen as yet another instance of this occurring. Previous revivals also involved the recapture of much (if not all) of the territory lost by Russia during its setback. Putin's annexation of Crimea in 2014 fits within this narrative.[20]

But in addition to the prevalent belief within Russia that the country can and will rise again after suffering any setback, there exists a fear that another catastrophic setback could occur again in the future. Conflating his own interests with those of Russia as a whole, Putin appears to take seriously the possibility that the United States could support a successful color revolution that would overthrow his regime and replace it with a democratic (actual or supposed) government that would be subservient to the United States.[21] In other words, while Russia may overcome all setbacks and rise like the phoenix afterward, Putin would prefer not to experience another such setback. Even if Russia would survive, his regime likely would not.

While firmly believing that the United States and the West (or powerful forces within them) seek to overthrow him via democratic color revolution, Putin also sees Washington, other Western governments, and Western institutions such as NATO and the EU as being weak and vulnerable.[22] There is something of a contradiction in holding these two beliefs simultaneously. If the United States and the West are powerful enough to overthrow Putin via

[19] Kadri Liik, "How to Talk with Russia," European Council on Foreign Relations, Commentary, December 18, 2015, http://www.ecfr.eu/article/commentary_how_to_talk_to_russia5055.

[20] For an elaboration of this argument, see Mark N. Katz, "Will Putin Lead Russia to Glory or Disaster?" *Moscow Times*, June 21, 2015, https://themoscowtimes.com/articles/will-putin-lead-russia-to-glory-or-disaster-op-ed-47552.

[21] Darya Korsunskaya, "Putin Says Russia Must Prevent 'Color Revolution,'" Reuters, November 20, 2014, http://www.reuters.com/article/us-russia-putin-security-idUSKCN0J41J620141120.

[22] Ben Judah, "Why Russia No Longer Fears the West," *Politico Magazine*, March 2, 2014, http://www.politico.com/magazine/story/2014/03/russia-vladimir-putin-the-west-104134.

color revolution, then they must not be all that weak. But if they are indeed weak, then they are hardly strong enough to bring about Putin's overthrow. Notwithstanding the apparent inconsistency between these two beliefs, holding them simultaneously would logically lead to the conclusion that Russia must act to further weaken the West before the West, which is still strong enough to threaten Russia, can actually do so.[23] And indeed, Putin has acted to undermine the United States and the West through promoting right-wing parties and politicians who question or even oppose both NATO and the EU.

Finally, Putin sees the United States and the West as a greater threat than either Sunni jihadists or China. For whatever threats Sunni jihadists actually and China potentially pose to Russia and its interests, they do not pose the threat of undermining his authoritarian regime through promoting democratic revolution as Putin (whether accurately or not) sees the United States and the West as doing. For all these reasons, then, the United States has been the dominant focus of Moscow's military strategy under Putin, just as it was during the Cold War. The actual strategy he has employed in response to this threat environment has been shaped by the resource constraints on Russian national power as well as by the mindset of Russian strategic culture.

Russia's Military Strategy during the Cold War and the Yeltsin Era

Before discussing Putin's military strategy something needs to be said about what came before it during both the Cold War and the immediate post–Cold War Yeltsin era. During the Cold War, the Soviet Union maintained very large conventional armed forces, the centerpiece of which was a largely conscript army. It also built up a large nuclear weapons capacity, which by the early 1970s exceeded that of the United States in number of delivery vehicles, if not in destructive capacity. With these large conventional and nuclear armed forces, the Soviet Union was able to deter a U.S. nuclear attack (just as the United States was able to do regarding a Soviet one), defend Soviet territory and occupy Eastern Europe, conduct interventions aimed at preserving faltering Marxist regimes (as it did in Hungary in 1956, Czechoslovakia in 1968, and Afghanistan in 1979), and project Soviet influence into other parts of the world. Indeed, the combination of strong conventional and nuclear forces gave rise to anxiety that the Soviet Union could launch an invasion of Western Europe that the United States and its NATO allies could not halt with conventional forces and would be too afraid to use nuclear forces against for

---

[23] For an elaboration of this argument, see Mark N. Katz, "Inside the Confused Mind of Vladimir Putin," *Moscow Times*, April 1, 2015, https://themoscowtimes.com/articles/inside-the-confused-mind-of-vladimir-putin-45355.

fear that this would lead to a general nuclear war. However, the enormous cost of maintaining such large-scale armed forces, as well as the constant effort needed to keep up with the West technologically, contributed to Mikhail Gorbachev's ill-fated economic reform efforts that led to the collapse of the Soviet economy as well as of the Soviet Union itself—neither of which the Soviet military, with all of its strength, could prevent.

Under Yeltsin, by contrast, the armed forces became smaller and weaker as a result of being downsized due to lack of funding as well as Russia's withdrawal from Afghanistan, Eastern Europe, and the newly independent former Soviet republics. The greatest fear that emerged about the Russian nuclear arsenal was not its strength but its weakness—particularly whether Moscow could even safeguard its massive stockpiles of weapons-grade fissile material. Further, the reputation of Russia's conventional armed forces suffered when they were unable to defeat even internal opposition within Chechnya and ended up withdrawing from there in a humiliating retreat in 1996. The poor performance of the Russian military in Chechnya also led to public opposition to this war and the casualties suffered by Russian conscripts. In addition, Russians became frustrated with how the weak state of the armed forces served (in their view) to encourage the United States and the West to undertake military actions (such as the expansion of NATO and intervention against Serbia) that Moscow objected to but was unable to prevent. This frustration only deepened in the years after Putin first came to power when the George W. Bush administration intervened in Iraq, despite Russian opposition, and supported color revolutions in Georgia, Ukraine, and Kyrgyzstan. Putin saw these color revolutions as efforts to install pro-Western governments allied with the United States against Russia. It was in response to this U.S. tendency to act unilaterally in ways to which Moscow objected that Putin implemented a military strategy aimed at thwarting U.S. unilateralism as well as building up Russia's own ability to act unilaterally.

Putin's U.S.-Focused Military Strategy

Putin had alternatives to adopting a military strategy prioritizing the United States as Russia's primary external adversary. Specifically, he could have adopted a more patient strategy focused on maintaining calm relations with the West while building Russia's economic strength until the country was in a much stronger position to challenge the United States, as China did from the 1970s until Xi Jinping became president in 2012. Several factors may have contributed to Putin's not adopting this approach, including (1) Russia's inability, or simply unwillingness, to undertake the sort of economic changes that Deng Xiaoping set in motion that enabled the Chinese economy to grow so successfully, (2) an immediate Russian sense (whether justified or not) of threats from an expansion of NATO and the EU on Russia's borders, (3) an urgent desire to immediately restore Russia's recently lost status as a superpower, and (4) Putin's simply being more impatient and less risk averse than China's leaders since Mao Zedong have been. But whatever the set of reasons (and these may have as much to do with individual leadership psychology as Russia's broader strategic culture), the fact remains that Putin has adopted a more confrontational military strategy.

Putin has not been alone in adopting this approach. It has received the full support of the Russian elite, including the armed forces, security services, and state-influenced business sector. As Rumer put it, "a rapprochement with the West and participation in its institutions would require the Russian elite to take steps that would be certain to diminish its hold on the country's domestic politics and economy. Thus, a rapprochement with the West would mean, as Putin and other elite members have correctly assessed, regime change in Russia."[24] Whether this is a correct assessment on the part of the Russian elite is very much in doubt. Much greater Western economic interaction with China has not had any such effect in that country. Not only are Western governments not seeking regime change in China, but the Chinese elite does not seem to be as fearful of this as the Russian elite.[25] But because this is what the Russian elite genuinely fears, its focus on the combined threat from the United States externally and a color revolution internally has understandably led to a more aggressive strategy.

One important aspect of Putin's military strategy has been a re-emphasis on the nuclear arsenal. Allowed to deteriorate during the 1990s, Russia's nuclear force has been modernized and updated by Putin. Russian commentary has discussed how at a time when Russia no longer appears to have many advantages over other nations, its status as one of the two leading nuclear weapons powers (along with the United States) is an advantage that Moscow should capitalize on. Precisely how Russia can make use of its modernized nuclear arsenal, however, is unclear given that actually employing nuclear weapons would undoubtedly have very high, unpredictable costs for Russia. Of course, if Moscow really did fear an attack from the West (or anywhere else), then modernizing the nuclear force could be meant to deter this threat. Putin's nuclear modernization program, though, may also

---

[24] Rumer, "Russia's China Policy," 18.

[25] In response to my asking about why the Russian elite is more fearful than the Chinese elite of a U.S.-backed color revolution, a Russian scholar I met with in Moscow in mid-2014 stated that this was because Russians believe that the United States and the West have higher expectations for democratization in Russia than in China due to their seeing Russians as white and Chinese as not white. In this regard, Russian elite fears would only subside when the United States and the West finally realize that, as this scholar put it, "Russians are not white."

be intended to intimidate NATO into not provoking Russia over an issue that is of more importance to Moscow than to the West. Even if he does not intend to ever launch any sort of nuclear attack, Putin may calculate that he benefits if his adversaries cannot be certain that he will not, or what would trigger him to do so.[26]

In addition, Putin has undertaken the modernization and upgrade of Russia's conventional forces.[27] These had fallen into a dire state during the 1990s. Even though successful, the Russian war against Georgia in 2008 revealed numerous deficiencies (including lack of coordination between ground and air forces, maintenance issues, air assault and airborne forces being inappropriately used in standard infantry roles, poor targeting, and limited capacity for air war) that Putin has energetically worked to overcome.[28] Since then, Putin has overseen an across-the-board buildup and modernization of Russia's conventional forces, including its ground forces, aerospace forces, navy, special operations forces, and intelligence services. Underpinning these efforts is the concept of non-nuclear deterrence, which was articulated in the 2014 *Military Doctrine of the Russian Federation*.[29] This includes an emphasis on anti-access/area-denial capacity aimed at deterring "any Western use of aerospace power against Russia."[30] That the most recent military deployments and construction activity are in western Russia (including near the border with Ukraine and in the Kaliningrad exclave) suggests that Moscow remains focused on the West.[31] It also began an ambitious, multiyear state armament program in 2011 to upgrade existing weapons systems as well as develop new ones.[32] In addition to relying increasingly on more professional contract

---

[26] For a discussion of current Russian nuclear strategy, see Stephen J. Cimbala and Roger N. McDermott, "Putin and the Nuclear Dimension to Russian Strategy," *Journal of Slavic Military Studies* 29, no. 4 (2016): 535–53.

[27] Nikolai Sokov, "Russia's New Conventional Capability: Implications for Eurasia and Beyond," PONARS Eurasia, Policy Memo, no. 472, April 2017, http://www.ponarseurasia.org/sites/default/files/policy-memos-pdf/Pepm472_Sokov_May2017.pdf.

[28] "Russia's Military Modernisation: Putin's New Model Army," *Economist*, May 24, 2014, http://www.economist.com/news/europe/21602743-money-and-reform-have-given-russia-armed-forces-it-can-use-putins-new-model-army. On the problems experienced by the Russian military in the 2008 Georgian war, see Ariel Cohen and Robert E. Hamilton, *The Russian Military and the Georgia War: Lessons and Implications* (Carlisle: Strategic Studies Institute, 2011), 35–41, http://ssi.armywarcollege.edu/pdffiles/pub1069.pdf.

[29] U.S. Defense Intelligence Agency, *Russia Military Power: Building a Military to Support Great Power Aspirations* (Washington, D.C., June 2017), 22, http://www.dia.mil/Portals/27/Documents/News/Military%20Power%20Publications/Russia%20Military%20Power%20Report%202017.pdf.

[30] Ibid., 32.

[31] International Institute for Strategic Studies (IISS), *The Military Balance 2017* (London: Routledge, 2017), 184–86. Moscow's military buildup in the Arctic also appears to be directed at the West, given that Russia does not face any challenge there from China, Sunni jihadists, or Putin's domestic opponents.

[32] Ibid., 193.

service personnel and less on conscripts, the Russian Defense Ministry has been conducting more large-scale training exercises and has instituted frequent "snap inspections" as a way both to improve readiness and to identify and remedy problems that these expose.[33]

Another important development was the formation of the National Guard in 2016, which incorporated a number of existing organizations such as the internal troops, police special forces, and rapid-response forces. The National Guard reports directly to the Russian president, and its stated role is to counter internal threats, including separatism and anti-government unrest. Although it can be deployed abroad, this new organization (consisting of 340,000 military and civilian personnel) appears designed to allow Putin to more rapidly quash any attempt at a color revolution.[34] What its creation shows is just how seriously he takes this threat.

Yet while doing much to revitalize Russian military forces, Moscow faces two important obstacles in this endeavor. One is maintaining large-scale conventional forces at a time when a smaller cohort of young, ethnically reliable (i.e., Russian) males is available as a result of Russia's changing demographics. Another is that decreased revenue resulting from prolonged low petroleum prices has constrained the financial resources available for modernizing the country's conventional (as well as nuclear) forces. Indeed, fiscal constraints have led to delays in implementing the state armament program.[35] As Andrew Kuchins concluded in his study of Russian national power for the 2015–16 volume of *Strategic Asia*, Putin's military modernization efforts have succeeded in some areas but not in others.[36]

Thus, despite the modernization they have undergone, Russia's conventional forces do not appear to be intended to fight a major land war in Europe. Jakub J. Grygiel and A. Wess Mitchell have argued that Putin wants to avoid this scenario because Russian forces would quickly run into serious problems in fighting against NATO over a prolonged period of time. Putin, they note, has instead opted for an aggressive military strategy just short of war that involves taking provocative actions designed to probe how NATO responds. This has involved Russian military aircraft flying near or even within the airspace of many European countries, as well as Japan, without

---

[33] IISS, *The Military Balance 2017*, 186–87.

[34] Ibid., 186.

[35] Ibid., 193.

[36] Andrew C. Kuchins, "Russian Power Rising and Falling Simultaneously," in *Strategic Asia 2015–16: Foundations of National Power in the Asia-Pacific*, ed. Ashley J. Tellis, Alison Szalwinski, and Michael Wills (Seattle: NBR, 2015), 125–58.

permission or warning. Russian warplanes have also flown perilously close to U.S. naval vessels and military aircraft.[37]

In addition to the modernization of nuclear and conventional forces under Putin, Russia has built up an impressive cyberwarfare capability.[38] Indeed, it appears to have actually utilized this capability on occasion— such as against Estonia in 2007 when that country's government moved a Soviet war memorial, an action to which many Russians took offense.[39] An advantage of launching a cyberattack is that if a state can do this in a way that allows it to plausibly deny responsibility for the attack (which Russia has done), support for retaliation within the targeted nation and its allies can be undermined.

With constraints on his ability to strengthen Russia militarily, Putin has sought to compensate through undertaking actions that weaken the West, including through support for politicians and parties that are pro-Russian as well as anti-NATO and anti-EU.[40] Putin, it must be emphasized, did not create the economic grievances, xenophobia, and nationalism that have led to the rise of these forces, but he has certainly sought to exploit them—as the U.S. intelligence community has concluded that Russia did most noticeably during the 2016 U.S. presidential election by taking actions designed to discredit Hillary Clinton.[41] The aim of this strategy seems clear: if the United States and the West are Russia's principal adversary, then Russia is better off if they are weak and divided.

Moscow has used force, however, on several occasions since Putin first rose to power: in Chechnya beginning in 1999, when he was Yeltsin's prime minister; against Georgia in 2008, when he was prime minister again; and then, after he resumed the presidency, in Crimea in 2014, in eastern Ukraine (Donetsk and Luhansk) beginning later that year, and in Syria beginning in 2015. The later interventions were all external ones that led to great concern in the West about the revival of Russian expansionism, the West's ineffectual response, and the fear that Russian success combined with the lack of an effective Western response would lead to more such

---

[37] Jakub J. Grygiel and A. Wess Mitchell, *The Unquiet Frontier: Rising Rivals, Vulnerable Allies, and the Crisis of American Power* (Princeton: Princeton University Press, 2016).

[38] Timothy Thomas, "Russia's Information Warfare Strategy: Can the Nation Cope in Future Conflicts?" *Journal of Slavic Military Studies* 27, no. 1 (2014): 101–30.

[39] Damien McGuinness, "How a Cyber Attack Transformed Estonia," BBC News, April 27, 2017, http://www.bbc.com/news/39655415.

[40] Fredrik Wesslau, "Putin's Friends in Europe," European Council on Foreign Relations, Commentary, October 19, 2016, http://www.ecfr.eu/article/commentary_putins_friends_in_europe7153.

[41] Office of the Director of National Intelligence and National Intelligence Council, "Assessing Russian Activities and Intentions in Recent U.S. Elections," Intelligence Community Assessment, ICA 2017-01D, January 6, 2017, https://www.dni.gov/files/documents/ICA_2017_01.pdf.

interventions. What is noteworthy, though, is the relatively limited nature of each of them.

Unlike the first Chechen War (1994–96), in which Russian forces fared poorly, Moscow was far more successful in the second Chechen War, which Putin oversaw. One of the reasons for this was that Putin was able to take advantage of conflicts among Chechen rebels to enlist an important segment of them, the Kadyrov clan, in the fight against others who insisted on Chechen independence. The deal Putin essentially made with the Kadyrovs was to allow them to run Chechnya as they saw fit so long as they remained loyal to Moscow and did not declare independence.[42] And this has largely worked, though it is not clear the extent to which the Chechen strongman Ramzan Kadyrov is dependent on Putin or Putin is dependent on him.[43]

In 2008, at a time when the United States and many of its allies were distracted by conflicts in Afghanistan and Iraq, the West was neither willing nor able to help Georgia militarily in its conflict with Russia. But while Russia might well have taken this opportunity to overrun all of Georgia, it contented itself with seizing control over Georgia's two breakaway regions—Abkhazia and South Ossetia—which, with Russian help, had already been largely outside Georgia's control ever since the breakup of the Soviet Union.[44]

When Russia seized Crimea from Ukraine in early 2014, it did so with a relatively small number of soldiers and little violence. At the time that the operation was occurring, Moscow even denied that its own troops were involved in the operation (the "polite men" who accomplished the task bore no Russian military insignia), though Putin later admitted that they were Russian soldiers.[45] Russian military involvement in eastern Ukraine since the latter part of 2014 has been much greater, but Moscow has denied (and continues to deny) that its forces are involved.[46] In both cases, Moscow could have pushed well beyond either Crimea or the far eastern part of the country and overrun much more of Ukraine but did not.

---

[42] John Russell, "Ramzan Kadyrov: The Indigenous Key to Success in Putin's Chechenization Strategy?" *Nationalities Papers* 36, no. 4 (2008): 659–87.

[43] Anna Arutunyan, "Why Putin Won't Get Tough on Kadyrov," European Council on Foreign Relations, Commentary, April 25, 2017, http://www.ecfr.eu/article/commentary_why_putin_wont_get_tough_on_kadyrov_7278.

[44] Roy Allison, "Russia Resurgent? Moscow's Campaign to 'Coerce Georgia to Peace,'" *International Affairs* 84, no. 6 (2008): 1145–71.

[45] Shaun Walker, "Putin Admits Russian Military Presence in Ukraine for First Time," *Guardian*, December 17, 2015, https://www.theguardian.com/world/2015/dec/17/vladimir-putin-admits-russian-military-presence-ukraine.

[46] "Kyiv Says Russia Has at Least 5,000 Troops in Eastern Ukraine," Radio Free Europe/Radio Liberty, November 29, 2016, https://www.rferl.org/a/ukraine-russia-troops-crimea/28146059.html; and "Vladimir Putin: 'No Russian Units in Eastern Ukraine,'" BBC News, April 17, 2014, http://www.bbc.com/news/av/world-europe-27063231/vladimir-putin-no-russian-units-in-eastern-ukraine.

Finally, the Russian intervention in Syria has been undertaken largely with air and naval units. Putin has indicated that he does not want Russian ground forces to become involved in the conflict there, and a significant number of the ground forces sent from Russia have come from Chechnya. On two occasions, Moscow has even announced that it is withdrawing Russian forces from Syria.[47] Although Putin did not actually do this, these announcements indicated that Russian forces were not going to undertake the brunt of the fighting that would be needed to fulfill Bashar al-Assad's ambition of restoring his regime throughout Syria.

The two shorter interventions during the Putin era (Georgia in 2008 and Crimea in 2014) were undertaken primarily with Russian forces. By contrast, the three longer interventions (Chechnya, eastern Ukraine since 2014, and Syria since 2015) have been undertaken with allies. In Chechnya, as noted above, these allies were the Kadyrov clan and the forces under their command. In eastern Ukraine, Moscow allied with the pro-Russian secessionist militia forces in Donetsk and Luhansk. In Syria, its allies are the Assad regime's armed forces plus units from the Iranian Revolutionary Guards Corps, Hezbollah, and Iraqi and Afghan Shia militia forces.

In Chechnya, turning over the task of suppressing the rebels to the Kadyrov clan allowed Putin to reduce the involvement of Russian armed forces in this battle—an important concern since it was the high level of Russian casualties that had contributed to the unpopularity of the first Chechen War with the Russian public and Yeltsin's withdrawal of Russian forces from Chechnya in mid-1996.[48]

In eastern Ukraine, there are some indications that the pro-Russian separatist militias began to seize control in various parts of the region on their own initiative. They did, however, receive support from Russia (which Moscow denied it was giving). But it was when the separatist militias encountered resistance and then pushback from Ukrainian government forces (as well as nationalist militias) that Russian troops (which were declared to be volunteers) became more heavily involved in the conflict.[49]

---

[47] Fatima Tlisova, "Russian Ground Troops, Including Chechens, Reportedly Fighting in Syria," Voice of America, December 13, 2016, http://www.voanews.com/a/russia-chechnya-ground-troops-syria/3634787.html; and Michael Kofman, "A Comparative Guide to Russia's Use of Force: Measure Twice, Invade Once," War on the Rocks, February 16, 2017, https://warontherocks.com/2017/02/a-comparative-guide-to-russias-use-of-force-measure-twice-invade-once.

[48] Joss Meakins, "The Other Side of the COIN: The Russians in Chechnya," Small Wars Journal, January 13, 2017, http://smallwarsjournal.com/jrnl/art/the-other-side-of-the-coin-the-russians-in-chechnya.

[49] Dmitri Trenin, "The Ukraine Crisis and the Resumption of Great-Power Rivalry," Carnegie Moscow Center, July 2014, http://carnegieendowment.org/files/ukraine_great_power_rivalry2014.pdf; and Adam Čech and Jakub Janda, "Caught in the Act: Proof of Russian Military Intervention in Ukraine," Wilfried Martens Centre for European Studies, July 2015, https://www.martenscentre.eu/sites/default/files/publication-files/russian-military-intervention-ukraine_0.pdf.

Putin's classification in 2015 of all military deaths, whether in peacetime or wartime, as state secrets indicates that the Kremlin does not want to see the revival of Russian public concern about casualties, which, as discussed above, could fuel opposition to his regime.[50]

Moscow began providing arms to the Assad regime long before the outset of the Arab Spring in 2011. Syria was important to Russia then not only for being one of its last allies in the region but also for being the location of what would become the last Russian naval base outside the former Soviet Union.[51] Yet it was only after it appeared that the Assad regime might fall, even with Iranian and Shia militia support, that Russian forces intervened in Syria in September 2015.[52] Moscow has succeeded not just in protecting the Assad regime but in helping it regain lost territory. However, Russia has mainly contributed air and naval forces, while the Syrian government, Iran, Hezbollah, and other Shia forces have continued to undertake the bulk of the ground war.[53]

If these past interventions under Putin are a guide to the future, what they indicate is that he has a preference both for short military operations (lasting one or two weeks) that by their very nature involve few Russian casualties and for longer ones undertaken with allies that bear the main burden of the fighting and thus relieve Russian forces from experiencing heavy casualties.

This trend in Russian interventions suggests that Putin has become increasingly aggressive about intervening outside Russia in countries that are not members of NATO or do not have a defense agreement with the United States. But if in fact Putin continues to limit Russia to very short interventions or long ones in which its allies do most of the fighting, it is not clear where there are other such "opportunities" for Putin to exploit. It is always possible, of course, that Moscow could miscalculate, especially about what it anticipates will be a short war. What may occur instead, though, is small seizures of territory—such as occurred in July 2017 when

---

[50] Alec Luhn, "Vladimir Putin Declares All Russian Military Deaths State Secrets," *Guardian*, May 28, 2015, https://www.theguardian.com/world/2015/may/28/vladimir-putin-declares-all-russian-military-deaths-state-secrets.

[51] While some Western observers have stressed the importance of the Russian naval facility in Syria to Moscow, others have pointed out how underdeveloped the base was prior to its buildup after the 2015 Russian intervention. For a discussion of both sides of this argument, see Frank Gardner, "How Vital Is Syria's Tartus Port to Russia?" BBC News, June 27, 2012, http://www.bbc.com/news/world-middle-east-18616191. These opposing arguments, though, are not mutually exclusive: despite its being in a poor state, the facility was still important to Moscow.

[52] Ian Black, "Wake-Up Call on Syrian Army Weakness Prompted Russian Intervention," *Guardian*, October 1, 2015, https://www.theguardian.com/world/2015/oct/01/syrian-military-weakness-russian-intervention.

[53] Aniseh Bassiri Tabrizi and Raffaello Pantucci, eds., "Understanding Iran's Role in the Syrian Conflict," Royal United Services Institute, Occasional Paper, August 2016, https://rusi.org/sites/default/files/201608_op_understanding_irans_role_in_the_syrian_conflict_0.pdf.

Russian forces unilaterally moved the border posts between Georgia and South Ossetia by 700 meters—that are individually too small to trigger a full-scale crisis.[54]

Yet while Putin has not been willing (at least so far) to intervene militarily in a NATO country, he has demonstrated a willingness to intervene politically—including in the United States itself—through efforts aimed at affecting the outcome of their elections. While perhaps not a purely military strategy, this appears to be part of a broader politico-military strategy that is more focused on weakening the West than on initiating additional Russian military interventions.

As was noted earlier, Putin prioritizes the threats he sees himself facing both from his internal opponents and from the United States and the West. He places less emphasis on the jihadist threat, which he sees as a challenge but not an existential threat to his regime. And while many in the West, as well as pro-Western Russians, think of China as a threat to Russia, Putin sees it as a partner instead. Not only has Russia continued to sell advanced weaponry to China, but the two countries also have been engaging in annual joint naval exercises since 2012—including in the Mediterranean in 2015, the South China Sea in 2016, and the Baltic Sea in 2017.[55] Although some Western observers predicted that the rise of Chinese influence in what has long been Moscow's bailiwick in Central Asia would lead to a Sino-Russian clash, "Russia and China appeared to belie these predictions, and to transform a potential source of tension into a means of cooperation and mutual reassurance."[56]

Even so, there have been some indications that Moscow does see China as a potential threat (even if it does not say so), and that it has undertaken some actions aimed at hedging against this possibility. Notably in this regard, Russia has deployed Iskander-M missile systems at four locations along its border with China. According to one analyst, while the Iskander-M missiles deployed to Kaliningrad are clearly aimed at NATO forces, those stationed in the Russian Far East have "very limited ability to threaten U.S. forces deployed in the region"; instead, their primary purpose is "containing China and responding to contingencies on the Korean Peninsula."[57] Those located further inland in Buryatia (near Mongolia) and Zabaykalsky Krai (near China's Inner Mongolia)

---

[54] Brian Whitmore, "The Daily Vertical: Strategic Salami Tactics in Georgia (Transcript)," Radio Free Europe/Radio Liberty, July 11, 2017, https://www.rferl.org/a/daily-vertical-georgia-ossetia-border-moved-russian-troops/28609829.html.

[55] Kathrin Hille, "Chinese Warships Join Russia in Baltic Naval Drill," *Financial Times*, July 25, 2017.

[56] IISS, *Strategic Survey 2016* (London: IISS, 2016), 220.

[57] Guy Plopsky, "Why Is Russia Aiming Missiles at China?" *Diplomat*, July 12, 2017, http://thediplomat.com/2017/07/why-is-russia-aiming-missiles-at-china.

can only be aimed at China.[58] Further, Moscow conducted large-scale military exercises involving over 100,000 soldiers in the Russian Far East in both 2010 and 2014. According to Roger McDermott of the Jamestown Foundation, the assets deployed in these two exercises "were more consistent with facing and preparing for the defense of the Russian Far East from a state actor: the only state actor that fits the bill in this strategic direction is China."[59] Finally, while Moscow would certainly claim that it is only acting in pursuit of its commercial interests, Russian arms exports to Asian states such as India and Vietnam that are more openly concerned about China have the practical effect of better enabling them to defend themselves against Beijing. As Evan Medeiros and Michael Chase have noted, "some Chinese scholars have already criticized Russian defense cooperation with Vietnam as a type of 'covert containment' of China inasmuch as Russian arms sales give Hanoi a 'stronger hand' to play against Beijing in the South China Sea."[60]

Each of these actions suggests that Moscow is concerned about a potential threat from Beijing. It is all the more remarkable, then, that Russia cooperates so much with China despite these concerns. What this shows is how much greater Putin's concerns about his internal opponents, as well as the United States and the West, must be for him to prioritize these over a potential threat from a neighboring state that is only growing stronger economically and militarily. This does not just reflect Putin's peculiarities. As Facon pointed out in *Strategic Asia 2016–17*, Russian strategic culture's prioritization of the threat to Russia from the West has influenced its perception of the East not only as less of a threat but also as an ally against the West: "Asia is important to Moscow primarily as a function of what the region can help Russia achieve in relations with the West. The secondary nature of Russia's interest in Asia has always been striking."[61]

Assessing the Durability, Adequacy, and Impact of the Dominant Russian Strategy

How durable is Putin's military strategy? The answer to this question may depend largely on how durable Putin's rule is. While it must obviously come to an end at some point, there is no doubt that he will win a fourth term as

---

[58] Plopsky, "Why Is Russia Aiming Missiles at China?"

[59] Roger McDermott, "Vostok 2014 and Russia's Hypothetical Enemies (Part One)," Jamestown Foundation, Eurasia Daily Monitor, September 23, 2014, https://jamestown.org/program/vostok-2014-and-russias-hypothetical-enemies-part-one.

[60] Evan S. Medeiros and Michael S. Chase, "Chinese Perspectives on the Sino-Russian Relationship," in "Russia-China Relations," 12.

[61] Facon, "Russian Strategic Culture in the 21st Century," 76.

president if he chooses to run for re-election in 2018, which seems highly likely. Although the Russian constitution says that he cannot run for a third consecutive term in 2024, Putin clearly has the power to either change the constitution or rule from the post of prime minister like he did after his first two consecutive terms as president ended in 2008. Either way, he could then run for president again in 2030 and 2036 if he is still alive and well. In other words, Putin could remain in power for many years.

This being the case, the immediate question about the durability of his military strategy hinges on the question of whether there is any reason that he would alter it. Since Putin has been steadily implementing this strategy that identifies the United States and the West as Russia's primary external opponents, and since he probably sees it as having been highly successful up to now, there is little reason to think that he will change his mind unless something happens that induces him to do so.

One possible scenario is a dramatic improvement in Russian relations with the United States and the West. There was actually some anticipation after the election of Donald Trump as president in 2016 that Russian-U.S. relations would improve at least somewhat, but even this limited expectation now appears unwarranted given continued differences over sanctions, Crimea, Ukraine, and NATO. And despite Trump's own relatively friendly tone toward Russia, several of his top appointees have taken a much tougher approach.[62] In his first phone conversation as president with Putin on January 28, 2017, Trump reportedly spurned Putin's offer to extend the New Strategic Arms Reduction Treaty (New START), declaring that it was a "bad deal" for the United States.[63] Putin's displeasure with Trump over this issue, as well as others, may go a long way to explaining why Russian media coverage of Trump went from being warm and friendly to being cold and distant in mid-February 2017.[64] Putin's expectations were clearly disappointed.

It is worth considering what these initial expectations for Trump might have been. As noted earlier, the preferred ordering of international relations for Putin, as was the case for his predecessors, is a world in which the great powers recognize one another's respective spheres of influence. But whatever

---

[62] On the rise and fall of Russian expectations for improved ties between Moscow and Washington since the election of Trump, see Neil MacFarquhar, "Russia, Feeling Slighted by Trump, Seeks a Reset," *New York Times*, May 3, 2017, https://www.nytimes.com/2017/05/03/world/europe/trump-putin-russia-relations.html.

[63] Jonathan Landay and David Rohde, "Exclusive: In Call with Putin, Trump Denounced Obama-Era Nuclear Arms Treaty—Sources," Reuters, February 9, 2017, http://www.reuters.com/article/us-usa-trump-putin-idUSKBN15O2A5.

[64] Steve Rosenberg, "Russian Media No Longer Dazzled by Trump," BBC News, February 17, 2017, http://www.bbc.com/news/world-europe-39004987. I personally saw the negative, even hostile, Russian attitude toward Trump on display when I was a participant in the Valdai International Discussion Club's conference on the Middle East in Moscow, February 27–28, 2017.

hopes Putin may have initially had that Trump, "the dealmaker," would go along with this approach have not been met. In fact, the publicity in the United States about allegations that Trump and his presidential campaign had close ties to Russia makes it difficult for Trump to cooperate closely with Putin without furthering suspicion about this issue.[65] While Putin would prefer an approach to world order by which great powers accept each other's spheres of influence, this requires that the leaders of other great powers—especially the United States—share it. Identifying the circumstances under which a U.S. president would do this are beyond the scope of this chapter, but the fact that Trump, who at first seemed amenable to this great-power bargain approach, turned away from it suggests that such an agreement is unlikely.

Another reason that Putin might change his mind about prioritizing the United States and the West as Russia's principal external adversaries is that he decides that the strategy has succeeded to the point where it is no longer necessary. This might occur as the result of the election of pro-Russian or anti-NATO/EU parties and leaders in enough Western countries that Western governments focus more on their own internal politics or differences with one another than on Russia. If those differences are severe enough, some governments may even turn to Russia for support against other Western countries. But while Putin may indeed be seeking to weaken the West through supporting the election of right- and left-wing parties and politicians, as well as promoting differences within the region, whether the Western alliance actually does weaken depends more on the strength of divisive forces inside the West than on Russian efforts to promote them. Indeed, these efforts may actually serve to discredit Moscow in the West, as demonstrated by negative public reaction in many countries (including the United States) to signs of Russian attempts to influence their elections.[66]

Yet another reason that Putin might change his mind about prioritizing the United States and the West as Russia's principal adversaries is he decides that an even greater threat to Russia, and his rule over it, has emerged. If, for example, something happens that leads him to view China or the Sunni Muslim world as more threatening, then Putin may well seek Western support

---

[65] Republican concern in Congress about Russia had grown to such an extent that a bill imposing additional U.S. sanctions on Russia (as well as on Iran and North Korea) that limited President Trump's ability to lift them was passed by overwhelming majorities in both the House and the Senate. Despite his opposition to it, Trump signed the bill (since a veto would have been easily overridden). See Kaitlan Collins, Jeremy Herb, and Daniella Diaz, "Trump Signs Bill Approving New Sanctions against Russia," CNN, August 3, 2017, http://edition.cnn.com/2017/08/02/politics/donald-trump-russia-sanctions-bill/index.html.

[66] For a discussion of this issue, see Yuval Weber, "Russia Looks Out for Own Interests in Europe's Elections but Risks Long-Term Blowback," Harvard Kennedy School, Belfer Center for Science and International Affairs, Russia Matters, April 19, 2017, https://www.russiamatters.org/analysis/russia-looks-out-own-interests-europes-elections-risks-long-term-blowback.

against what he will portray as (and may actually be) a common threat. In this case, a strong and united West will be of far greater value to Russia than a weak and divided one.

It does not seem likely, though, that Putin will change his mind about the military strategy he is now pursuing. Subsequent Russian leaders, of course, may take quite a different view. This would be especially true if the Putin regime were replaced by a democratic one. Yet much like the Franco-U.S. relationship, the relationship between a democratic Russia, on the one hand, and the United States and various European governments, on the other, still might be somewhat contentious instead.[67] A democratic Russian government, however, would presumably not share Putin's fear of a Western-backed color revolution (especially if this post-Putin government resulted from just such a revolution, whether supported by the West or not). A democratic Russian government, moreover, might share Western concerns about threats emanating from the Muslim world and from China. On the other hand, a democratic Russia would also want to maintain good relations with both the Muslim world and China for fear of what bad relations with either might lead to, particularly given their close proximity.

While the emergence of a democratic Russia might offer the best prospect for a shift in the country's current focus under Putin on the United States and the West as being the main threat to Russia, the prospects for a democratic government replacing Putin do not appear to be at all good. It is far more likely that he will be succeeded, ousted, or otherwise replaced by someone inside his regime. In such a scenario, there is a strong possibility that another authoritarian leader who similarly fears democratization would continue the strategy of focusing on the United States and the West as being the main external threat to Russia. But this is not the only possibility, or even the most likely one.

In looking back at Russia's leaders over the past century, it is noteworthy that each one has changed significant aspects of the foreign or domestic policies of the leader he replaced. Shifting circumstances drove some of these changes, but so did personal preference as well as each leader's desire to distinguish himself from the previous one. Indeed, each new Kremlin leader usually criticizes the one he replaced.[68] It would not be surprising,

---

[67] For a further elaboration of this argument, see Mark N. Katz, "What Would a Democratic Russian Foreign Policy Look Like?" *New Zealand International Review* 37, no. 2 (2012): 2–6, http://digilib.gmu.edu/jspui/bitstream/handle/1920/7540/What%20Would%20a%20Democratic%20Russian%20Foreign%20Policy%20Look%20Like.pdf?sequence=1&isAllowed=y.

[68] For example, Khrushchev denounced Stalin, Brezhnev denounced Khrushchev, Gorbachev denounced Brezhnev, Yeltsin denounced Gorbachev, and Putin criticized Yeltsin. The fact that Medvedev did not criticize Putin after replacing him as president was an indicator that he had not actually replaced him in power. For an elaboration of this argument, see Mark N. Katz, "Imagining the Post-Putin Era," LobeLog, July 17, 2014, https://lobelog.com/russia-imagining-the-post-putin-era.

then, if a successor that even Putin himself had chosen became critical of Putin and altered significant aspects of his policies. This could occur if the state of Russia's economy continues to stagnate or even deteriorate under Putin, and his successor were to decide that improved relations with the West are a necessity for appeasing not just the Russian public but also elites more concerned about their own well-being than whether Moscow is more influential than the West in places such as Syria or eastern Ukraine. In other words, there may be not only an opportunity for his successor to change Putin's defense policy but compelling domestic political reasons to do so—such as heightened Russian threat perceptions about China or the Islamist challenge (from both within and without).

Yet while it is quite possible that even Putin's own hand-picked successor might well alter his defense policy, Putin might yet remain in power (as was noted earlier) for many more years, and he seems unlikely to alter his belief that the United States and the West are the main external threat that he faces. Indeed, events like the surprise anti-Putin demonstrations that broke out across Russia in late March 2017 only confirm his views on this challenge.[69] But with a U.S.- and Western-focused defense policy likely to remain durable so long as Putin remains in power (and perhaps longer), the question that arises is whether this strategy is adequate for satisfying Russia's principal geopolitical aims.

The answer to this question depends on an assessment of whether Putin has accurately identified and prioritized the threats facing Russia as well as whether he has fashioned a strategy to deal with them effectively. If indeed the United States and the West are not only a threat to Russia but a greater threat than either China or the Sunni jihadists, then Putin's military strategy is not only sensible but successful. But are the United States and the West really a threat? They hardly seem likely to invade, as this could lead to a nuclear conflagration as catastrophic for them as for Russia. Putin does not seem to fear a Western invasion; rather, he fears the West's promotion of a democratic color revolution against him. But is the West really trying to democratize Russia? There was a period after the end of the Cold War when many in the West and elsewhere thought that Russia was on the road to democratization, and Western governments sought to encourage this process. However, they did not do much to stop Putin from reversing whatever progress toward democracy Russia had made and reviving authoritarianism. His belief that the color revolutions in former Soviet republics, the Arab Spring, and the

---

[69] Putin declared that "such unsanctioned protests" risked plunging Russia into violence as happened in Arab countries in 2011 and Ukraine in 2013–14. See Henry Meyer, Stepan Kravchenko, and Anna Andrianova, "Putin Takes Tough Stance on Protests, Warns of Arab Spring Chaos," Bloomberg Politics, March 30, 2017, https://www.bloomberg.com/politics/articles/2017-03-30/putin-takes-tough-stance-on-protests-warns-of-arab-spring-chaos.

demonstrations against him inside Russia in 2011–12 were all instigated by the West underestimates popular support for these movements in each country where they took place. The fact that widespread demonstrations against Putin broke out in Russia in March 2017 over two months after Donald Trump—who is definitely not trying to promote a color revolution—took office raises the possibility that Putin will view Trump as no different from previous U.S. presidents in seeking to undermine him.

It is possible that Putin will succeed in undermining (or perhaps more accurately, encouraging trends within the West that undermine) the strength and cohesion of the Western alliance. But if he has overestimated the extent to which the United States and the West actually pose a threat to Russia, then his efforts to neutralize that threat have been completely unnecessary. It is also possible that Putin does not really see the West as a threat but merely says so to justify the pursuit of an aggressive and offensive strategy to undermine it. But whether Putin's prioritization of this threat is defensively or offensively motivated, his success in weakening the West does nothing to enhance Russian capacity for dealing with other external threats that might arise from China and the Sunni jihadists. In fact, his success in weakening the West will lessen Western capacity to aid Russia if it faces growing threats from either source. Moreover, a weakened West will be less able (not to mention less willing) to provide the investment and trade that Putin needs to bolster the Russian economy and placate both the general population and the elite, on whose support he especially depends. The strategic prioritization of the United States and the West, then, is a huge bet either that China and the Sunni jihadists will not become a serious threat to Russia or that Moscow can manage them (along with maintaining internal stability) without the aid of the West. Of course, if Putin's efforts to weaken the West do not succeed, then perhaps these other threats will not grow stronger than they are. Another possibility is that the West will overlook Putin's efforts against it if it deems China or the Sunni jihadists as common threats to both the West and Russia. In other words, Russia's own security may be enhanced if Putin's efforts to undermine the West do not succeed.

But whatever the inadequacy of his strategy, as well as the risks to which it exposes Russia, Putin himself now appears to be quite satisfied with it. Regardless of the successes or failures of this strategy vis-à-vis the United States and the West, Russia's relations with the West are likely to remain contentious so long as Putin is in power, which could be a long time. Additional geopolitical gains for Russia that Putin makes in Ukraine, Belarus, or elsewhere will not result in reduced Western sanctions on Russia but probably in increased ones instead. Hostile Russian actions vis-à-vis the Baltic states risk the possibility of a larger conflict between Russia and

NATO—or of NATO being seen as irrelevant if it does not act to defend the Baltics. Either way, Russia's economic relationship with the West is likely to decline further, and so will the Russian economy.

What Putin does not seem capable of accomplishing is simultaneously making geopolitical gains for Russia, on the one hand, and persuading the West to accept this situation and return to doing business as usual, or preferably increasing its economic interaction, with Russia, on the other. Further, whatever success Putin has in helping nationalist, anti-EU/NATO, and pro-Russian politicians and parties gain power in the West does not mean that they will be willing or able to do Putin's bidding once in power. In fact, his success in expanding Russia's geopolitical reach and weakening the West may eventually result in his successors facing the choice between expending scarce resources to defend Putin's territorial gains, which have done little to enhance Russia's actual security, or withdrawing from this territory. The latter course could very well become necessary to reduce costs as well as improve relations with a West with which Russia needs good relations economically and perhaps even militarily to manage the threat from a rising China or Sunni jihadism.

The Implications for the United States

Even if Putin's U.S.- and Western-focused military strategy ultimately proves harmful to Russian interests, the United States and the West will have to either devote considerable energy and resources to countering, or at least containing, Russia for as long as Putin pursues this strategy, or face internal disarray within the West if they do not do so. Moreover, the United States and the West's need to respond to Putin's strategy targeting them only distracts from their ability to respond to other threats. His strategy certainly does not promote cooperation between Russia and the West against common threats to both.

Although there are thus no easy policy options for how Washington should respond to this situation, one possibility is to try to do again what it successfully did before: pursue a strategy of containment toward Russia that focuses on Europe (presuming that a containment effort against Russia in Asia would not be needed since Moscow is unlikely to undertake actions there that Beijing would strongly object to). Such a policy, however, would encounter some serious obstacles. First, the U.S. military presence in Europe has been greatly reduced in the years since the end of the Cold War and would be time-consuming and expensive to rebuild. Whether there is sufficient political will in both the United States and Europe for such an undertaking, and whether the two sides can agree on how to share the costs, is highly uncertain. Second, whereas the Soviet Union was the primary threat faced by the United States during the Cold War, Russia is now one of many challenges alongside China, North Korea, Iran, and Sunni jihadists such as al Qaeda and ISIS. In order to mount an effective containment effort against Russia, the U.S. political process would have to be willing either to obtain additional resources through increased taxation or borrowing, or to reduce spending on current priorities in order to free up resources for dealing with Russia. Neither option seems likely at present. Third, however the resources for containing Russia are obtained, focusing more on this goal would probably entail reducing the time and attention that the United States now devotes toward other threats—something that many policymakers would be loath to do.

Another possibility, as President Trump and some of his close associates have suggested, is negotiating a grand bargain that eases the ongoing tensions between Washington and Moscow. Since regime preservation is Putin's main concern, Washington would need to provide reassurances that it is not threatening this. And even if it did not do so formally, the United States would have to accept Russia's acquisition of Crimea, eastern Ukraine, Abkhazia, and South Ossetia. Washington may also need to privately convey to Moscow that neither Ukraine, nor Georgia, nor any other former Soviet republic would join NATO. In exchange for these concessions, Russia would need to agree to cease all further hostile action against its neighbors as well as its intimidating air and naval maneuvers in Europe and elsewhere.

Achieving any such grand bargain would be extremely difficult. Russian interference in the 2016 U.S. presidential election would make it imperative for Trump to obtain meaningful concessions from Putin in order to avoid appearing to be under the latter's influence. And Putin, it appears, may actually prefer a state of hostility with the United States and the West, given his fears that friendly relations are more likely to undermine him. Finally, even if Washington were to agree to not support Putin's internal opponents, this would not stop their activity—which Putin would undoubtedly see as being instigated by the United States in violation of the agreement. Thus, an attempt to achieve a grand bargain with Russia seems highly unlikely to succeed.

Another sort of great-power grand bargain may be possible, though. Many have observed that hostile relations between Russia and the West have resulted in Russian dependence on China increasing to the point of Moscow becoming Beijing's junior partner. Yet there may well be a limit to Beijing's willingness to bail out its junior partner if Russia either gets into more conflicts or becomes more isolated from the West economically. If this is the case, then the key to reining in Russian behavior may not be a grand bargain with Moscow but with Beijing. Whatever its differences with the United

States, China certainly wants to continue its profitable trade relations with the West. If Washington could help Beijing understand how Russian activity that undermines the West ultimately limits Chinese trade and investment opportunities, perhaps Beijing would be willing to help persuade Putin to behave more constructively for everyone's benefit. It is not clear, of course, whether China would be in a position to do this even if it were willing. Beijing's lack of success in persuading North Korea to behave constructively does not instill confidence in its ability to persuade Russia to do so. Still, U.S. policymakers should keep in mind this possibility if circumstances more favorable to it ever arise.

Perhaps, though, the best strategy that the United States could pursue is one of strategic patience. After all, a leader who focuses on gaining every tactical advantage he can vis-à-vis the West and not on building up the Russian economy, who is so determined to counter the Western "threat" that he is willing to allow Russia to increasingly become a junior partner to China, who really believes that any internal opposition against him is caused by the United States rather than his own policies (and so persists in them), and who has not institutionalized leadership transition like the post-Mao Chinese Communist Party has done (at least up to the present) is not strengthening but weakening Russia in the long run. This, of course, may be the end result of Putin's actions, whether Washington seeks it or not.

EXECUTIVE SUMMARY

This chapter argues that Japan's grand strategy—responding to evolving security pressures and material constraints—is exploring a shift from the old certainties of the Yoshida doctrine to an Abe doctrine characterized by a new level of military commitment and stronger integration of the U.S.-Japan alliance.

MAIN ARGUMENT

For most of the postwar period, Japan has opted for the Yoshida doctrine's minimalist defense posture and dependence on the U.S. as the best fit for navigating an uncertain regional security environment. Other debated options of neutralism, autonomy, and multilateralism have largely been rejected as lacking feasibility. Consequently, in the post–Cold War era, the Yoshida doctrine has been adapted to meet unfolding strategic needs while still delimiting defense commitments. However, the rise of China and uncertainties over U.S. power and commitment have forced Japanese policymakers to reconsider their grand strategy. The emerging Abe doctrine now commits Japan to move beyond minimalism in its national defense posture and to cease much of the hedging around the U.S.-Japan alliance. But the transition to the Abe doctrine is not yet complete, given residual domestic antimilitarism and potential strains to the U.S.-Japan alliance.

POLICY IMPLICATIONS

- Japan is intent on shifting its grand strategy and fulfilling a greater commitment to the U.S.-Japan alliance. This presents opportunities for the U.S., with Japanese support, to strengthen its own strategic position in the region vis-à-vis rising challenges.

- The Trump administration may find Japan a responsive partner in its quest for greater burden-sharing among East Asian allies and should continue close U.S. engagement on strategic priorities.

- To avoid tilting the Abe doctrine toward traditions of autonomy, the U.S. needs to manage the alliance carefully, especially given Japan's recent concerns about abandonment and resurgent concerns about entrapment.

Japan's Grand Strategic Shift: From the Yoshida Doctrine to an Abe Doctrine?

Christopher W. Hughes

Japan's grand strategy and concomitant choice of military doctrines and capabilities have proved remarkably durable in the post–World War II era. This is the result of the strong confluence of, and careful mediation among, contending international structural factors and domestic ideational and material drivers. Japan's policymakers and citizenry, as a consequence, have defaulted pragmatically to the Yoshida doctrine as a grand strategy and largely avoided exploration of potential alternative or more radical options. Devised in outline by Shigeru Yoshida, who served as prime minister in 1946–47 and again in 1948–54, this doctrine advocates a minimalist defense posture and dependence on the U.S.-Japan security relationship.

Much of this chapter is devoted to explaining the reasons for the evolution, growing acceptance, and continued resilience of Japan's postwar grand strategy. Yet it also considers whether, given the gradual shifting of underlying international and domestic drivers, avenues are opening up for resultant shifts in this strategy overall. Specifically, this chapter argues that a changing mix of international security challenges, accompanied by domestic political upheavals, economic constraints, and, crucially, the resurgence of ideological intent in policy discourse, has given impetus to the emergence of the Abe doctrine as a new grand strategy. Put forward by Prime Minister Shinzo Abe, who began his second stint as prime minister in 2012, this doctrine might be cast in some of its features as just a more ambitious extension of the Yoshida doctrine. In other ways, though, the Abe doctrine could overturn the status quo in security policy and set Japan on a

Christopher W. Hughes is Professor of International Politics and Japanese Studies in the Department of Politics and International Studies at the University of Warwick. He can be reached at <c.w.hughes@warwick.ac.uk>.

new strategic direction—one that integrates Japanese and U.S. military efforts and ceases hedging, while taking a more independent line. It thus carries important implications for regional security relations and the development of the U.S.-Japan alliance.

This chapter builds on the previous two *Strategic Asia* volumes to explain how the interaction of Japan's material capabilities and strategic culture influences its grand strategy and military stance.[1] The chapter proceeds in four main sections. The first section outlines the key international and domestic strategic drivers throughout the postwar era and into the contemporary period that have shaped the formulation of Japan's grand strategy. The policy discourse around Japan's strategic choices, including the predilection for the Yoshida doctrine and emergence of the Abe doctrine, needs to be understood with reference to these parameters and baselines. The second section considers the principal strategic options—neutralism, autonomy, multilateralism, and the Yoshida doctrine—that have been pondered by Japanese policymakers at different stages in the postwar era. This section provides the context for the deeper examination in the third section of why Japan's policymakers and public have actively pursued, or at a minimum acquiesced in, the Yoshida doctrine as a grand strategy throughout most of the postwar era. In comparison with the other options debated, the Yoshida doctrine charted the most effective course for navigating international and domestic challenges and ensuring national security. Yet this section also demonstrates how Japan's shifting international and domestic parameters have opened the space for the emergence of the Abe doctrine and the potential displacement of the Yoshida doctrine. The fourth section of the chapter examines the durability of Japan's existing grand strategy, the possibility of strands of past options re-entering the debate on the country's strategic trajectory, and the transition from the Yoshida doctrine to the Abe doctrine. Finally, the conclusion considers the potential impact of the shift in Japan's grand strategy and military stance on regional stability and relations with the United States, especially with the advent of the Trump administration.

---

[1] See Michael Auslin, "Japan's National Power in a Shifting Global Balance," in *Strategic Asia 2015-16: Foundations of National Power in the Asia-Pacific*, ed. Ashley J. Tellis, Alison Szalwinski, and Michael Wills (Seattle: National Bureau of Asian Research [NBR], 2015), 56–88; and Alexis Dudden, "Two Strategic Cultures, Two Japans," in *Strategic Asia 2016-17: Understanding Strategic Cultures in the Asia-Pacific*, ed. Ashley J. Tellis, Alison Szalwinski, and Michael Wills (Seattle: NBR, 2016), 90–111.

Japan's Strategic Drivers and Culture: International and Domestic Challenges

Japan's external and internal strategic drivers, even though steadily evolving and subject to some fluctuation, during most of the postwar era have provided a consistent set of parameters for grand strategy and military policy. Japanese policymakers, in addition to encountering a difficult set of international security challenges, have experienced particularly stringent domestic constraints around security policy that have tended to inhibit discussion, let alone pursuit, of a full range of strategic options.

Regional Instability and Alliance Dilemmas

In terms of international structural drivers, throughout premodern history and the emergence of the modern state system, Japan's policy elites have traditionally perceived their nation as inherently vulnerable due to limitations in comprehensive national strength and strategic depth in terms of natural resources, geographic area, and population. These shortcomings are compounded by Japan's location at the juncture of a uniquely disadvantageous set of regional and global security flashpoints. With the onset of the Cold War after World War II, Japan's overall objective as a defeated power under the U.S.-led occupation was to recover national independence, reconstruct its economy, and navigate a generally hostile region. Japan's principal direct security challenge during the Cold War was the Soviet Union's conventional and nuclear threat, expanding by the 1980s to encompass even the risk of Soviet invasion of Japanese territory. The creation of the People's Republic of China (PRC) as a Communist regime, bouts of deep political instability in mainland China, and the procurement of nuclear weapons by the People's Liberation Army (PLA) posed some concerns for Japanese security but were perceived as secondary concerns. Similarly, although Japan's policymakers continued throughout the Cold War to be concerned about North Korea's military buildup and general instability on the Korean Peninsula, this threat was judged to be indirect and limited. In Southeast Asia, even though few direct risks were posed to Japanese security, concerns revolved around intrastate and interstate conflicts that might have an impact on wider regional stability and Japanese economic interests. Meanwhile, this hazard-strewn regional security situation was compounded by the legacy of Japan's own colonial history that predisposed many of the new regional states toward hostility. Japan was thus faced in this period with the need to find a foreign policy that would ensure its own security and help stabilize the region. Japanese policymakers' responses involved deeper diplomatic and economic re-engagement with the region but necessitated difficult choices about the military aspects of grand strategy.

In the post–Cold War period, Japan's international strategic drivers and overall objectives have exhibited a high degree of continuity. The country's security situation had improved by the end of the Cold War through a combination of shifts in the international system and its own efforts but has gradually deteriorated since then. The Soviet threat has been increasingly substituted for by China's rise in not entirely comparable, yet sometimes nearly as challenging, ways.[2] Japanese policymakers have expressed anxieties since the late 1990s about China's growing defense expenditures and capacity for military power projection. Japan fears that China's rising military power no longer is focused simply on access denial and the prevention of Taiwan independence but now is looking to pursue the longer-term goal of area control over the first island chain in the East and South China Seas by transgressing established international norms relating to freedom of navigation and exclusive economic zones (EEZ) and gradually levering out the Japanese and U.S. naval presence. Moreover, in Southeast Asia the expansion of China's naval power is now seen to pose a direct threat to Japanese sea lines of communication and economic interests. Hence, the threat from China has become direct and immediate, challenging both Japan's territorial integrity and ability to function as a maritime nation.[3]

This threat is compounded by a host of other security challenges. Although North Korea is second to China in terms of the long-term threat it poses, the regime's development of its nuclear and ballistic missile programs over the last two decades presents a clear and present danger to Japan. North Korea's frequent missile tests in 2017 as tensions with the United States have risen, including the reportedly successful launch of an intercontinental ballistic missile in July 2017 and the testing of intermediate-range missiles with trajectories passing over northern Japan in August and September of the same year, have only served to increase Japanese policymakers' awareness of these dangers. The result is that North Korea has joined China in presenting new and direct security threats to Japan. Furthermore, in the post–Cold War period, Japan's strategic horizons have expanded to include an increasing recognition of global concerns. The Gulf War of 1990–91 first indicated the potential impact of conflicts outside the Asia-Pacific on Japan's own security, and Japanese awareness of the need to respond to new global security challenges was heightened further in the aftermath of the events

---

[2] Sheila A. Smith, *Intimate Rivals: Japanese Domestic Politics and a Rising China* (New York: Columbia University Press, 2015); and June Teufel Dreyer, *Middle Kingdom and Empire of the Rising Sun: Sino-Japanese Relations, Past and Present* (Oxford: Oxford University Press, 2016).

[3] Dudden, "Two Strategic Cultures, Two Japans," 99–103.

of September 11, 2001, and with the onset of the "war on terrorism." Consequently, Japanese policymakers have started to acknowledge the new interdependencies of their own nation's security with global security as a whole.

In addition to these regional and global security threats, the other external constant influencing Japan's strategic parameters has been the role of the United States. During the Cold War, Japanese policymakers were able to draw comfort from the United States' hegemonic presence as an overall stabilizer of East Asian security. At the same time, their analysis of the costs and benefits of alignment and later an alliance with the United States was crucial. In evaluating their security options, Japanese policymakers calculated the risks both of entrapment if aligning too closely with the U.S. security orbit for protection and of abandonment if becoming too distant.[4] In the post–Cold War period, Japan's alliance with the United States has remained a constant and increasingly dominant external variable in shaping national security preferences. The perceived waxing and waning of the United States' relative hegemonic power and commitment to Asia-Pacific security, and the rise of China as a potential pole in the international order, has caused Japanese policymakers to speculate at times on available security options. Similarly, the accompanying impulses to strengthen the military alliance with the United States have remained heavily conditioned by the strategic risks of entrapment and abandonment, especially as different U.S. administrations have seemed to fluctuate in their willingness to deter or accommodate China.

Domestic Political Fissures, Antimilitarism, and Material Factors

Regarding the internal drivers of Japan's security strategy and military policy, domestic politics and economic development prospects have functioned throughout the postwar era to determine the policy parameters for responding to external challenges. In the post–Cold War period, domestic politics have possibly declined in significance as a constraint, while the role of economics has gradually increased. Japanese policymakers in the immediate postwar period had to negotiate their way through a party system characterized by deep cleavages over security policy. On the left of the political spectrum, the then electorally strong Japan Socialist Party (JSP) insisted on adhering to the so-called peace clause of Article 9 of the 1947 constitution. By contrast, conservatives in the eventually dominant Liberal Democratic Party (LDP) and its mainstream factions were more willing to consider Japan's re-engagement with issues of military power

---

[4] Daniel M. Kliman, *Japan's Security Strategy in the Post-9/11 World: Embracing a New Realpolitik* (Westport: Praeger, 2006), 12–14.

and international security. In a related fashion, policymaking institutions were decentralized and of limited effectiveness, given the policy divides and competition among central ministries and agencies, strong oversight of the Japan Defense Agency (JDA) by larger ministries such as the Ministry of Foreign Affairs and Ministry of International Trade and Industry, and firm civilian control of the Japan Self-Defense Forces (JSDF) by the JDA.[5] These political and bureaucratic constraints both reflected and were reinforced by Japanese society's broader sentiment of antimilitarism, characterized by attachment to the principles of Article 9 and suspicion of the utility of military power for security ends.[6]

The political and bureaucratic obstacles to Japan mobilizing national resources for security were reinforced in the early post–Cold War period by the need to focus on economic reconstruction. As the Japanese "economic miracle" took hold from the 1960s to 1980s, Japan's massively enhanced material and technological potential enabled significant investment in the JSDF's capabilities, both quantitatively and qualitatively, and sparked discussions of the country moving to utilize its new economic superpower status to establish a commensurate position as a military superpower.[7] But despite Japan's considerable material potential, the ability of policymakers to mobilize these resources remained constrained by the broader national security culture. Political leaders preferred modest defense budgets to reassure domestic and international opinion about Japanese military intentions and to utilize economic power for "comprehensive security" ends focused on resource procurement and the development and stabilization of the political economy of East Asia's emerging states.[8]

In the post–Cold War period, Japan's domestic political, institutional, and societal cleavages over security policy have become significantly less entrenched, reflecting greater fluidity in the party political regime. A result of this shift has been greater political instability, including the rapid turnover of administrations, but also greater space for discussions over future security policy. The LDP has largely dominated Japan politically from the Cold War into the contemporary period, but its competency to govern has been deeply challenged by Japan's relative economic malaise over the last quarter of a

---

[5] Andrew L. Oros and Yuki Tatsumi, *Global Security Watch: Japan* (Santa Barbara: Praeger, 2010), 47–70.

[6] Thomas U. Berger, *Cultures of Antimilitarism: National Security in Germany and Japan* (Baltimore: Johns Hopkins University Press, 1998); and Andrew L. Oros, *Normalizing Japan: Politics, Identity, and the Evolution of Security Practice* (Stanford: Stanford University Press, 2008).

[7] Kenneth N. Waltz, "The Emerging Structure of International Politics," *International Security* 18, no. 2 (1993): 55–70.

[8] John M.W. Chapman, Reinhard Drifte, and Ian T. M. Gow, *Japan's Quest for Comprehensive Security: Defence, Diplomacy, Dependence* (London: Pinter, 1983); and Christopher W. Hughes, *Japan's Security Agenda: Military, Economic and Environmental Dimensions* (Boulder: Lynne Rienner, 2004).

century, or "lost decades."[9] The consequence has been the LDP's increasing orientation away from the mainstream toward the more radical elements of the party fixed on neoliberal economic remedies and revisionism in defense and security. The gradual collapse of the JSP and its successor, the Social Democratic Party of Japan (SDPJ), as the main opposition party enabled the LDP to see off one competitor. However, the LDP then encountered more serious opposition from the more center-right Democratic Party of Japan (DPJ), even losing power to its rival from 2009 to 2012. The result for Japanese politics has been periods of relative stability during the long-running premierships of Junichiro Koizumi (2001–6) and most recently Abe, punctuated with rapid instability during the five years between 2006 and 2011 when the country was led by five prime ministers. In addition, the DPJ itself split and reformed as the Democratic Party (DP) in 2016.

Nevertheless, even in the midst of this political uncertainty, there has been the potential for a new convergence on security policy. LDP and DPJ members, although often at loggerheads over Japan's precise security orientation, have strongly overlapped in perspectives at times and generally converged on the view that Japan should boost its security efforts.[10] In turn, LDP and DPJ administrations have looked to reform domestic security institutions, enhance political control over the bureaucracy, and loosen heavy civilian control of the military. Japan's citizenry has also broadly followed in the trail of its political leaders. For while residual antimilitaristic sentiment remains a potential obstacle, the public appears increasingly, if still grudgingly, accepting of the need for Japan to undertake greater efforts for the defense of its own territory and in support of U.S. and international security.[11] For instance, Cabinet Office opinion polls demonstrate over the long term the increase in support for the JSDF in the postwar period. In 1965, only 15% of respondents viewed the JSDF's role as national defense compared to 40% who emphasized domestic disaster relief. But in 2015, not long after the March 2011 disasters, 74% of respondents acknowledged the JSDF's national defense role, nearly as much as the 82% who recognized its role in disaster relief. Support for the U.S.-Japan alliance has also increased over time, with the percentage of respondents answering that the U.S.-Japan security treaty functions effectively for Japan's security rising from 66% in

---

[9] T.J. Pempel, *Regime Shift: Comparative Dynamics of the Japanese Political Economy* (Ithaca: Cornell University Press, 1998).

[10] Amy Catalinac, *Electoral Reform and National Security in Japan: From Pork to Foreign Policy* (Cambridge: Cambridge University Press, 2016).

[11] Paul Midford, *Rethinking Japanese Public Opinion and Security: From Pacifism to Realism?* (Stanford: Stanford University Press, 2011), 170–86; and Paul Midford, "The GSDF's Quest for Public Acceptance and the 'Allergy' Myth," in *The Japanese Ground Self-Defense Force: Search for Legitimacy*, ed. Robert D. Eldridge and Paul Midford (New York: Palgrave Macmillan, 2017), 314–17.

1978 to 83% by 2015. Meanwhile, the same poll indicates that support for maintaining the JSDF and the U.S.-Japan alliance working in combination for Japan's security rose from 41% in 1969 to 85% by 2015.[12]

In contrast, if political barriers to Japan's security role have declined to some degree as a constant in setting parameters, then material factors have risen in policymakers' considerations.[13] Japan's poor economic performance since the early 1990s, massive government pump-priming, and the racking up of a debt-to-GDP ratio of 250% by 2016, along with rising social and health budget demands, have constrained the finances available for defense expenditure.[14] Similarly, Japan's demographic decline—with the population forecast to fall from 128 million in 2007 to 95 million in 2050—poses questions for the country's long-term standing as an economic superpower and the ability of the JSDF to recruit sufficient personnel.[15] The relative shift of Japan's economic power vis-à-vis China as a key regional competitor is also noteworthy. In 2010, China overtook Japan to become the second-largest economy in GDP terms at $6.1 trillion, compared with Japan's $5.7 trillion. By 2015, China's GDP had increased to $11.1 trillion, while Japan's had shrunk to $4.4 trillion.[16]

Japan still has considerable economic, technological, and budgetary capabilities to expand its military power, but it increasingly needs to weigh such a move against other budgetary choices. Regardless, it would still fall far short of any expectations to match the resource inputs of the United States and the double-digit increases of China. Hence, even though the current Abe administration has increased Japan's defense budget, it has remained around 5% of the government budget, whereas social welfare and public works have expanded their share of total expenditure.[17] The proportion of the defense budget available for the procurement of weapons systems has also fallen. Over the last twenty years up to 45% has been directed toward personnel and provisions (given rising salary and pension costs), whereas the proportion directed to equipment acquisition declined from around 23% of the budget in 1988 to around 16% in 2016.[18]

---

[12] "Jieitai boei ni kansuru yoron chosa" [Opinion Poll Regarding the JSDF and Defense], Naikakufu Daijin Kanbo Seifu Kohoshitsu, January 2017, http://survey.gov-online.go.jp/h26/h26-bouei/index.html.

[13] Auslin, "Japan's National Power in a Shifting Global Balance," 59–67.

[14] "IMF Warns of Higher Debt-GDP Ratio in Japan," Japan Times, April 16, 2015.

[15] Lynann Butkiewicz, "Implications of Japan's Changing Demographics," NBR, October 10, 2012, http://www.nbr.org/downloads/pdfs/ETA/ES_Japan_demographics_report.pdf.

[16] "Countries and Economies Data," World Bank, http://data.worldbank.org/country.

[17] Boei handobukku 2016 [Defense Handbook 2016] (Tokyo: Asagumo Shinbunsha, 2016), 283.

[18] Ibid., 285.

Japan's Strategic and Military Options: The Yoshida Doctrine by Process of Elimination

In seeking to respond to this complex mix of international and domestic challenges and parameters, Japan's policymakers and analysts have in the past considered a range of potential strategic and military options for ensuring national security. These options have jostled for policymakers' attention to different degrees throughout the postwar era and, as will been seen in later sections, have returned in modified form for consideration again in the contemporary period. However, during the Cold War, and in the process of setting the dominant grand strategy and security trajectory that largely continues to date, Japanese leaders rejected most of these options as lacking feasibility in their own right, although components did find their way into the dominant grand strategy. The exception, of course, was the Yoshida doctrine.

Neutralism

The first of Japan's security options that was considered but essentially discarded early in the Cold War period was a stance of neutralism, echoing General Douglas MacArthur's initial recommendation at the time of the occupation in 1950 that Japan should be akin to a "Switzerland of the Far East." The JSP was the principal advocate of unarmed neutralism (*hibuso churitsu*), which it viewed as congruent with the interpretation of Article 9 as prohibiting even the right of self-defense.[19] In line with this view, the JSDF is unconstitutional, and Japan instead should seek to provide for its security through regional diplomacy and economic cooperation, eschewing any form of alignment with the United States or involvement in Cold War politics. The Japan Communist Party (JCP) promoted a variant of neutralism, again refusing alignment with the United States or embroilment in Cold War tensions, but supported Japan's maintenance of its own limited conventional armed forces.[20] Although Japan's consideration of neutralism appears unorthodox today, given the 65-year history of the U.S.-Japan security treaty, for the parties on the left of the political spectrum during the Cold War years it appeared to be a viable means to resolve Japan's defense *problématique*. Neutralism was thought to offer Japan a means to recover its autonomy, reassure its East Asian neighbors over its intentions in the aftermath of colonialism, enable concentration on economic recovery, avoid exacerbating the emerging Cold War security dilemmas in the region, and

---

[19] Glenn D. Hook, *Militarization and Demilitarization in Contemporary Japan* (London: Routledge, 1996), 31–4.

[20] *Boei handobukku 2003* [Defense Handbook 2003] (Tokyo: Asagumo Shinbunsha, 2003), 762–64.

escape entrapment dilemmas involved with alignment toward either side of the bipolar divide.[21]

Nevertheless, even though many policymakers from other parties acknowledged similar risks in Japan's international position to those pointed out by the JSP and JCP, and the broader Japanese public was not entirely unsympathetic, neutralism was rejected as a credible national policy. The JSP was never able to gain sufficient political strength to challenge the LDP's grip on power, and the majority of conservative politicians and government bureaucrats did not view neutralism as an appropriate policy for addressing the realities of the Cold War, given the lack of potential partner states in East Asia and the requirement for a superpower sponsor.

Japanese Autonomy and Revisionism

At the other end of the spectrum of strategic options, from the early Cold War period onward a significant caucus of Japanese conservative policymakers argued for full remilitarization as a feasible route to autonomy and security. These "Gaullists" or "revisionists" advocated that Japan should revise Article 9, which was an alien imposition constraining its national identity.[22] Instead, these thinkers advocated that Japan should rearm, re-enter great-power politics, form shifting alliances, play the international balance of power, and reject the presence of foreign troops on Japanese territory.[23] Figures such as Hitoshi Ashida, Ichiro Hatoyama, and Nobusuke Kishi (Abe's grandfather), and later Yasuhiro Nakasone and Shintaro Ishihara—anti-mainstream representatives of the LDP—argued that only in this way could Japan free itself of foreign domination and protect its national interests. They also argued that rearmament would stimulate the economy. In the latter stages of the Cold War, Japanese Gaullists were also comfortable proposing the procurement of an indigenous nuclear deterrent to fully guarantee Japan's autonomy.[24] Moreover, many of these Gaullists espoused the need for Japan to revisit

---

[21] Ivan Morris, "Japanese Foreign Policy and Neutralism," *International Affairs* 36, no. 1 (1960): 7–20.

[22] Japan's revisionist or neo-autonomist strategic thinkers share similarities with, and were to an extent inspired by, the tradition of Gaullism in France. This tradition is characterized by a strong state, reliance on realpolitik rather than internationalist principles, the avoidance of reliance on allies and multilateral security frameworks if not coinciding with national interests, and the development of a strong military posture, including an independent nuclear deterrent. For more detail on the Gaullist tradition in Japan, see H.D.P. Envall, "Transforming Security Politics: Koizumi Jun'ichiro and the Gaullist Tradition in Japan," *Electronic Journal of Contemporary Japanese Studies*, July 20, 2008, http://www.japanesestudies.org.uk/articles/2008/Envall.html.

[23] Mike M. Mochizuki, "Japan's Search for Strategy," *International Security* 8, no. 3 (1983–84): 166–68; and Richard J. Samuels, *Securing Japan: Tokyo's Grand Strategy and the Future of East Asia* (Ithaca: Cornell University Press, 2008), 30–31.

[24] John Welfield, *An Empire in Eclipse: Japan in the Postwar American Alliance System* (London: Athlone, 1988), 364–8.

and ultimately cast off historical judgments on its colonial past in order to exercise freedom of action in the international arena rather than submitting to pressure from China and other East Asian states on historical issues.

Gaullism struggled to gain full traction in Japan during the Cold War. This option was rebuffed as highly expensive in terms of the expenditure on armaments and likely to provoke security dilemmas with the Soviet Union, China, and even the United States, as well as counterreactions in East Asia over concerns of Japanese revanchism. All the same, Japan's conservatives never fully abandoned consideration of Gaullism. As will be seen in later sections, this view was able to once again penetrate and influence the mainstream LDP and Yoshida doctrine after the Cold War.

Multilateralism, Regionalism, and Internationalism

Japan's third traditionally debated option—although arguably only emerging as a potential option in its own right toward the end of the Cold War—has revolved around a multilateral, regional, and liberal internationalist approach. Japan has always declared a strong internationalist bent in its security policy. The 1957 Basic Policy on National Defense stated as its first objective cooperation with the United Nations for the realization of world peace and as its fifth objective security cooperation with the United States until such a point that the United Nations can take on responsibility for preventing aggression.[25] Japanese policymakers and analysts have thus advocated fuller UN cooperation in various forms, including proposals for the Cold War deployment of a UN police force in Japan as a deterrent against international aggression and for early post–Cold War participation in support of UN collective security and peacekeeping operations.[26] In addition, Japan has been thought to have opportunities to work with its East Asian neighbors to stabilize regional security by cooperating on economic issues, building regional multilateralism, and acting as a "civilian power."[27]

However, for most of the Cold War, these liberal internationalist approaches failed to enter Japan's policy mainstream given the perceived ineffectiveness of the United Nations and the depth of regional political and security divisions. As noted in later sections, it was not until the end of the Cold War that elements of the DPJ were able to articulate more fully multilateral and East Asia–oriented security plans.

---

[25] *Boei handobukku 2003*, 88.

[26] Sakamoto Yoshikazu, *Kaku jidai no kokusai seiji* [International Politics in the Nuclear Age] (Tokyo: Iwanami Shoten, 1982), 3–29.

[27] Yoichi Funabashi, "Japan and the New World Order," *Foreign Affairs*, Winter 1991/92, 58–74.

The Yoshida Doctrine

Instead, during the Cold War and into the early stages of the post–Cold War period, it was the LDP mainstream that came to dictate and implement Japanese security policy through the fourth strategic option, the Yoshida doctrine, which at that point was alone capable of reconciling Japan's array of international and domestic challenges.[28] Prime Minister Yoshida and the other "pragmatists" or "political realists" of the eventual LDP mainstream, although committed to restoring Japan's position among the ranks of the great powers, rejected ideological positions, military spending increases, and large-scale rearmament as unfeasible given the generally precarious state of the Japanese economy and political opposition from the JSP and JCP. The pragmatists instead perceived that the reconstruction of the civilian economy and technological prowess were future prerequisites for ensuring national autonomy, and that national wealth would be rebuilt through maritime trade and regaining markets in the United States, Europe, and, most crucially, East Asia. The pragmatists did not reject altogether the role of military power in ensuring national autonomy. They were prepared to contemplate more significant rearmament and Japan's re-emergence as an autonomous military power in the future once economic strength had been restored.[29]

To implement this highly expedient new grand strategy, known initially as the "Yoshida line," Prime Minister Yoshida chose the mechanism of alignment—although not necessarily alliance—with the United States by seeking and signing the 1951 Security Treaty between the United States and Japan, concurrent with the signing of the San Francisco Peace Treaty. The bilateral security treaty initiated an implicit grand strategic bargain between Japan and the United States. In line with the treaty, Japan was obliged to provide the United States with bases to enable the projection of U.S. power onto continental East Asia. In separate agreements, Japan committed itself to assume some responsibility for national self-defense through light rearmament and eventual foundation of the JSDF in 1954. In return, it gained effective guarantees of superpower military protection, including forward-deployed forces and the deterrence provided by the extended U.S. nuclear "umbrella." In accepting these security arrangements, Japan further gained U.S. assent for ending the occupation and thus the restoration of its independence (although the United States would retain administrative control of Okinawa Prefecture until 1972). Additionally, Japan's postwar

---

[28] J.W. Dower, *Empire and Aftermath: Yoshida Shigeru and the Japanese Experience, 1878–1954* (Cambridge: Harvard University Press, 1988), 371–77; and Richard J. Samuels, *Machiavelli's Children: Leaders and Their Legacies in Italy and Japan* (Ithaca: Cornell University Press, 2003), 203–11.

[29] Kenneth B. Pyle, *Japan Rising: The Resurgence of Japanese Power and Purpose* (New York: PublicAffairs, 2007), 230.

alignment with its former principal adversary brought economic security guarantees in the form of special economic dispensations by the United States, including access to the U.S. market, financial aid and international economic institutions such as the General Agreement on Tariffs and Trade (GATT), and technology transfers. Hence, through U.S. sponsorship, Japan was able to regain its place in the international community and, equipped with U.S. military protection, was free to pursue economic reconstruction. As well as meeting the challenges of the nation's postwar international vulnerabilities, Yoshida's decision to largely entrust military security to the United States enabled the suppression and management of domestic controversies over Japan's military stance. Left-wing Japanese still objected to the U.S.-Japan security treaty but were robbed of significant political leverage by the avoidance of large-scale rearmament; and the revisionists acquiesced in Japan's more gradual rearmament, seeing the U.S.-Japan security treaty as necessary for reviving national economic strength.[30]

The Sustainability of Japan's Grand Strategy

Consolidation of the Yoshida Doctrine as Grand Strategy

The choices of Yoshida and the LDP mainstream were able to set Japan's long-term strategic direction, and indeed evolve from a "line" (*Yoshida rosen*) to an approximation of a full doctrine (*Yoshida dokutorin*), partly because of Yoshida's own farsighted leadership but mainly due to the doctrine's remarkable capacity to satisfy competing strategic, political, and economic demands and constituencies.[31] The doctrine enabled Japan in the early Cold War period to largely marginalize domestic political and ideological concerns over security and to instead focus on the expedient task of economic reconstruction while relying on U.S. security guarantees.

As the Cold War developed, the Yoshida doctrine was further consolidated as a grand strategy, again partly due to the political and diplomatic skills of Yoshida's successors in the LDP mainstream who were able to focus the Japanese polity on economics rather than on entangling security issues. Fundamentally, this was a result of the doctrine's ability to accommodate changing security demands. Japan's security situation, as noted in earlier sections, became more complex as the Cold War wore on, with the persistent rise of the Soviet threat and increasing U.S. pressure

---

[30] Michael J. Green, *Japan's Reluctant Realism: Foreign Policy Challenges in an Era of Uncertain Power* (New York: Palgrave, 2001), 14–15.

[31] Soeya Yoshihide, "Yoshida Rosen to Yoshida Dokutorin—Jo ni kaete" [The Yoshida Line and Yoshida Doctrine: Changing to an Order], *Kokusai Seiji* 151 (2008): 6–10.

on Japan to undertake more responsibility for its own defense and share the burden of security obligations. Consequently, the Yoshida doctrine underwent a number of adjustments to enable an expansion of security responsibilities. The revised "mutual" 1960 security treaty made more explicit U.S. obligations to defend Japan under Article 5, as well as indicating the importance of the treaty for the wider peace and security of East Asia in Article 6. Moreover, as noted earlier, the JSDF undertook a major quantitative and qualitative expansion of capabilities in response to the Soviet buildup and began to explore for the first time bilateral military coordination with the United States under Article 6 to contribute to its own and wider regional security through the formulation of the U.S.-Japan Defense Guidelines in 1978. In 1981, for the first time in the 30 years since the signing of the treaty, Japan's leaders began to refer to the U.S.-Japan security arrangement as an "alliance."[32]

Even if stretching the Yoshida doctrine, Japanese policymakers nevertheless preserved its essential tenets through carefully managing the demands of the international security environment and the developing U.S. alliance against the constant dilemmas of abandonment and especially entrapment. They proved highly adept at hedging security obligations to continue a minimalist defense stance while at the same time staying strategically close to the United States. The JSDF concentrated on developing capabilities that were designed solely for the defense of national land and sea space, including large numbers of Maritime Self-Defense Force (MSDF) advanced destroyers, Air Self-Defense Force interceptors, and Ground Self-Defense Force (GSDF) main battle tanks. Although these capabilities could help act as a defensive shield for U.S. forces projecting power from bases in Japan, they were not integrated tactically or in command and control with the U.S. military and were highly limited in their own power projection so as to avoid involvement in U.S. expeditionary warfare.

Japan's hedging through complementary but essentially separate forces with those of the United States was reinforced by the range of constitutional prohibitions and antimilitaristic principles derived from Article 9 of the constitution that helped simultaneously to minimize international and alliance security obligations and reassure the domestic political opposition and public over the military's intentions. Japan promoted an "exclusively defense-oriented policy." Most crucially, from 1954 to 2014, it held to the interpretation that while it possesses the right to collective self-defense as a sovereign nation under the UN Charter, the exercise of this right was prohibited by Article 9 of the Japanese constitution as exceeding the

---

[32] Akihiko Tanaka, *Anzen hosho: Sengo 50-nen no mosaku* [Security Policy: 50-Year Exploration in Postwar Japan] (Tokyo: Yomiuri Shimbunsha, 1997), 265–304.

necessary use of force for self-defense and instead only the right of individual self-defense was permitted. Japan was thus barred from using armed force to assist its U.S. ally or other states outside its own territory. Similarly, Japan has expounded the "three non-nuclear principles" (not to produce, possess, or introduce nuclear weapons) since 1967, a complete ban on the export of military technology (with the exception of a limited number of technological projects with the United States) since 1976, the "peaceful" use of outer space since 1969, and a 1% GNP limit on defense expenditure since 1976. Individually and in combination, these principles made for a highly restrained military stance during the Cold War period, although none of them, despite originating from the spirit of the Japanese constitution, were legally binding so as to maximize policymakers' future strategic freedom.[33]

International and Domestic Challenges

The Yoshida doctrine thus proved extraordinarily flexible and resilient throughout the Cold War. In the post–Cold War period, however, the doctrine has come under increasing stress as Japan's security challenges, both regional and global, have mounted and its domestic politics and economy have begun to transform. Japan's grand strategy and security policy still demonstrate considerable continuity, reflecting the adaptability of the doctrine. But questions have now arisen as to whether a revamped or "post-Yoshida consensus" may emerge, or even whether other past strategic options might return that lead to a more radical direction in security.[34]

The first set of challenges to the traditional strategic pathway emerged in the wake of the Gulf War of 1990–91 as Japan was confronted with global security issues that it had previously been largely shielded from by the United States. Japanese policymakers now perceived a demand from the United States and the international community to provide a "human contribution" to the war effort in the form of an overseas dispatch of the JSDF. In the end, Japan only provided a financial contribution—totaling $13 billion—to support the coalition forces. The Gulf War reopened domestic fissures in the debate over national security, with the SDPJ working to block LDP plans to dispatch the JSDF to the Gulf on noncombat logistical support missions. After the cessation of hostilities, Japan was able to dispatch MSDF minesweepers to the Gulf in 1991, but a full-scale domestic debate still ensued on the country's future international security role. Japan eventually passed a new International

---

[33] Christopher W. Hughes, *Japan's Re-emergence as a "Normal" Military Power* (Oxford: Oxford University Press, 2004), 31–35.

[34] Richard J. Samuels, "Japan's Goldilocks Strategy," *Washington Quarterly* 29, no. 4 (2006): 111–27.

Peace Cooperation Law in June 1992 to allow the dispatch of the JSDF on noncombat UN peacekeeping operations for the first time.

The Japanese consensus over grand strategy was shaken further by a second set of global security challenges associated with the war on terrorism. Japanese policy elites perceived the need to demonstrate solidarity with the United States and international community to expunge the threats of terrorism and weapons of mass destruction, and to do so through the dispatch of the JSDF. Moreover, despite risks of entrapment in U.S.-led expeditionary coalitions in the Indian Ocean and Gulf regions, policymakers feared that if Japan did not show a sufficient response, there was an even higher risk of abandonment as an unreliable ally.

Japan's concerns over regional security in the post–Cold War period have proved to be the third major test of policymakers' previous confidence about grand strategy. These concerns were focused originally on North Korea's nuclear and ballistic missile programs but then far more on China's rise and military modernization. The North Korean nuclear crisis of 1993–94 provided a key reality check for Japanese policymakers in exposing the U.S.-Japan alliance's inability to respond to regional contingencies. Concentration on Article 5 rather than bilateral cooperation under Article 6 of the 1978 U.S.-Japan Defense Guidelines meant that Japan was unprepared to respond to U.S. requests for military logistical support in the event of a conflict on the Korean Peninsula. The specter was thus again raised of abandonment as an unreliable ally.[35] Continuing fears of abandonment have compounded Japan's growing concerns over North Korea since the mid-1990s. The principal anxiety is that the United States might not fulfill its security guarantees to Japan in the event that North Korea acquires a nuclear strike and blackmail capability against U.S. forces in the Asia-Pacific or the U.S. homeland (a scenario of whether Washington would sacrifice Los Angeles for Tokyo). China's rising power has only exacerbated Japan's concerns over the offense-defense balance starting to swing in China's favor. Japan fears becoming caught in the middle of Sino-U.S. strategic competition or, even more dangerously, being left exposed in the event that the United States does not maintain the military capability or political will to provide security guarantees.

---

[35] Sheila A. Smith, "The Evolution of Military Cooperation in the U.S.-Japan Alliance," in *The U.S.-Japan Alliance: Past, Present, and Future*, ed. Michael J. Green and Patrick M. Cronin (New York: Council on Foreign Relations, 1999), 69–93.

Stretching the Doctrine

As Japanese policymakers have debated and responded to these challenges, the prime impulse has been to further stretch the Yoshida doctrine in the direction of Japan's becoming a "normal" military power rather than fundamentally revisit the doctrine's continued utility. Japan's mainstream discourse has shifted to ensuring the normalization of the country's security role—involving stronger measures not only for the defense of the homeland but also for a range of "international peace cooperation activities," encompassing more active support regionally and globally for the United States as an ally and engagement in UN and other international security operations.

Japan's renewed seriousness of purpose in the defense realm has been demonstrated by the establishment in 2004 of the Japan Ministry of Defense, replacing the former Japan Defense Agency that had been created in 1954. The JDA had already been very much under the domination of the other ministries in the formulation of security policy, but its elevation to full ministerial status provided it with greater autonomy and a place alongside the Ministry of Foreign Affairs and U.S. Departments of State and Defense in managing the alliance in the bilateral "2+2" Security Consultative Committee.

Japan's revision of its security policymaking structures has facilitated important changes in doctrines and capabilities. The National Defense Program Guidelines (NDPG), the document that sets out doctrine and necessary capabilities, has been revised four times since its inception in 1976. Although, as with most developments in Japanese security policy, change has been incremental so as to obscure overall trajectories, the versions of the NDPG from the mid-1990s onward have moved to essentially overturn many elements of the postwar doctrine. The 2010 NDPG abandoned the previous doctrine of the Basic Defense Force and instituted a new Dynamic Defense Force concept.[36] This latter concept moved away from the minimal defense posture of the Basic Defense Force concept, which was designed to help repulse a Soviet land invasion. Mindful of the North Korean and Chinese threats, the new concept stressed a more proactive JSDF posture in and around Japanese territory, with increasing deployments of forces southward and the capability of power projection. In turn, the accompanying midterm defense programs that lay out military procurement priorities have emphasized for the JSDF the characteristics of readiness, flexibility, sustainability, versatility, and jointness. In practice, this has meant continuing to reduce the number of main battle tanks and artillery in the GSDF and switching to investments in lighter,

---

[36] Ministry of Defense (Japan), "National Defense Program Guidelines for FY 2011 and Beyond," December 17, 2010, http://www.mod.go.jp/e/d_act/d_policy/pdf/guidelinesFY2011.pdf.

more mobile and technologically advanced forces capable of responding to regional contingencies.

The Air Self-Defense Force has sought to slow any adverse movement in the balance of air defense power by investing in fifth-generation fighters to trump China's current fourth-generation inventory. Japan's decision in December 2011 to procure 42 F-35As with stealth capabilities indicates that it is interested not only in restoring its traditional superiority in air interception but also in adding air defense penetration to strike against North Korean missile bases and even the Chinese mainland in a contingency. After the United States, Japan now deploys the most sophisticated ballistic missile defense (BMD) capabilities in the Asia-Pacific, as well as contemplating deterrence by denial through the use of F-35As and the possible acquisition of a cruise missile capability.

The MSDF, however, has embarked on the most significant buildup of capabilities, many of which are designed to negate both China's access-denial and blue water naval strategies. The MSDF under the 2010 NDPG increased its submarine fleet by more than 30% from 16 to 22 boats.[37] It maintains 48 destroyers and continues to introduce helicopter destroyer warships (DDH). The MSDF has taken delivery of two 20,000-ton Hyuga-class DDHs, with a regular complement of four helicopters but the capability to carry up to eleven. It has further procured two 27,000-ton Izumo-class DDHs, which are capable of carrying up to fourteen helicopters. MSDF DDHs are the largest vessels built for the service in the postwar period and are light helicopter carriers in all but name. Their prime function is to provide a very powerful antisubmarine warfare capability, clearly aimed against China's access-denial strategy. But Japan's venture back into carrier technology is resonant of a possible carrier arms race between China and Japan. The suspicion of analysts is that the MSDF might eventually attempt to operate fixed-wing aircraft from the Izumo-class DDHs, such as the maritime variant of the F-35. Japan's maritime air and antisubmarine warfare capabilities have been further strengthened through an indigenously developed P-1 patrol surveillance aircraft, procured to replace the P-3Cs, that is able to sweep over an 8,000-kilometer range and thus deep into the South China Sea.

Japan's transformation of its national defense doctrines and capabilities has been accompanied by significant shifts in its external military commitments. The exposure in the mid-1990s of the lack of interoperability in the U.S.-Japan alliance to respond to regional contingences has led to attempts to consolidate bilateral military cooperation. Japan and the United States revised the Guidelines for Defense Cooperation from 1996 to 1997,

---

[37] Ministry of Defense (Japan), *Defense of Japan 2012* (Tokyo, 2012), 115, http://www.mod.go.jp/e/publ/w_paper/pdf/2012/21_Part2_Chapter2_Sec2.pdf.

thereby clarifying the extent of Japanese rear-area logistical support for the United States in a regional contingency under Article 6.

U.S.-Japan cooperation has been further promoted through Japan's response to global security issues. In order to support the U.S.-led international coalition in Afghanistan after September 11, the Diet passed an Anti-Terrorism Special Measures Law, which enabled the dispatch of the MSDF to conduct noncombat refueling operations for coalition ships in the Indian Ocean from 2002 to 2009. Furthermore, in response to expectations for allied support in the U.S. intervention in Iraq, Japan passed an Iraqi Reconstruction Law that enabled the dispatch of the JSDF on noncombat logistical and reconstruction missions in southern Iraq from 2004 to 2008.

Finally, Japan's experimentation with enhanced bilateral cooperation with the United States outside traditional geographic and functional parameters has opened the way for new external commitments with other U.S. allies and partners. Japan, for example, has forged closer cooperation with Australia through the announcement in 2007 of a Joint Security Declaration, and the conclusion in 2010 of a bilateral acquisition and cross-servicing agreement to provide logistical support in peacetime operations.[38] Japan has also sought to strengthen military ties with South Korea, India, and the states of Southeast Asia. Japan has also maintained its first overseas base in the postwar period through the stationing of MSDF patrol aircraft and the GSDF Central Readiness Force personnel in Djibouti on the Horn of Africa since 2011.

Japan's security policy in the post–Cold War period thus has been far from immutable and has shifted considerably from the initial baselines of the Yoshida doctrine toward assuming a normal military role and military realism.[39] Nevertheless, despite the expansion of military capabilities and the functional and geographic scope of alliance cooperation, the intent has often been to maintain the evolution of security policy within the essential tenets of the Yoshida doctrine. Hence, in undertaking U.S.-Japan security cooperation, Tokyo has been careful to maintain its hedging tactics where possible. In the case of regional contingencies, Japan was anxious to ensure that the JSDF's role under the revised Defense Guidelines of 1997 remains one of logistical support. Policymakers have been careful not to specify the exact geographic extent of this support, preferring to stress a "situational" rather than a strict geographic definition of the scope of the U.S.-Japan security treaty. Their reason for doing so was to avoid a commitment to provide support in particular contingencies such as the Taiwan Strait that might drag Japan into a conflict with China. Similarly, in the case of the

[38] Corey J. Wallace, "Japan's Strategic Pivot South: Diversifying the Dual Hedge," *International Relations of the Asia-Pacific* 13, no. 3 (2013): 488–95.

[39] Mochizuki, "Japan's Search for Strategy," 168–75.

Indian Ocean and Iraq dispatches, Japan was careful to ensure that the JSDF missions were noncombat and time-bound by different sets of legislation to delimit operations and avoid problems of entrapment.[40]

In addition to seeking to still utilize the Yoshida doctrine to satisfy international security demands, policymakers have remained attached to the doctrine in order to cope with domestic political and economic pressures around security. Japanese administrations have been quick to stress to domestic audiences that security policy changes over the last two decades have been implemented within the same constitutional and legal frameworks put in place in the postwar era. Hence, Japan has remained committed to an exclusively defense-oriented posture—one that eschews the exercise of collective self-defense and maintains most of the antimilitaristic prohibitions. These prescriptions have enabled the LDP to defuse most domestic political criticism of its security policy, including from its dovish coalition partner Komeito; reassure the public; and also cut military policy to the cloth of a constrained defense budget. Indeed, even the SDPJ allowed itself to be co-opted into supporting the doctrine in essence. By agreeing to join a coalition government with the LDP from 1993 to 1996, and in return for its leader Tomiichi Murayama (1994–96) assuming the premiership, the SDJP agreed to accept the constitutionality of the JSDF and the U.S.-Japan security treaty.

It seems, therefore, that the genius of the Yoshida doctrine in governing Japanese security policy is its sheer resilience, adaptability, and ability to reassure domestic and international audiences.[41] However, as the next section argues, the convergence of ever more challenging international security drivers and changing domestic political forces suggests that the doctrine may be reaching the limit of its flexibility. As a result, Japan may need to reconsider past options or strike out in a more radical direction from the current foundations of its security practice.

Japan's Reconsideration of Strategic Options and the Emergence of the Abe Doctrine

Japan's security situation since the late 2000s onward, as noted above, is perceived to have entered a new stage of peril. North Korea's nuclear and missile programs and China's rise have remained constants influencing Japan's security behavior but have seemingly ramped up in intensity. In particular,

---

[40] Hughes, *Japan's Re-emergence as a "Normal" Military Power*, 126–36.

[41] Paul Midford, "The Logic of Reassurance and Japan's Grand Strategy," *Security Studies* 11, no. 3 (2002): 1–45.

Sino-Japanese security tensions have reached an unprecedented level since the Japan Coast Guard's seizure of a Chinese trawler in late 2010 around the disputed Senkaku/Diaoyu Islands and China's subsequent diplomatic reaction and alleged economic embargo on rare earth materials, resulting in heightened maritime activities by both sides. Japan's policymakers and broader society have read these developments as manifestations of China establishing itself as a power genuinely capable of challenging for regional dominance, and even more worryingly as now intent on pursuing its territorial claims by force if necessary.[42]

Japanese security concerns centered on North Korea and China have been compounded by new uncertainties in the old constant of the U.S. security commitment to Japan and the Asia-Pacific. Policymakers have drawn comfort from the strong cooperation that the U.S. military offered to Japan through Operation Tomodachi in the aftermath of the triple disasters in March 2011—the Great East Japan Earthquake, tsunami, and meltdown of the Fukushima Daiichi nuclear power plant—and from the Obama administration's policy of the "rebalance" of diplomatic, economic, and military power to the region.[43] Japan has also managed to extract more reassurances from the United States regarding Article 5 as encompassing defense of the Senkaku Islands. Nevertheless, nagging doubts remain, not only regarding potential entrapment in any struggle for regional dominance between China and the United States but more likely regarding abandonment by a United States that is no longer equipped with the material and military capabilities and political will to defend Japan, especially over an issue of relatively minor U.S. strategic importance such as the Senkaku Islands.[44]

Meanwhile, Japan's sense of a shifting international landscape has been accompanied by renewed domestic regime changes, encouraging a review of strategic options. Koizumi represented the resurgence of the LDP's revisionist wing and was followed by two even stronger revisionists, Abe and Taro Aso (2008–9), with the more mainstream Yasuo Fukuda (2007–8) in between. The DPJ's displacement of the LDP from 2009 to 2012 further opened up room for fundamental strategic debate. Abe's return to power placed the LDP firmly in the grip of the party's revisionist wing, whose members were prepared

---

[42] Christopher W. Hughes, "Japan's 'Resentful Realism' and Balancing China's Rise," *Chinese Journal of International Politics* 9, no. 2 (2016): 109–50.

[43] Richard J. Samuels, *3.11: Disaster and Change in Japan* (Ithaca: Cornell University Press, 2013), 94–99.

[44] Magosaki Ukeru, *Fuyukai no genjitsu: Chugoku no taikokuka, Beikoku no senryaku tenkan* [The Uncomfortable Truth: China's Rise to Great Power, the U.S.'s Strategic Change] (Tokyo: Kodansha Gendai Shinsho, 2012), 130–34.

to reject the expediency and limited ambition of the Yoshida doctrine and reinject Japan's security stance with a new sense of political ideology.

In totality, therefore, changing international and domestic parameters have started to transform the parameters of Japan's strategic trajectory and accompanying security policy. Japanese policymakers of all stripes, even if differing over the precise policy prescriptions, have become increasingly conscious of the need for Japan to enhance its own defense efforts, consider the appropriate degree of security cooperation with the United States, and participate in international and multilateral cooperation to respond to diverse threats. All this has raised questions about the Yoshida doctrine's continued ability to meet new security challenges.

No Mileage in Alternatives?

If the Yoshida doctrine is matched against the other long-considered main strategic options, then no serious competition now arises from the arguments of the political left and neutralism. As noted earlier, the SDPJ had essentially accepted the status quo of the doctrine by the mid-1990s and the compromise of its pacifist principles led to its eventual decline as the largest opposition party. Similarly, the JCP's arguments have failed to gain hold beyond its traditional electoral core. Moreover, despite the continuing misgivings of large sections of the Japanese public about the utility of military power and risks of Japan's involvement in military conflicts, there is an increasing recognition of the international security threats posed to Japan, acquiescence in the need to strengthen the JSDF, and acceptance of arguments both that the alliance has contributed to Japan's security and that Japan as an advanced industrial democracy has international security interests and responsibilities.[45] All of this spells no easy return to considerations of pacifism and neutralism as strategic options. The Cabinet Office opinion polls in 2015 found that only 3% of respondents supported this option.[46]

The most serious alternative to the Yoshida doctrine emerged briefly in the mid to late 2000s from the DPJ, particularly its center-left elements, with its revival of regional and multilateral options for security. The DPJ has often been mistakenly portrayed as weak on national security issues or as opposed to the U.S.-Japan alliance. This perception was reinforced by the initial tussles of Prime Minister Yukio Hatoyama (2009–10) with the Obama administration over the relocation of the U.S. Marine Corps Futenma Air Station within Okinawa Prefecture and the seemingly pro-China stance reflected in his

---

[45] Andrew L. Oros, *Japan's Security Renaissance: New Policies and Politics for the Twenty-First Century* (New York: Columbia University Press, 2017), 154–58.

[46] "Jieitai boei ni kansuru yoron chosa."

talk of the creation of an East Asian Community that excluded the United States. In fact, under Hatoyama and his successors Naoto Kan (2010–11) and Yoshihiko Noda (2011–12) the DPJ continued to pursue similar policies to those of the LDP. These aimed to strengthen Japan's national defense capabilities and the U.S.-Japan alliance, even though many of the party's key members did differ from the LDP in their analysis of the evolving international security environment and the most feasible response.[47] While predominantly vested in its center-left groups and even drawing in more conservative elements, the DPJ increasingly concluded that Japan was confronted by a fundamental transformation in the international system characterized by the United States' relative decline and China's concomitant rise. The party realized that Japan risked the ground shifting under its feet in this emerging multipolarity if it became overreliant on the United States. Thus, the country needed to not only expand its support for the U.S. presence in East Asia but also engage China more actively. Japan's attempts to restore a degree of autonomy and to rebalance ties as a trilateral arrangement in turn indicated that it should promote regional frameworks for diplomacy and cooperation such as the East Asia Summit, multilateral security dialogues, and UN peacekeeping operations.[48]

In the end, however, the DPJ's pursuit of this regional and multilateral strategic option quickly foundered due to its falling outside the parameters of what was possible, both domestically and internationally. The administration's plans collapsed due to its own domestic political incompetence, the United States' intransigence over the Futenma issue and flat rejection of any strategy that might risk diminishing alliance ties (even if this was not the DPJ's actual intent), and ultimately the Sino-Japanese confrontation over the Senkaku Islands. The latter demonstrated that China could not become a viable security partner but rather posed a threat to Japan's territorial integrity. The result was that Hatoyama's successors cleaved even more strongly toward the alliance. Japanese policymakers' hopes to promote multilateral regional security dialogues and peacekeeping operations clearly continue from the past into the current LDP administration. But the ending of the DPJ's alternative vision of foreign and security policy almost as soon as the administration had begun, followed by the party's own electoral demise, demonstrated that this type of strategy was unlikely to ever serve as a full stand-alone option and would more likely only supplement other options.

---

[47] Jeffrey Hornung, "With a Left Like This, Who Needs the Right?" Center for Strategic and International Studies (CSIS), February 11, 2011, http://csis.org/files/publication/110211_Hornung.pdf.

[48] Christopher W. Hughes, "The Democratic Party of Japan's New (but Failing) Grand Security Strategy: From 'Reluctant Realism' to 'Resentful Realism?'" *Journal of Japanese Studies* 38, no. 1 (2012): 113–19; and Paul O'Shea, "Overestimating the 'Power Shift': The U.S. Role in the Failure of the Democratic Party of Japan's 'Asia Pivot,'" *Asian Perspective* 38, no. 3 (2014): 435–59.

At the other end of the spectrum of strategic options, Japanese Gaullism and revisionism have seen a degree of revival, but again not as a full-fledged, or fully revealed, movement. The China threat and concerns over U.S. security commitments have encouraged "neoautonomists" to advocate casting off the past constraints of history and a minimalist military stance that have limited Japan's strategic freedom. According to this view, Japan should no longer be encumbered by the need to apologize for the colonial past that has made it subservient in the face of U.S., Chinese, and East Asian pressure. Instead, it should reject the postwar constitution and Article 9, which have deprived the country of its true national identity as a great power, and seek full rearmament commensurate with its economic standing in order to once again engage in the international balance of power. The JSDF should be recast as a normal national military with the complete panoply of power-projection and, if necessary, offensive capabilities, and even a nuclear *force de frappe* to deter North Korea and China.[49]

This neoautonomist or revamped Gaullist stance still has limited traction given that it is not seen as providing any easy solutions to extant security challenges. The majority of Japanese still believe that full autonomy would only worsen security dilemmas with China and North Korea and invite the United States to see Japan as a destabilizing security presence. Japan's major rearmament would also be extremely costly and divert budgetary resources required for other economic and social priorities. An indigenous nuclear deterrent might be technologically feasible, although Japan is thought to lack the strategic depth for anything other than a submarine-deployed deterrent that would require a massive budgetary commitment. Most importantly, the political barriers to Japan's possession of nuclear weapons remain high, given the three non-nuclear principles and the legacy of the attacks on Hiroshima and Nagasaki. Policymakers and the public might only contemplate such a move in the direst of security situations.[50] In 2015, Cabinet Office opinion polls suggested that only 7% of respondents considered Japan's assumption of full responsibility for its own security as feasible.[51]

Abe and the Revisionists' Capture of the Yoshida Doctrine

While Gaullism and neoautonomism cannot function as full strategic options, they have played a crucial role in the repurposing of the Yoshida

---

[49] Samuels, *Securing Japan*, 120–23.

[50] Richard J. Samuels and James L. Schoff, "Japan's Nuclear Hedge: Beyond 'Allergy' and Breakout," in *Strategic Asia 2013–14: Asia in the Second Nuclear Age*, ed. Ashley J. Tellis, Abraham M. Denmark, and Travis Tanner (Seattle: NBR, 2013), 233–64; and Mark Fitzpatrick, *Asia's Latent Nuclear Powers: Japan, South Korea and Taiwan* (London: Routledge, 2016), 65–125.

[51] "Jieitai boei ni kansuru yoron chosa."

doctrine in new directions by Abe and the revisionists of the LDP. This resurgence has thus far been depicted by these leaders and many analysts as a further evolution of the Yoshida doctrine rather than as a break with it.[52] However, the evidence suggests that Abe and his revisionist supporters, while not breaking entirely free of the Yoshida doctrine and still using it as a vehicle to reassure domestic and international audiences, hope to refashion it into an Abe doctrine. This doctrine would provide a new strategic option and look to eventually remove past security constraints. Indeed, it is arguable that for Abe and his supporters, the Yoshida doctrine cannot be allowed to stand, given that it was a strategy formulated by a defeated power to deal with the conditions of defeat and has perpetuated this lowly status for Japan into the post–Cold War era.

The Abe doctrine's first departure from the Yoshida doctrine is its view that the rise of China does indeed presage the possibility of multipolarity and a diminishing ability to count on the U.S. commitment to Japanese and East Asian security. As Abe has noted, the risk is that China may reduce the influence of the United States and turn the South China Sea into "Lake Beijing."[53] This view is not entirely divorced from the analyses of the neoautonomists and even the DPJ. Abe's diagnosis of the necessary response to China's rise is, however, different from the Yoshida doctrine in that it implies that Japan should shift the emphasis of its China policy away from engagement and toward active power balancing. Such a shift would involve a degree of diplomatic "soft balancing" but entail increasing internal and external military "hard balancing."[54] In turn, Abe's prescription to respond to the changing balance of power is for Japan to invest more heavily in supporting the continuation of U.S. hegemony and accept that the country's security is increasingly indivisible from that of its alliance partner. Abe and his supporters are now talking more than ever before—and certainly in ways that were never envisaged by the originators and proponents of the Yoshida doctrine even up until the mid-2000s—about the nature of contemporary

[52] Linus Hagström and Jon Williamsson, "'Remilitarization,' Really? Assessing Change in Japanese Foreign Security Policy," *Asian Security* 5, no. 3 (2009): 246–59; Adam P. Liff, "Japan's Defense Policy: Abe the Evolutionary," *Washington Quarterly* 38, no. 2 (2015): 79–99; and Oros, *Japan's Security Renaissance*, 128–29.

[53] Shinzo Abe, "Asia's Democratic Security Diamond," Project Syndicate, December 27, 2012, http://www.project-syndicate.org/commentary/a-strategic-alliance-for-japan-and-india-by-shinzo-abe.

[54] Bjørn Elias Mikalsen Grønning, "Japan's Shifting Military Priorities: Counterbalancing China's Rise," *Asian Security* 10, no. 1 (2014): 1–21; Jeffrey W. Hornung, "Japan's Growing Hard Hedge against China," *Asian Security* 10, no. 2 (2014): 97–122; Jeffrey W. Hornung, "Japan's Pushback of China," *Washington Quarterly* 38, no. 1 (2015): 167–83; and Yomiuri Shimbun Seijibu, *Abe kantei vs Shu Kinpei: Gekika suru Nicchu gaiko senso* [Prime Minister Abe's Administration Versus Xi Jinping: Intensifying the Sino-Japanese Diplomatic War] (Tokyo: Shinchosha, 2015).

military technologies and regional and global threats as posing security challenges that can only be solved collectively.[55]

Abe's program of reshaping Japanese strategy is also far more ideologically driven than Yoshida's was, which essentially preached expediency above all as the means to pursue national interests. Abe and the revisionists, in the same way as the Gaullists and neoautonomists, are intent on freeing Japanese security policy from the postwar constraints of history and the constitution to ensure Japan's place as a "tier one" nation, whereas the Yoshida doctrine accepted a more lowly status for Japan.[56] Abe has exhibited a willingness to shelve his ideological stance on historical issues in the name of pragmatism after the initial diplomatic faux pas of visiting the Yasukuni Shrine in December 2013 that invited criticism from East Asia and the United States. His statement in August 2015 on the 70th anniversary of the end of World War II and the agreement in December 2015 between Japan and South Korea over the "comfort women" issue demonstrated a degree of adherence to the Kono Statement of 1993 and Murayama Statement of 1995. Yet although Abe's statement attempted to avoid stirring historical tensions, it in essence conceded nothing with respect to his revisionist historical perspective that Japan's colonialism had not been exceptional in nature and that the country should no longer be bound by this legacy.[57] Meanwhile, he has sought to tackle historical legacies domestically by revising the Basic Law on Education in 2007 to restore a sense of national patriotism and by moving toward attempts to revise Article 9 of the constitution from 2018 onward. Finally, on top of this historical revisionism, Abe has propounded a "values-oriented diplomacy." The administration has argued that Japan should promote liberal market democracy and the rule of law, in implicit contradistinction to China's set of illiberal values. It should thus seek to forge new bonds among Japan, the United States, and other partners such as Australia and India.

This ideologically charged strategy has provided the Abe administration thus far with the resilience and the dynamism to implement substantive changes to security policy that have moved beyond the core tenets of the Yoshida doctrine. It has moved rapidly to overcome much of the fragmentation of security policymaking that characterized the postwar period, finally bringing to fruition plans for the establishment of Japan's National Security Council (NSC) in December 2013 to serve as the "control tower" for security

---

[55] Cabinet Secretariat (Japan), "Cabinet Decision on Development of Seamless Security Legislation to Ensure Japan's Survival and Protect Its People," July 1, 2014, http://www.cas.go.jp/jp/gaiyou/jimu/pdf/anpohosei_eng.pdf.

[56] Shinzo Abe, "Japan Is Back" (speech presented at CSIS, Washington, D.C., February 22, 2013), http://www.mofa.go.jp/announce/pm/abe/us_20130222en.html.

[57] Shinzo Abe, "Statement by Prime Minister Shinzo Abe," Prime Minister of Japan and His Cabinet, August 14, 2015, http://japan.kantei.go.jp/97_abe/statement/201508/0814statement.html.

policy and concentrating crisis management among the four key positions of the prime minister, chief cabinet secretary, and foreign and defense ministers. The creation of the NSC has also enabled the JSDF to attain a greater formal role in military planning and thus represents another diminution of the strict civilian control of the postwar era.[58] The NSC was then able to release Japan's very first National Security Strategy in December 2013.[59]

Abe's reform of Japan's security institutions has been accompanied by further extension of the JSDF doctrines and capabilities. The revised 2013 NDPG modified the Dynamic Defense Force to produce the concept of a Dynamic Joint Defense Force, which this time emphasized the need for improved joint operations between services. The 2013 NDPG and Medium-Term Defense Program were notable for increasing the number of MSDF destroyers from 48 to 54, and stating that the GSDF would for the first time acquire a full amphibious capability for the retaking of remote islands. This force will consist of around three thousand personnel, equipped with the GSDF's first 52 amphibious armed personnel carriers, and Japan will further procure seventeen MV-22 Osprey transports, which are used by the U.S. Marine Corps. Under Abe, Japan also appears more willing than in the past to fund this defense buildup.[60] Shortly after taking power, Abe initiated the first, if modest, rise in national defense spending in over a decade. The defense expenditure of the Ministry of Defense has since increased at rates of 1%–2% over the last five years.[61]

Abe's administration has subsequently worked to further erode Japan's antimilitaristic principles, many of which have remained in place for most of the postwar period. The 1% GDP limit on defense expenditure has remained broadly intact as a military constraint, although it was overtly breached with the JSDF's buildup in the mid-1980s and, depending on how it is calculated, has been consistently breached by small margins since then. However, Abe announced in the National Diet in March 2017 that his administration had no intention of suppressing defense expenditure below 1% of GDP and that in fact no such budgetary policy ceiling existed.[62] He also moved to abandon fully the 1976 total ban on the export of military technology.

---

[58] Oros, *Japan's Security Renaissance*, 133–37.

[59] Kokka Anzen Hosho Kaigi, "Kokka anzen hosho ni tsuite" [Concerning National Security], December 17, 2013, http://www.cas.go.jp/jp/siryou/131217anzenhoshou/nss-j.pdf.

[60] Ministry of Defense (Japan), "National Defense Program Guidelines for FY2014 and Beyond," http://www.mod.go.jp/j/approach/agenda/guideline/2014/pdf/20131217_e2.pdf.

[61] Ministry of Defense (Japan), "Waga kuni no boei to yosan: Heisei 28nendo gaisan yokyu no gaiyo" [Japan's Defense and Budget: Outline of the Budget Request for 2016], August 2015, http://www.mod.go.jp/j/yosan/2016/gaisan.pdf.

[62] "Boeihi '1% ni osaeru kangaekata nai'" [Defense Spending "Not Thought to Be Restrained to 1%"], *Asahi Shimbun*, March 3, 2017.

The Noda administration had already made plans to overturn this ban in 2011 in order to help sustain Japan's defense industrial base under pressure from constrained JSDF budgets and develop economies of scale and access to export opportunities.[63] Japan has reverted to a policy akin to the original 1967 ban, which permitted military exports on a licensed basis to states not involved in conflicts or Communist in nature, and is already exploring the export of equipment to Southeast Asia and India as well as basic military technology exchange agreements with the United Kingdom and France.

As for the three non-nuclear principles, these were consistently breached from the 1960s onward with the United States' transport of nuclear weapons on ships transiting Japanese ports. Japan has long maintained, in fact, that the acquisition of nuclear weapons is constitutional if it is undertaken for defensive purposes. As prime minister, Abe has steered clear of commenting on Japan's nuclear status, although in the past he publicly toyed with the need to reconsider this stance in the face of North Korea's nuclearization and China's military modernization.[64] Tomomi Inada, minister of defense until August 2017, has also called in the past for Japan to investigate the benefits of possessing nuclear weapons but argues at present that there is no need for an indigenous deterrent.[65] Hence, for Abe and the revisionists, the three non-nuclear principles are not the main obstacle to the acquisition of a nuclear deterrent; instead the question revolves more around military necessity than the need to pay lip service to these principles.

In addition to strengthening national military capabilities, the other crucial aspect of Abe moving beyond and starting to discard the central tenets of the Yoshida doctrine concerns the U.S.-Japan alliance. As noted above, Abe has diverged from Yoshida in no longer seeing the security relationship with the United States as one of expedience; instead, he now sees it as a full-fledged alliance based on indivisible interests and values. Consequently, the administration's 2015 revision of the Defense Guidelines greatly expanded—far beyond that of the 1978 and 1997 versions—the range of Japanese support for the United States in contingencies. First, the functional range of support was increased to specify intelligence, surveillance, and reconnaissance; BMD; protection of maritime security assets; joint use of facilities; peacekeeping operations; humanitarian

[63] Christopher W. Hughes, "The Slow Death of Japanese Techno-Nationalism? Emerging Comparative Lessons for China's Defense Production," *Journal of Strategic Studies* 34, no. 3 (2011): 451–79.

[64] Christopher W. Hughes, "North Korea's Nuclear Weapons: Implications for the Nuclear Ambitions of Japan, South Korea, and Taiwan," *Asia Policy*, no. 3 (2007): 77–85.

[65] Reiji Yoshida, "Japan's New Defense Chief Dodges Questions on Yasukuni, Reverses Position on Nuclear Weapons," *Japan Times*, August 4, 2016, http://www.japantimes.co.jp/news/2016/08/04/national/politics-diplomacy/japans-new-defense-chief-dodges-questions-on-yasukuni-reverses-position-on-nuclear-weapons/#.WOY9qGd1rDA.

assistance and disaster relief; and now defense activities in cyberspace and outer space. Second, the revised guidelines stress "seamless cooperation," removing the previous rigid separation of bilateral cooperation into "Japan" and "regional" contingencies. The intention is that military cooperation will operate more smoothly across all potential scenarios and levels of conflict escalation. Third, the revised guidelines emphasize that bilateral cooperation should be global and not necessarily be restricted geographically, as in past formulations, to Japan or the surrounding region. Fourth, and most significantly, the revised Defense Guidelines outline the areas where the JSDF can now use force to defend U.S. operations, such as the protection of shipping lanes, interdiction of illegal shipments, deployment of BMD, and provision of logistical support during conflicts.[66] This revision is designed to interlink with the breach of the ban on the exercise of collective self-defense.

Indeed, the most important element of the Abe doctrine for changing the nature of U.S.-Japan security cooperation and shifting radically from the Yoshida doctrine has been the breach on the ban of collective self-defense. In July 2014, the Abe government issued a cabinet decision formally contravening the near 60-year-old ban and enabling a "limited" form of collective self-defense. In the face of considerable political and public opposition, Abe then pushed on to pass a raft of security bills in the National Diet in September 2015. The Law on Response to Contingencies enables Japan's exercise of the right of collective self-defense under "three new conditions": where an attack on another state in a close relationship with Japan poses a clear danger to overturning the Japanese people's right to life, liberty, and the pursuit of happiness; where there is no other appropriate means to repel an attack; and where the use of force is restricted to the minimum necessary to repel the attack. The Law to Ensure Security in Contingencies Significantly Affecting Japan replaces the 1999 Regional Contingencies Law and is designed to boost Japanese noncombat logistical support for the United States and now other states regionally and even globally. The International Peace Support Law removes the need to enact separate laws for each JSDF dispatch that provides logistical support to multinational forces; and revisions to the International Peace Cooperation Law enable the JSDF to use force during UN peacekeeping operations in pursuing certain duties rather than just defending JSDF personnel. The GSDF peacekeeping operation in South Sudan had this collective self-defense element added to its mission from late 2016 until early 2017, although the right was never exercised.

---

[66] Ministry of Foreign Affairs (Japan), "The Guidelines for Japan-U.S. Defense Cooperation," April 27, 2015, http://www.mofa.go.jp/mofaj/files/000078188.pdf.

The Abe administration argues that the three new conditions still significantly circumscribe the likelihood and extent of military actions to exercise collective self-defense in support of the United States. However, these constraints appear to be largely hollow in reality. The Abe administration has consistently avoided defining in detail the actual conditions that might constitute a clear danger to Japan's existence and trigger a military response (potentially even encompassing economic threats). It also has not made clear what the threshold is for deciding when there is no alternative to military action, nor has it clarified what might constitute the minimum use of force. The government has thus retained considerable flexibility to interpret the need for military action as it sees fit when responding to U.S. calls for assistance.[67]

In this way, by finally breaching the ban on collective self-defense and presenting a blueprint for operationalizing military action in support of the United States through the revised Defense Guidelines, the Abe administration has largely abandoned the cautious hedging and minimalist military commitments embodied in the Yoshida doctrine from its inception until the early 2000s. Japan under Abe has indicated a new resolve to function as a more capable and willing U.S. ally, in the sense of being willing not just to provide support but now even in certain contingencies to fight alongside its ally. In this sense, Abe and other revisionist security policymakers, while building on the Yoshida doctrine, have also hijacked it in their determination to redress the balance of power in the region, gain greater status alongside the United States, exercise collective self-defense, and increasingly unfetter Japanese military power. By doing so, they have sought to transform the Yoshida doctrine into a full Abe doctrine and new strategic option.[68]

Implications for Regional Security

The triumph of the Abe doctrine over the Yoshida doctrine is not yet complete or entirely certain, but it does appear relentless in its progress. The Abe administration still has to contend with a degree of domestic opposition and residual antimilitarism. The Japanese public has only grudgingly

---

[67] Christopher W. Hughes, "Japan's Strategic Trajectory and Collective Self-Defense: Essential Continuity or Radical Shift?" *Journal of Japanese Studies* 43, no. 1 (2017): 93–126; and Bryce Wakefield and Craig Martin, "Reexamining 'Myths' about Japan's Collective Self-Defense Change: What Critics (and the Japanese Public) Do Understand about Japan's Constitutional Reinterpretation," *Asia-Pacific Journal: Japan Focus*, September 8, 2014, http://apjjf.org/-Bryce-Wakefield/4803/article.html.

[68] Hugo Dobson, "Is Japan Really Back? The 'Abe Doctrine' and Global Governance," *Journal of Contemporary Asia* 47, no. 2 (2016): 199–224; and Christopher W. Hughes, *Japan's Foreign and Security Policy Under the 'Abe Doctrine': New Dynamism or New Dead End?* (New York: Palgrave Macmillan, 2015).

accepted reforms such as collective self-defense, as was underscored by the large-scale protests in the late summer of 2015, and remains suspicious of Abe's revisionism and often strong-arm methods of advancing his security agenda. Abe furthermore must contend with increased opposition from Okinawa Prefecture against his plan to move ahead with the relocation of the U.S. Marine Corps Futenma facility within the prefecture. In addition, the LDP must continue to negotiate around any limits imposed on security policy by its coalition partner, Komeito, while Abe has been challenged by his critics within the party both on the right and within the former mainstream.

Nonetheless, his agenda will not be easily derailed domestically. Despite public disquiet over security policy, Abe has proved in his second administration to be a master of "bait and switch" by timing elections to avoid security controversies and then utilizing the renewed National Diet mandate to forge ahead with reforms. But even then, he has demonstrated resolve in overriding public and political opposition, as with the issue of collective self-defense.[69] Abe has continued with plans for relocating the Futenma air station, despite stiffening prefectural opposition. The LDP-Komeito coalition has stood strong during these security controversies, and, barring an unforeseen domestic political scandal fully taking hold, Abe may be able to remain as prime minister until 2021. This would make him the longest-serving Japanese prime minister in postwar history and enable him to continue to remold Japanese security policy and possibly even achieve his ultimate goal of revision of Article 9. In any case, even if Abe were to fall, there is no guarantee that the LDP would spring back to the mainstream on security, given that the party is increasingly dominated by leaders of a similar revisionist ilk to Abe. Abe's agenda also does not seem likely to encounter serious opposition outside the governing parties, given the DP's lack of credibility.

In the international environment, moreover, there are few signs that Abe and the revisionists will need to slow or diverge. North Korea's raising of the security ante in its recent ballistic missile tests, coupled with China's relentless rise and provocative actions in the East and South China Seas, is only likely to force Japan to up its security game and follow the trajectory set by Abe, as few other options appear palatable. The advent of the Trump administration has thrown a potential wildcard into Japanese and East Asian security. On the one hand, the quixotic nature of the new administration might pose issues of entrapment for Japan, as the United States now seems more willing to confront China over the South China Sea and North Korea, and perhaps

---

[69] Robert J. Pekkanen, Steven R. Reed, and Ethan Scheiner, "Introduction: Take a Second Look at the 2014 Election, It's Worth It," in *Japan Decides 2014: The Japanese General Election*, ed. Robert J. Pekkanen, Steven R. Reed, and Ethan Scheiner (New York: Palgrave Macmillan, 2016), 2.

even Taiwan. On the other hand, the Trump administration's "America first" policies, determination to push U.S. allies on increasing their own defense budgets and contributions to burden-sharing, and discussion of scenarios in which Japan and South Korea possibly possess their own nuclear deterrents hint at a policy of offshore balancing and potential abandonment of Japan.[70] President Donald Trump's jettisoning of the Trans-Pacific Partnership (TPP) has also not instilled confidence in the United States' engagement in the region and capability to counter China's rising influence, given that the TPP was a major plank in the U.S. rebalance.

Japan's Gaullists and strongest revisionists might be encouraged to see space opening up to attain greater autonomy in security policy. However, the Abe administration looks set to continue a similar but even more assertive line in seeking above all to avoid abandonment by moving ever closer to the United States. Abe's early visits to the United States to meet with Trump in November 2016 and February 2017, their agreement on a tough stance toward North Korea, and his talk of enhancing Japan's commitments under collective self-defense all suggest a continuation of the Abe doctrine. This is not to say that Japanese policymakers are entirely sanguine and have ruled out strategic adjustments and other options. Since the start of the Trump administration, reports from the LDP and Japanese policy think tanks have argued that Japan, while needing to strengthen the alliance where possible as a *sine qua non*, should also look to supplement its position by building up more autonomous counterstrike capabilities against North Korea, such as through the procurement of cruise missiles.[71] Nevertheless, the revisionists still see Japan's most feasible security option as developing greater capabilities to work alongside the United States.

Moving beyond the Yoshida doctrine and into the realm of an Abe doctrine carries important implications for the United States and regional security. Japanese policymakers' new readiness to expand the scope of alliance cooperation functionally and geographically, to make more definite security

---

[70] "Tainichi hatsugen shingi wa" [Truth and Falsehoods of Statements Regarding Japan], *Asahi Shimbun*, February 6, 2017; and "Amid North Korea Threat, Tillerson Hints That 'Circumstances Could Evolve' for a Japanese Nuclear Arsenal," *Japan Times*, March 19, 2017, http://www.japantimes. co.jp/news/2017/03/19/national/amid-north-korea-threat-tillerson-hints-circumstances-evolve-japanese-nuclear-arsenal/#.WOjEGFfw-b8.

[71] Henbo Suru Beikoku Shakai to Rejiriento na Nichibei Kankei Purojekuto, "Teigen hokokusho rejiriento na Nichibei kankei kochiku ni muketa teigen" [Proposal Report for Creating Resilient U.S.-Japan Relations], Seisaku Shinkutanku PHP, January 2017, http://thinktank.php.co.jp/wp-content/uploads/2017/01/resilient170118.pdf, 18, 28–29; Japan-U.S. Alliance Study Group Report, "The Trump Administration and Japan: Challenges and Visions for Japan's Foreign and Security Policy in the New Era," Institute for International Policy Studies, January 2017, http://www.iips. org/en/research/usjr2017en.pdf; and "Kichi kogeki noryoku no kento, teigen, Jimin, taikitachosen Minshin 'jijitsujo no kaiken'" [LDP Proposal to Investigate Base Counterstrike Capability, DP "De Facto Constitutional Revision"], *Asahi Shimbun*, March 30, 2017.

commitments, to exercise collective self-defense, and if necessary to balance against China makes Japan a far more cooperative ally for the United States. The Abe administration has also shown a willingness to work with other key U.S. partners in the region to buttress the U.S.-led alliance network and security system. Japan thus still remains the key to the U.S. security presence in the Asia-Pacific and to the prospects for wider regional stability.

However, this emerging security doctrine and the relationship with the United States require careful management on all sides. Japan's more capable military stance is probably a reassurance for many U.S. allies, if supporting a steady U.S. policy toward the region. For potential U.S. adversaries, though, a resurgent Japanese military, undergirded by strong revisionism, could either restore the security balance in Asia or fuel new security dilemmas. For U.S. allies, partners, and adversaries alike, however, a stronger Japan that is less engaged with the United States or is working in tandem with a more unpredictable U.S. administration is of equal concern.

The Trump administration thus needs to work carefully to manage security ties with Japan, while reassuring external observers that the alliance is not one of pairing revisionist states looking to upset the security balance in the region. Secretary of Defense James Mattis's visit to the region in early 2017 struck the right tone.[72] In addition, the Trump administration must surely pay close attention to managing the internal politics of the alliance. Japan's principal alliance dilemma focuses on abandonment by the United States, and it is this fear that would be most likely to fuel revisionism and lead to a swing away from the Abe doctrine toward full-blown Gaullism. The Trump administration would thus do well to continue to reassure Japan on U.S. security commitments while still reining in Japanese revisionist ambitions.

---

[72] "Mattis Wraps Up Japan Visit with U.S. Pledge to Maintain Alliance 'For Years to Come,'" *Japan Times*, February 4, 2017, http://www.japantimes.co.jp/news/2017/02/04/national/politics-diplomacy/inada-says-hopes-mattis-visit-strengthens-regional-security-ties-south-korea/#.WOjFQVfw9PM.

EXECUTIVE SUMMARY

This chapter examines the development of South Korea's grand strategy, with special reference to the military dimension, and argues that it is critical for South Korea to undertake structural military reforms and create a new bipartisan national security paradigm.

MAIN ARGUMENT

Several facets of South Korea's grand strategy remain constant, such as the goals of achieving peaceful reunification of the Korean Peninsula, deterring and defending the country's territorial and political integrity from a range of North Korean threats, ensuring its global economic competitiveness, and sustaining its democratic foundations. Yet even as these pillars remain the same, South Korea must now adapt this strategy to address an unprecedented range of threats. It not only must contend with a growing spectrum of North Korean threats and nonlinear scenarios; it also must consider China's anti-access/area-denial capabilities around the Korean Peninsula in an acute military crisis. These challenges will test the ability of the political leadership in Seoul to break out of its constant political infighting and build a new national security consensus.

POLICY IMPLICATIONS

- The South Korean government and military must anticipate hybrid conflict scenarios and the growing possibility of volatile transformations on the Korean Peninsula. The National Assembly should create a new national security committee to ensure bipartisan approaches to critical diplomatic, military, and intelligence issues.

- The U.S. must ensure the credibility of extended deterrence by demonstrating its military, political, and economic commitment to Asia as a critical superpower counterbalance vis-à-vis China.

- Despite outstanding historical differences and lingering legacies, it is important for South Korea and Japan to enhance their bilateral security, defense, and intelligence cooperation.

South Korea's Grand Strategy in Transition: Coping with Existential Threats and New Political Forces

Chung Min Lee

South Korea's grand strategy, particularly in the context of its military capabilities, doctrines, and strategies, has gone through several phases since the Republic of Korea (ROK) was founded in 1948. Its traditional goals remain the same: pursuing reunification, prevailing in the event of major North Korean attacks, and maintaining a decisive and irreversible economic and technological edge over the North. More recently, however, other major factors have come into play that will significantly affect South Korea's grand strategy, including North Korea's rapidly progressing nuclear and missile programs, the accelerated rise of China's power-projection capabilities in the East and South China Seas and throughout Northeast Asia, the potential for the People's Liberation Army (PLA) to intervene during a severe North Korean crisis, and accelerating Sino-U.S. strategic competition.

The range of threats now confronting the ROK is unprecedented and shows no signs of abating. Conceptualizing and implementing a viable grand strategy under omnidirectional pressures will place massive burdens on the political leadership. Moreover, the government's ability to fund much higher defense budgets in an era of rising social welfare costs and to push forward the development and deployment of critical asymmetrical assets will require sustained defense budget increases to respond more effectively to North Korea's expanding asymmetrical threats.

Chung Min Lee is a Professor of International Relations in the Graduate School of International Studies at Yonsei University and Nonresident Senior Fellow at the Carnegie Endowment for International Peace. He can be reached at <chungminlee@gmail.com>.

To examine these strategic challenges in greater detail and assess the attendant policy ramifications for both the U.S.-ROK alliance and U.S. security policy, the chapter is divided into four main sections. The first section outlines the major strategic problems and threats confronting the ROK. Second, the chapter provides an overview of South Korea's grand strategy with an emphasis on the development of Seoul's military strategy, capabilities, and missile programs. The third section analyzes thorny issues in South Korea's current military strategy, including reliance on U.S. extended deterrence and coordination with the United States and U.S. allies, the hitherto taboo subject of developing an indigenous nuclear weapons capability, defense modernization, and the regaining of wartime operational control (OPCON). Fourth, the chapter evaluates ROK and joint U.S.-ROK capabilities and plans for executing South Korea's grand strategy and concludes by analyzing the policy implications for the alliance and U.S. policy toward the Korean Peninsula.

Major Strategic Challenges Confronting the ROK

Three main forces—rapidly expanding North Korean nuclear and missile threats, intensifying domestic and regional political pressures on South Korea, and China's increasingly aggressive and robust power-projection capabilities—have altered South Korea's strategic landscape and reshaped its grand strategy. The burden on the political leadership and the ROK Armed Forces to successfully manage all three challenges is high today but will progressively worsen depending on internal dynamics in North Korea and the extent to which Pyongyang continues to threaten the United States.

North Korea's Growing WMD Arsenal and South Korean Responses

On September 3, 2017, North Korea conducted its sixth nuclear test and the most potent to date. While estimates vary on the bomb's yield, the consensus was that it ranged between 100 and 120 kilotons—six times as large as North Korea's nuclear test on September 9, 2016, and approximately eight times the yield of the atomic bomb dropped on Hiroshima.[1] According to reports from North Korea's state news agency, the hydrogen bomb tested "was adjustable to hundreds of kilotons in explosive power and could be detonated at high altitudes, with its indigenously produced components allowing the

---

[1] "North Korea's Sixth Nuclear Test: A First Look," 38 North, September 5, 2017, https://www.38north. org/2017/09/punggye090517.

country to build as many nuclear weapons as it wants."[2] The growing consensus in the intelligence communities in Seoul, Washington, and Tokyo is that the September 2017 nuclear test was a thermonuclear bomb. Coming on the heels of North Korea's intercontinental ballistic missile (ICBM) tests on July 4 and July 29, the nuclear test significantly increased tensions in South Korea, Japan, and especially the United States. On September 14, North Korea tested an intermediate-range ballistic missile that flew over Japan in defiance of the latest round of UN sanctions. One senior U.S. military official called it "a test shot that was also meant as a warning that the primary American bomber base in the Pacific, which would be central to any military action on the Korean Peninsula, was within easy reach of the North's intermediate-range missiles."[3]

With these tests, Pyongyang has demonstrated considerable progress toward developing the capability to launch a nuclear-tipped missile at countervalue and counterforce targets in the continental United States.[4] While the statement by the North American Aerospace Defense Command that "the missile launch from North Korea did not pose a threat to North America" was technically true, the ICBM was estimated to have a range of nine thousand to ten thousand kilometers (km), which would have allowed it to target the United States.[5] Equally worrisome for South Korea is the North Korean navy's development of submarine-launched ballistic missile (SLBM) capabilities, given the absence of any realistic early warning should North Korea opt to target U.S. and South Korean military and civilian sites. To date, North Korea has tested at least four Pukguksong-1 (KN-11) SLBMs. In addition to the test barge at Sinpo, satellite imagery has discovered a second test barge at Nampo.[6]

Following the September 2017 nuclear test, Secretary of Defense James Mattis briefed President Donald Trump on potential military options and affirmed that if North Korea took very aggressive action, the United States would respond with a "massive military response" that would be "effective

---

[2] Justin McCurry, "North Korean Nuclear Test Confirmed in Major Escalation by Kim Jong-un," *Guardian*, September 3, 2017, https://www.theguardian.com/world/2017/sep/03/north-korean-nuclear-test-confirmed-in-major-escalation-by-kim-jong-un.

[3] Choe Sang-hun and David E. Sanger, "North Korea Launches Another Missile, Escalating Crisis," *New York Times*, September 14, 2017, https://www.nytimes.com/2017/09/14/world/asia/north-korea-missile.html.

[4] William J. Broad et. al., "This Missile Could Reach California. But Can North Korea Use It with a Nuclear Weapon?" *New York Times*, August 22, 2017, https://www.nytimes.com/interactive/2017/08/22/world/asia/north-korea-nuclear-weapons.html.

[5] David E. Sanger, Choe Sang-hun, and William J. Broad, "North Korea Tests a Ballistic Missile That Experts Say Could Hit California," *New York Times*, July 28, 2017, https://www.nytimes.com/2017/07/28/world/asia/north-korea-ballistic-missile.html.

[6] "North Korea's Submarine-Launched Ballistic Missile Program: Are the Tests Poised to Accelerate?" 38 North, May 1, 2017, https://www.38north.org/2017/05/nampo050117.

and overwhelming."[7] South Korea responded by undertaking tests with its own land-based Hyunmu ballistic missile to simulate an attack on North Korean nuclear sites. The South Korean Joint Chiefs of Staff stated that the target was set according to the distance of North Korea's nuclear test site and to augment the ROK military's precision-strike capabilities and cut off North Korean reinforcements.[8]

Taken together, North Korea's accelerating nuclear and ballistic missile capabilities pose an existential threat to South Korea. Although South Korea and the United States were surprised at the pace of North Korea's nuclear weapons program, the September 2017 nuclear test appears to be a critical tipping point in South Korea. Public perceptions of the North Korean nuclear threat have reflected growing alarm, even under a progressive government. How Seoul responds militarily, politically, and economically remains a highly politically charged issue, given the ruling Democratic Party's inclination to downplay North Korea's array of threats while continuing to stress dialogue and engagement with Pyongyang.[9]

This represents a significant shift in public thinking. Decades of North Korean provocations and even successive nuclear tests since 2006 were not really perceived as "existential" threats by a significant portion of South Koreans. Complacency was one factor, but another was the enthusiasm for inter-Korean cooperation and dialogue following the first South-North summit in June 2001. President Kim Dae-jung stated that North Korea had neither the capability nor the will to make nuclear weapons.[10] Even after its first nuclear test in October 2006, Kim continued to insist that North Korea did not have malicious intentions toward the South.[11] The sinking of the ROK Navy corvette *Cheonan* in April 2010, killing 47 sailors, and the bombing of Yeonpyeong Island in December 2010 marked the first

---

[7] David E. Sanger, "How the U.S. Could Respond to Another North Korean Missile Test," *New York Times*, September 7, 2017, https://www.nytimes.com/2017/09/07/world/asia/north-korea-missile-test-us-options.html.

[8] "South Korea Simulates Attack on North Korea's Nuclear Site after Test," NBC News, September 4, 2017, https://www.nbcnews.com/news/world/north-korea-claims-h-bomb-test-experts-urge-trump-talks-n798431.

[9] For example, when Choo Mi-ae became head of the then main opposition Minju (Democratic) Party in August 2016, she stated that "I will make opposition to THAAD battery the party's official position [and that] we cannot let China and the U.S. clash on the Korean Peninsula." See "South Korea's Main Opposition Party 'Takes Stand Against THAAD,'" *Time*, August 28, 2016, http://time.com/4470154/south-north-korea-thaad-missiles-minjoo-party.

[10] Goh Sung-hyuk, "Kim Dae-jung–Roh Moo-hyun bukhek ohngho baleon moeum" [Compilation of Kim Dae-jung's and Roh Moo-hyun's Remarks Defending North Korea's Nuclear Weapons], *New Daily*, February 5, 2013.

[11] "South Korea's Kim Dae-jung Believed North Would Disarm," Reuters, August 18, 2009, http://www.reuters.com/article/us-korea-president-kim-comments-sb/south-koreas-kim-dae-jung-believed-north-would-disarm-idUSTRE57H16A20090818.

time since the Korean War that North Korea bombed South Korea. Despite reports by an international fact-finding commission and by the Ministry of National Defense (MND) concluding that North Korea was responsible for the attack,[12] a significant number of progressive politicians believe that there is no definitive proof that a North Korean torpedo sank the *Cheonan*.[13]

The September 2017 nuclear test, however, is being seen by the South Korean public as a qualitatively different military threat. Survey results from Gallup Korea conducted during the first week of September 2017 revealed that 76% of respondents perceive the sixth nuclear test as a threat, with 53% characterizing it as very serious.[14] Only 20% replied that it was either not really a threat or not a threat at all, while 4% responded that they had no opinion.[15] In addition, 60% of respondents agreed with the statement that South Korea should develop its own nuclear weapons, while only 35% disagreed.[16] According to the same poll, 65% of respondents stated that if North Korea does not give up its nuclear weapons, all assistance and aid should be cut off, while only 35% said that humanitarian aid should be continued.[17]

New Political Pressures

President Moon's maneuverability in coping with North Korea's growing WMD threats is heavily affected by two opposing demands. First, there is an urgency to respond by effectively using all the capabilities available and significantly accelerating South Korea's own offensive weapons systems that could be used against the North. At the same time, Moon must placate his progressive and left-of-center political base even as he pursues a more pragmatic and realistic stance on a range of critical national security issues. For example, although he has taken steps to bolster South Korea's defense capabilities after the North's sixth nuclear test and successive ICBM launches,

---

[12] Bard Lendon, "S. Korea's Final Report Affirms *Cheonan* Was Sunk by N. Korean Torpedo," CNN, September 14, 2010, http://edition.cnn.com/2010/WORLD/asiapcf/09/13/south.korea.cheonan. report/index.html; and Joint Civilian-Military Investigation Group, *Investigation Result in the Sinking of the ROKS "Cheonan"* (Seoul: Ministry of National Defense, 2010), 5.

[13] For example, former minister of unification Jeong Se-hyun and former head of the Justice Party Lee Jung-hee asserted that there was no conclusive evidence that the *Cheonan* was sunk by a North Korean mini-submarine. In addition, former prime minister Han Myung-sook maintained that she could not believe in the credibility of the multinational committee's findings owing to the hiding of critical facts. See Seo Yook-shik, "Cheonanham pokchimae daehan jwaik 50myung-eui mangeon" [50 Reckless Remarks by Leftists on the Sinking of the *Cheonan*], AllinKorea.net, March 24, 2014, http://allinkorea.net/sub_read.html?uid=29494&section=section12.

[14] Gallup Korea Daily Opinion, September 5–7, 2017, 10.

[15] Ibid.

[16] Ibid., 12.

[17] Ibid., 12.

he has also been firm that humanitarian assistance should continue (to the consternation of Washington and Tokyo).

Heightened tensions between the two Koreas, strains between the United States and both North Korea and China, and mixed signals between Seoul and Washington mean that the North Korean nuclear threat will dominate the agenda of Moon's single five-year term. To the dismay of his core supporters on the left, Moon has come out in favor of the rapid deployment of the Terminal High Altitude Area Defense (THAAD) system after hedging on the issue during the presidential campaign. In a statement issued on September 8, Moon said that "the government has decided that it is no longer possible to delay the temporary deployment of the THAAD units to prevent the outbreak of war and to safeguard our citizens' livelihood and security...[though] the ultimate decision to deploy THAAD will be made after a thorough environmental impact study has been finished."[18] Moon stressed the importance of upgrading South Korea's military capabilities as soon as possible in order to respond to North Korea's growing nuclear and missile threats. Specifically, he noted the importance of implementing fundamental military reforms while pursuing a more autonomous defense posture.[19] During a meeting with Vladimir Putin in Vladivostok on September 6, 2017, Moon also asked for Russian support in implementing extremely tough sanctions on North Korea, such as cutting off Russian oil supplies, but Putin firmly disagreed.[20]

China's Looming Shadow

China now possesses much more sophisticated power-projection capabilities, which could encumber and mitigate U.S. and South Korean military actions—a factor that will become even more crucial in the years and decades ahead. There is an increasing possibility that the PLA would become involved in a major crisis in North Korea, including through intervening militarily in case of regime collapse, actively undertaking counter-military operations against ROK and U.S. forces, or cooperating with Russia to prevent the ROK and the United States from taking proactive measures.

---

[18] Heo Wan, "Moon Jae-in daetongryeong, 'THAAD baechineun hyun sanghwang-eso chwihalsoo itneun choeseoneui jochi,' iphang jeonmun" [President Moon Jae-in, "Deployment of THAAD Is the Best Response under Current Circumstances," Full Statement], Huffington Post Korea, September 8, 2017, http://www.huffingtonpost.kr/2017/09/08/story_n_17936336.html.

[19] Jeong Eun-hye, "Moon Jae-in daetongryung 'bukhek-misail dae-eung jeolryeok hwakbo shikeub'" [President Moon Jae-in "Urgent Need to Acquire Military Capabilities to Respond to North Korea's Nuclear and Missile Threats"], Joongang Ilbo, August 8, 2017, http://news.joins.com/article/21828589.

[20] "Moon Presses Putin over North Korea Oil Supplies but Russian Leader Is Reluctant," South China Morning Post, September 6, 2017, http://www.scmp.com/news/asia/diplomacy/article/2110039/moon-presses-putin-over-north-korea-oil-supplies-russian-leader.

In particular, Beijing has been extremely vocal in its opposition to South Korea's decision to deploy THAAD. It has not only responded with vitriolic and shrill denouncements but also implemented partial sanctions on Korean companies and urged its citizens to boycott Korean goods and pop culture. In early March 2017, Chinese Ministry of Foreign Affairs spokesperson Geng Shuang stated that "our position on THAAD is very clear. We are firmly opposed to the deployment of THAAD [in South Korea]."[21] China's vehement opposition is based on the fear that the THAAD radars can see deep into Chinese military installations and denigrate China's deterrence capabilities.[22] On September 7, a Ministry of Foreign Affairs spokesperson reiterated China's stance on THAAD.[23] China's position makes little sense, however, given that there are already two THAAD radars in Japan that can see into China and that the THAAD radars in South Korea are configured not to peer into China.[24] Moreover, "China has state-of-the-art radars in the northeastern province of Heilongjiang with a maximum range of 5,500 km, while operating S-400 anti-aircraft radars with a detection range of 700 km in Shandong Province overlooking the Korean Peninsula across the West Sea."[25] Chinese media reported in March 2017 that the PLA was installing over-the-horizon radars with a range of 3,000 km that cover all of South Korea and Japan.

More importantly, if a major crisis were to erupt in North Korea, China could intervene militarily to install and bolster a new regime, shore up the Korean People's Army (KPA), safeguard North Korea's nuclear and ballistic missile sites to prevent U.S. or South Korean forces from acquiring them, and signal to Seoul and Washington that Beijing will not stand idle if they mount operations to decapitate the North Korean regime or assume de facto control over the North. China has never revealed its contingency plans relating to North Korea, but several insights can be gained from open sources. According to press reports, the PLA has deployed some 150,000

---

[21] Seema Mody, "China Lashes Out as South Korea Puts an American Anti-missile System in Place," CNBC, April 28, 2017, https://www.cnbc.com/2017/03/17/thaad-anti-missile-system-makes-china-lash-out-at-south-korea.html.

[22] "China, Russia, Share Opposition to U.S. THAAD in South Korea: Xi," Reuters, July 2, 2017, https://www.reuters.com/article/us-china-thaad-russia/china-russia-share-opposition-to-u-s-thaad-in-south-korea-xi-idUSKBN19O0N8.

[23] "Foreign Ministry Spokesperson Geng Shuang's Regular Press Conference," Ministry of Foreign Affairs of the People's Republic of China, September 7, 2017, http://www.fmprc.gov.cn/mfa_eng/xwfw_665399/s2510_665401/2511_665403/t1490884.shtml.

[24] "Why China Is Wrong to Be Furious about THAAD," Economist, May 23, 2017, https://www.economist.com/news/asia/21719485-deployment-american-anti-missile-system-south-korea-does-not-threaten-chinas-nuclear.

[25] Lee Kil-seong, "China Sets Up More Long-Range Radars," Chosun Ilbo, March 14, 2017, http://english.chosun.com/site/data/html_dir/2017/03/14/2017031401319.html.

troops near the 1,400 km border it shares with North Korea.[26] The PLA Air Force conducted drills on September 5, 2017, for a "surprise attack" and shot down several missiles in Bohai Bay, the innermost gulf between North Korea and China.[27] Other reports suggest that China is preparing for a range of contingencies along the North Korean border, including the creation of a new border defense brigade, bunkers against nuclear and chemical attacks, and full-time surveillance using drones.[28]

South Korea's Grand Strategy and the Primacy of Countering Asymmetrical Threats

What will shape the ROK's grand strategy heading into the 2020s is the expanding spectrum of threats confronting it, the need to maintain and strengthen the critical alliance with the United States, and political and military leaders' ability to skillfully manage growing strategic pressures from China. At the same time, efforts must be made to craft a new bipartisan national security consensus and modernize the bureaucratic machinery in a way that would enable Seoul to meet current and increasingly potent over-the-horizon threats. The following discussion will examine the development of South Korea's grand strategy, with special reference to its military dimension.

The Development of South Korea's Grand Strategy

Until the restoration of democracy in 1987, South Korea's grand strategy was characterized by three key elements: (1) the preponderance of presidential power, with no real checks and balances by the National Assembly and a heavy emphasis on the armed forces and key intelligence agencies, both civilian and military, (2) the highly limited role of the media and public opinion in the formation of strategy (especially military strategy, doctrines, and defense R&D), and (3) tension between the push for a more "self-reliant defense" (*jaju kukbang*) posture and the desire to ensure

---

[26] Kelly McLaughlin, "China Deploys 150,000 Troops to Deal with Possible North Korean Refugees over Fears Trump May Strike Kim Jong-un Following Missile Attack on Syria," *Daily Mail* (London), April 10, 2017, http://www.dailymail.co.uk/news/article-4399076/China-deploys-150-000-troops-North-Korea-border.html.

[27] Charlotte Gao, "China's Air Force Tests Missile Defense Near North Korea Border," *Diplomat*, September 7, 2017, https://thediplomat.com/2017/09/chinas-air-force-tests-missile-defense-near-north-korea-border.

[28] Matthew Dunn, "China's Military Preparing for a Potential Crisis in North Korea," News.com.au, July 26, 2017, http://www.news.com.au/technology/innovation/inventions/chinas-military-preparing-for-a-potential-crisis-with-north-korea/news-story/531eb0a06df3468290ceecffdacc4441.

sustained military and political support from the United States.[29] This basic structure survived even after the restoration of democracy during the term of President Roh Tae-woo (1988–93), who himself was a career soldier.

The process of formulating grand strategy began to shift during the term of President Kim Young-sam (1993–98), who was a lifelong democracy advocate and a giant in Korean politics. Kim sharply curtailed the military's influence on key national security decisions, including South Korea's policies toward the North. His biggest contribution to civilian control was publicizing and then abolishing an elite and powerful secret society within the army, known as Hanahoe (Group of One), that selectively recruited the best and brightest graduates of the Korean Military Academy.[30] On March 8, 1993, just two weeks into his term, Kim asked for the resignation of all of his top generals, including the army chief of staff and head of the Defense Security Command (army intelligence).[31]

But it was not until the administration of Kim Dae-jung (1998–2003) and the introduction of his Sunshine Policy that South Korea's national security paradigm ceased to be dominated by conservative forces. After the first inter-Korean summit in June 2001 and the second in November 2007 during the Roh Moo-hyun administration (2003–8), the ROK began to push the envelope by attempting to balance the U.S. alliance, inter-Korean "détente," and the ROK's rapidly expanding economic and political ties with China since the normalization of relations in 1992.

The progressive leadership of Kim and Roh was followed by a decade of conservative governments under Lee Myung-bak (2008–13) and Park Geun-hye (2013–17). Progressives regained the presidency in May 2017 after a snap election was held to replace Park, who was impeached in March. On the one hand, South Korea's single, five-year presidential terms have resulted in significant fluctuations in military and national security policies

---

[29] South Korea's prevailing security dilemma is characterized by the need to emphasize its alliance with the United States so that Washington will not abandon Seoul, while also expanding its own deterrence and defense capabilities should the United States' commitment to South Korea's defense waver. The announcement of the Nixon Doctrine in 1969, the removal of the U.S. 7th Infantry Division in 1971, the downfall of South Vietnam in 1975, and the Carter administration's initial decision to phase out U.S. ground forces from South Korea all contributed to growing uncertainty about the alliance. Managing this "tension of opposites" remains a priority today, especially since 1987 and subsequent changes in governments from the right to the left and vice versa.

[30] "YS: 'Hanahoe cheungsan eopseoteumyun DJ-Roh daetonrgyong an duetseul-keot'" [Kim Yong-sam: "If Hanahoe Was Not Abolished, Kim Dae-jung and Roh Moo-hyun Wouldn't Have Become Presidents"], SBS News, April, 20, 2009, http://news.sbs.co.kr/news/endPage.do?news_id=N1000579552.

[31] See Nam Jae-hee, "Kim Young-sam jeon daetongryeong-eul bonemyeo…tong keuko keonkanghan bosu jeongdo kuleun keo san…damdaehetdon Hanahoe cheok-kyul keun eopjeok" [Bidding Farewell to President Kim Young-sam…A Healthy Conservative with Broad Strokes…Biggest Achievement Was Disbanding the Arrogant Hanahoe], Kyunghyang Shinmun, November 23, 2015, http://news.khan.co.kr/kh_news/khan_art_view.html?artid=201511232256485&code=910100.

depending on the ideological orientation of the incoming government, which has limited continuity. On the other, changes in power from the left to the right and vice versa have increasingly convinced South Koreans about the merits of more centrist policies. In this sense, while President Moon is from the progressive wing of the ideological spectrum, his term in office will likely be different from any previous government. He cannot afford to cater solely or even primarily to his liberal base because he must address the widest array of security threats faced by any South Korean president.

It is too early to tell how the Moon administration will craft South Korea's grand strategy. When he became president, Moon proposed a number of dialogues with North Korea, such as holding bilateral meetings to lower military tensions and ascertain possible areas of cooperation. For example, the government decided on an $8 million aid package to North Korea, although the timing has been postponed due to rising military tensions. North Korea's sixth nuclear test and ICBM tests compelled Moon to react much more realistically, to the consternation of his core left-of-center political base. He has emphasized that while there must be no war or preemptive attack on the North, it is imperative to accelerate South Korea's military capabilities such as the "kill chain" and to begin discussion about reverting wartime operational control to South Korea as soon as it is politically, technologically, and strategically feasible. For the moment and so long as North Korea continues to push the threat envelope, Moon is unlikely to press for unilateral engagement with the North. Even as he has stressed the importance of securing peace, he has reiterated the centrality of the ROK's alliance with the United States.

South Korea's Military Strategy

Since the end of the Korean War in 1953, and especially since the 2000s, the ROK's basic military strategy has been shaped by four critical factors. First, it confronts an enemy—North Korea—that is not only the most militarized nation on the planet but also the most dangerous given the potent mix of formidable conventional and special forces matched with WMD capabilities. Second, South Korea must defend Seoul at all costs, including through developing the capability to launch massive counterattacks, given the capital's proximity to the demilitarized zone (DMZ) that separates the two Koreas and the primordial need for massive counterattacks owing to the impossibility of a defense-in-depth strategy. The third factor is the critical role of extended deterrence provided by the United States, including the 28,000-strong U.S. Forces Korea (USFK) and the capacity for rapid augmentation from U.S. bases in Japan, Guam, Hawaii, and the continental United States. The fourth factor is cohesion and jointness between the ROK military and USFK, which is without parallel in any other multilateral or bilateral alliance, coupled with the ROK military's sustained modernization since the 1970s.

Faced with the North's growing nuclear and missile capabilities, South Korea's military strategy has shifted from one that emphasizes absorbing a North Korean assault and mounting a counterattack to a proactive deterrence posture. Although the reversion of wartime operational control to the ROK is seen by the Moon administration as an essential part of augmenting South Korea's defense posture, the preservation of jointness and combined operations with the USFK and other U.S. military forces remains the *sine qua non* of South Korea's deterrence and defense posture. Given the growing asymmetrical nature of threats from North Korea—such as more advanced long-range artillery, nuclear-tipped ballistic missiles, and accelerating SLBM capabilities—ROK and U.S. forces must be prepared to fight beyond the forward edge of the battle area. This requires enhancing early-warning capabilities and devising a plan to mount rapid counterattacks or even a preemptive strike in case of definitive evidence of an impending North Korean ballistic missile or nuclear attack. Other key elements of the ROK's robust deterrence posture against the North are the capabilities to take out North Korea's critical command-and-control centers and nuclear and WMD sites and to mount an aggressive campaign to decapitate North Korea's leadership:

> During Phase 1, U.S.-ROK forces would conduct a vigorous forward defense aimed at protecting Seoul. Their campaign would be dominated by combined-arms ground battles waged with infantry, artillery, and armor. U.S. air and naval forces would conduct close air support, interdiction, and deep strike missions. After Phase 1, U.S.-ROK operations in Phase 2 would probably focus on seizing key terrain, inflicting additional casualties on enemy forces, and rebuffing further attacks. Phase 3, to start when the U.S. ground buildup was complete and ROK forces were replenished, would be a powerful counteroffensive aimed at destroying the DPRK's military power. The war plan envisions amphibious assaults into North Korea by U.S. Army and Marines at the narrow waist of North Korea. The entire resources of the U.S. Marine Corps would flow there to establish a beachhead, with substantial Army resources quickly conducting over-the-shore operations.[32]

As a result of the primacy of threats from the North, the South Korean military has prepared for a range of North Korea–centric war and conflict scenarios. With the rapid growth of the nuclear threat, the ROK Armed Forces have placed greater emphasis on acquiring the requisite weapons systems, expanded intelligence platforms, and modernized C4ISR (command, control,

---

[32] "OPLAN 5027 Major Theater War—West," GlobalSecurity.org, http://www.globalsecurity.org/military/ops/oplan-5027.htm.

communications, computers, intelligence, surveillance, and reconnaissance) capabilities and systems. The government has also increased defense spending: the defense budget for fiscal year 2017 is $36 billion, which is a 4% increase from 2016, and includes the procurement of 40 F-35 joint strike fighters (with options for 20 more), missile defenses, accelerated development of next-generation ballistic and cruise missiles, and improvements to C4ISR. In 2016 the ROK MND estimated that it must add $200 billion to the defense budget from 2016 to 2020 to effectively respond to North Korean threats.[33] Moon announced in July 2017 that he plans to increase South Korea's defense budget from 2.4% of GDP to 2.9%—or by up to $51 billion—during his term, emphasizing that "there must never be a gap in national defense regardless of changes in governments or commanders."[34] Yet current ROK and USFK frameworks will need to change in response to North Korea's hydrogen bomb test and growing ability to target U.S. bases in the Pacific and parts of the continental United States with nuclear-armed intermediate-range ballistic missiles and ICBMs.[35]

As shown in **Table 1**, North Korea's conventional forces significantly outnumber those of South Korea. In addition, the ROK and the USFK must also prepare for a wide range of lethal but limited attacks from both North Korea and China (see **Table 2**). Another key factor that the ROK and the

TABLE 1   South-North military balance, 2016

Category	South Korea	North Korea
Army	490,000	1,100,000
Navy	70,000 (including 29,000 marines)	60,000
Air force	65,000	110,000
Strategic forces	0	10,000
Total	625,000	1,280,000

SOURCE: Ministry of National Defense (ROK), *2016 Defense White Paper* (Seoul, 2017), 268.

---

[33] Vivienne Machi, "Record Defense Budget Ahead for South Korea," *National Defense*, February 15, 2017, http://www.nationaldefensemagazine.org/articles/2017/2/15/record-defense-budget-ahead-for-south-korea.

[34] Kim Jae-deuk, "Moon Jae-in daetongryeong imkine kukbang yesan GDP daebi 2.4%->2.9%ro ol-lil kot" [President Moon Jae-in Will Increase Defense Budget as Percentage of GDP from 2.4% to 2.0% during His Term], *Joongang Ilbo*, July 18, 2017, http://news.joins.com/article/21768963.

[35] Broad et al., "This Missile Could Reach California."

TABLE 2 Critical North Korean and Chinese asymmetrical threats

Category	Threats	Likelihood	Magnitude	Impact
North Korea				
WMD attacks	• Limited nuclear attack, blackmail, and electromagnetic pulse attack	• Unlikely unless Kim Jong-un believes that his regime's survival is at stake or a preemptive or preventive war is imminent	• Rapid escalation into a major conflict involving nuclear and conventional forces	• Extremely wide military, political, economic, and social repercussions
Nuclear demonstration (i.e., offshore detonation in South Korean waters)	• Taking Seoul hostage or forcing South Korea to bargain for peace under North Korea's conditions	• Not very high, given that even a nuclear demonstration would be perceived as a de facto nuclear attack	• Perceived as a major escalation calling for requisite military responses	• Unparalleled political tensions and dilemmas over appropriate military responses
Conventional and irregular forces	• Rear-area attacks • Decapitation of ROK leaders • Massive cyberattacks • Attacks on ROK naval vessels and forward-island bases behind the Northern Limit Line • Mining of major South Korean harbors	• Likely methods of choice to test South Korea's resolve and responses, given North Korea's track record	• Would not be seen as existential threats but as attacks that will spike public fears, sink markets, and cause massive evacuations	• Perception of South Korea as being on the brink of a major war

Table 2 continued.

Category		Threats	Likelihood	Magnitude	Impact
China	PLA's warning not to interfere in "internal" North Korean developments, including regime collapse	• Categorical Chinese warnings against U.S.-ROK joint operations in North Korea following military actions	• If the Kim Jong-un regime collapses, China will activate its own contingency plans, including ones to deal with an onslaught of refugees	• Would lead to increased forces along the Sino–North Korean border	• Would add significant political challenges and hurdles for the United States and South Korea with little leverage to stop Chinese actions
	Partial military intervention by the PLA	• Tailored threats against U.S.-ROK forces	• If U.S. or ROK forces cross the 38th parallel, the PLA will take action	• Could quickly escalate into a U.S.-China military showdown	• Depending on U.S. actions, different signals would be sent to key allies and influence China's next moves

s o u r c e : Adapted and modified from Duk-ki Kim, "The Republic of Korea's Counter-Asymmetric Strategy: Lessons from ROKS *Cheonan* and Yeonpyeong Island," *Naval War College Review* 65, no. 1 (2012): 61.

United States must consider is China's growing military power and the high probability of Chinese military intervention during an acute North Korean crisis. While China opposes North Korea's nuclear weapons program, it continues to believe that an unstable Pyongyang that could lead to the downfall of Kim Jong-un poses a greater national security risk. It also believes that a nuclearized North Korea—as much as it hurts Chinese interests by compelling South Korea and Japan to beef up their defense capabilities—buys time for China to catch up militarily with the United States.

Preparing for Korean War 2.0

In the event of an outbreak of war on the Korean Peninsula, North Korea's principal strategy would be to launch a blitzkrieg, beginning with over five hundred long-range artillery pieces, and occupy Seoul prior to the augmentation of U.S. forces beyond the 28,000 currently deployed in South Korea. Given that the population of Seoul and the surrounding area is over 20 million people, any major attack would be devastating. As the political, economic, cultural, and social heartland of South Korea, if Seoul falls to the KPA or is the target of North Korea's nuclear weapons, then for all practical purposes it would be the end of the ROK as we know it. North Korea would also suffer huge casualties. By one estimate, North Korea would suffer 20,000 casualties daily as U.S. and ROK forces begin massive bombing campaigns.[36]

As the North Korean nuclear and ballistic missile threats have assumed a new urgency, some high-level U.S. officials and politicians have advocated preventive surgical strikes to take out North Korea's nuclear sites. Although there is every reason to bolster the deterrence and defense capabilities of the ROK military and USFK, a preventive or preemptive strike by the United States would quickly escalate into a full-blown war between the two Koreas. In this scenario, South Korea would suffer millions of civilian casualties and its economy would grind to a halt. In the event of war, U.S. and ROK forces would attempt to track down and destroy as many targets as possible, but there is no assurance that a preemptive attack against North Korean WMD facilities would be fully successful. Real-time intelligence would be limited, and how the Kim Jong-un regime might decide to

---

[36] For an account of how a war with North Korea might unfold, see Rob Givens, "What War with North Korea Would Look Like: 20K NK Dead a Day," Breaking Defense, September 6, 2017, http://breakingdefense.com/2017/09/what-war-with-north-korea-would-look-like-20k-nk-dead-a-day.

retaliate is unknown.[37] But it is important to understand that even under the best of circumstances, U.S. and ROK forces would be likely to confront significant challenges, including the following:

> (1) locating, isolating and eliminating WMD program elements; (2) managing the consequences (to include humanitarian assistance, decontamination, disaster relief, etc.) of possible WMD attacks; (3) missile defense; (4) locating, seizing and securing weapons depots; (5) rendering constituted WMD safe through dismantlement of the warhead or weapon delivery mechanism; (6) maritime interdiction to prevent leakage off the peninsula; (7) stopping movement of people and materials of concern along land borders; and (8) dismantlement of possible proliferation networks so that materials of concern or even weapons do not move out of the theater in the midst of a chaotic security environment.[38]

The ROK's Kill Chain Program

To address the threat from North Korea, the ROK military has focused on building up its counter-asymmetrical capabilities, including more advanced intelligence platforms to target and destroy the North Korean command-and-control system (including Kim Jong-un and his immediate inner circle) with South Korea's ballistic and cruise missiles. The Kill Chain is a South Korean triad system consisting of the following components. The first piece of the system is detecting, targeting, and destroying North Korean missiles by incorporating advanced surveillance assets such as high-altitude reconnaissance unmanned aerial vehicles, developing and deploying a full range of ballistic and cruise missiles, and operationalizing joint direct-attack munitions and laser-guided missiles into the force structure.[39] During the 46th Security Consultative Meeting (the highest-level annual bilateral defense review) in 2014, South Korea and the United States agreed on a tailored "4D" strategy (detect, disrupt, destroy, and defend) to counter North Korea's growing array of ballistic missiles. In 2015, both sides began to define operational guidelines that included diplomacy, information, and economic

---

[37] David Wroe, "North Korea: A Terrifying Glimpse into What War with Kim Jong-un's Military Would Look Like," *Sydney Morning Herald*, July 15, 2017, http://www.smh.com.au/federal-politics/political-news/north-korea-a-terrifying-glimpse-into-what-warwith-kim-jonguns-military-would-look-like-20170713-gxadej.html.

[38] Robert J. Peters, "The WMD Challenges Posed by a Collapse of North Korea," 38 North, April 14, 2015, http://www.38north.org/2015/04/rpeters041415.

[39] Ministry of National Defense (ROK), *2016 Defense White Paper* (Seoul, 2017), 69–70, http://www.mnd.go.kr/cop/pblictn/selectPublicationUser.do?siteId=mndEN&componentId=51&categoryId=0&publicationSeq=777&pageIndex=1&id=mndEN_031300000000.

capabilities at the outermost ring, followed by related military components in the second ring, and finally counter-missile capabilities at the inner core.[40]

The second component of the triad system is the Korea Air and Missile Defense system, with advanced early-warning, command-and-control, and interception capabilities; deployment of the PAC-3 missile defense system; and development of medium-range surface-to-air missiles and long-range surface-to-air missiles designed to intercept North Korean missiles at the terminal phase.[41] The third component is operationalizing the Korea Massive Punishment and Retaliation (KMPR) plan. This plan was initially announced after North Korea's fifth nuclear test in September 2016, and defense sources note that it includes launching "pre-emptive bombing attacks on North Korean leader Kim Jong-un and the country's military leadership if signs of their impending use of nuclear weapons are detected or in the event of a war."[42] In addition, "every Pyongyang district, particularly where the North Korean leadership is possibly hidden, will be completely destroyed by ballistic missiles and high-explosive shells as soon as the North shows any signs of using a nuclear weapon."[43] In July 2017, the *National Interest* described the KMPR plan as follows:

> Unlike Kill Chain, which involves only precision-guided missile strikes and a handful of special operations forces, KMPR actually involves a seemingly suicidal invasion of the north by three thousand Republic of Korea marines. The brigade-sized unit, dubbed "Spartan 3000," is reportedly trained to "remove the North's wartime command and paralyze its function if war breaks out." Given the centralized nature of the North Korean government, that sounds an awful lot like an amphibious raid on Pyongyang.[44]

Following North Korea's sixth nuclear test, Defense Minister Song Young-moo informed the National Assembly that a special forces brigade would be set up by the end of 2017—a "decapitation unit" tasked with preparing for cross-border raids and detecting and killing high-value targets. According to one report, "the South's increasingly aggressive posture is meant to help push North Korea into accepting President Moon Jae-in's offer

---

[40] Ministry of National Defense (ROK), *2016 Defense White Paper*, 68.

[41] Ibid., 71.

[42] "S. Korea Unveils Plan to Raze Pyongyang in Case of Signs of Nuclear Attack," Yonhap, September 11, 2016, http://english.yonhapnews.co.kr/national/2016/09/11/65/0301000000AEN20160911000500315F.html.

[43] Ibid.

[44] Kyle Mizokami, "This Is How South Korea Plans to Stop a Nuclear Attack from North Korea," *National Interest*, July 10, 2017, http://nationalinterest.org/blog/the-buzz/how-south-korea-plans-stop-nuclear-attack-north-korea-21472.

of talks."[45] But for the KMPR plan to be successful, the special units would need accurate and real-time intelligence, surveillance and reconnaissance capabilities, and extremely well-coordinated support systems under war or near-war conditions.

Lifting Constraints on South Korea's Missile Development Capabilities

From the early 1980s to the mid-2000s, South Korea was heavily constrained in developing ballistic and cruise missiles after being pressured to sign an agreement on missile development guidelines with the United States in 1979. The initial agreement limited South Korea's ballistic missile range to 180 km, which was increased to 300 km in 2001 and to 800 km, with a payload of up to 500 kilograms, in 2010. These guidelines were put into place by the United States after intelligence reports revealed that South Korea was working on a nascent nuclear weapons program, which did not go beyond the conceptual phase before it was killed by the United States. It was only when North Korea's ballistic missile arsenal began to pose a serious military threat that Washington agreed to incrementally relax the restrictions on South Korean missile programs.

One of the deepest ironies in the U.S.-ROK alliance is that even though the United States provided indispensable defense support for South Korea during and after the Korean War, it worried about whether the ROK military would have asymmetrical capabilities against North Korea that would create a strategic imbalance. During the Park Chung-hee era (1961–79), the United States agreed to provide assistance in modernizing the ROK Armed Forces only after Park agreed to send three South Korean infantry divisions to South Vietnam to support the U.S. war effort. Even then, however, Washington was wary of Seoul developing more indigenous systems, including ballistic missiles. But at the same time, North Korea was embarking on an ambitious ballistic missile program with the ultimate goal of developing ICBM capabilities to directly threaten the United States.

According to assessments made by the Nuclear Threat Initiative based on U.S. sources, North Korea is estimated to have deployed various versions of the Scud missile (300 km range), approximately 200 Nodong missiles (1,300 km range), fewer than 50 Musudan missiles (3,500 km range), and

---

[45] Choe Sang-hun, "South Korea Plans 'Decapitation Unit' to Try to Scare North's Leaders," *New York Times*, September 12, 2017, https://www.nytimes.com/2017/09/12/world/asia/north-south-korea-decapitation-.html.

a small number of Taepodong missiles.[46] The Taepodong-1 has a range of 2,000–2,900 km, while the Taepodong-2 has an estimated range of 6,000–9,000 km.[47] North Korea also possesses an ICBM known as the KN-14 (or Hwasong-14 or KN-08 Mod 2) with a range of 10,000 km and the KN-08 (also known as the Hwasong-13) with a range of 11,500 km.[48] Scud missiles are deployed 100 km from the DMZ and intended exclusively for hitting targets throughout South Korea, while the longer-range Nodong missiles are likely to be employed against U.S. military bases in Japan as well as Japanese targets.

South Korea currently deploys the Hyunmu-2A and -2B surface-to-surface missiles (SSM), with ranges of 300 and 500 km.[49] Its ballistic and cruise missile arsenal includes the aforementioned Hyunmu SSMs and the Haeseong (SSM-700K) anti-ship cruise missile with a 200 km range. The ROK Navy has also deployed the Haeseong-2 ship-to-surface cruise missiles and the Haeseong-3 submarine-to-surface cruise missiles, with a range of up to 1,000 km.[50]

The MND announced in April 2017 that it will develop and deploy hypersonic anti-ship missiles (with speeds of Mach 3–4) by 2020. Although details have not been revealed, these new missiles are expected to have a range between 200 and 500 km.[51] Additionally, as tensions rose over the course of 2017, the United States reportedly deployed AGM-158 joint air-to-surface standoff missiles at Kunsan Air Base "designed to destroy hostile air defenses and high value, well defended, fixed and relocatable targets while keeping aircraft safely out of range from hostile air defense systems. Armed with a penetrator/blast fragmentation warhead, the operational range of the missile is estimated at over 370 kilometers."[52]

---

[46] "North Korea: Missile," Nuclear Threat Initiative (NTI), July 2017, http://www.nti.org/learn/countries/north-korea/delivery-systems; and Han Sang-mi, "Bukhan tando misail 1cheonyeo ki… Hankuk 'Kill Chain-KAMD-THAAD-ro daeung'" [About 1,000 North Korean Ballistic Missiles… South Korean "Kill-Chain-KAMD-THAAD Response"], Voice of America (Korean), July 20, 2016, https://www.voakorea.com/a/3426832.html.

[47] "North Korean Ballistic Missile Models," NTI, March 21, 2016, http://www.nti.org/analysis/articles/north-korean-ballistic-missile-models.

[48] Ibid.

[49] Franz-Stefan Gady, "South Korea Test Fires New Ballistic Missile," *Diplomat*, April 7, 2017, http://thediplomat.com/2017/04/south-korea-test-fires-new-ballistic-missile.

[50] Kim Jong-won, "Haegun, hamdaeji Haeseong-2-jamdaeji Haeseong-3 misail baechi" [Korean Navy Deploys Ship-to-Surface Haeseong-2 and Submarine-to-Surface Haeseong-3 Missiles], *Asia Today*, March 23, 2015, http://www.asiatoday.co.kr/view.php?key=20150322010013247.

[51] "Kun, choeumsok daham misail kaebal 2020nyunke siljeon baechi mokpyo" [Military Plans to Deploy Supersonic Anti-ship Missiles by 2020], Yonhap, April 20, 2017, http://www.yonhapnews.co.kr/bulletin/2017/04/19/0200000000AKR20170419168800014.HTML.

[52] Franz-Stefan Gady, "U.S. Deploys 10 Long-Range Air-to-Ground Missiles to South Korea," *Diplomat*, June 26, 2017, http://thediplomat.com/2017/06/us-deploys-10-long-range-air-to-ground-missiles-to-south-korea.

As a result of successive North Korean missile tests and Pyongyang's ability to miniaturize nuclear warheads, Washington finally began to incrementally shift its position on South Korea's need for a more proactive defense posture. After North Korea's two ICBM tests in July 2017 and its thermonuclear test of a hydrogen bomb in September 2017, President Moon told President Trump that it was imperative to remove the constraints placed on South Korea's missile programs. After the phone consultation between the two leaders, the White House announced that Trump "gave his in-principle approval to South Korea's initiative to lift restrictions on their missile payload capabilities...[and] also provided his conceptual approval for the purchase of many billions of dollars' worth of military weapons and equipment from the United States by South Korea."[53]

Following the agreement to enhance South Korea's missile capabilities, the MND is planning to develop a new SSM with a two-ton payload. Dubbed the "Frankenmissile," it is the Korean version of the United States' MOAB (massive ordinance air blast but more frequently referred to as the "mother of all bombs") and would be the most lethal ballistic missile developed by South Korea.[54] The missile would be designed to destroy North Korea's underground military facilities, wartime commands, and other critical military targets. After North Korea's sixth nuclear test, the ROK also conducted the first live-fire drill with its advanced air-launched cruise missiles—the Taurus system made in Germany, which has a maximum range of 500 km.[55]

Assessing the ROK's Current Military Strategy

While North Korea's growing nuclear and missile threats to South Korea and the region have fundamentally altered the strategic landscape on the Korean Peninsula, the primacy of defending Seoul remains as the backbone of the ROK's dominant military's strategy. But precisely because of North Korea's nuclear capabilities and South Korea's vulnerabilities, the ROK military has shifted its strategy of initially absorbing the brunt of North Korean assaults and mounting a counterattack to a proactive deterrence posture that entails a

[53] Mallory Shelbourne, "Trump Agrees to Lift Limits on South Korean Missile Payloads," *Hill*, September 4, 2017, http://thehill.com/homenews/administration/349137-us-south-korea-agree-to-end-missile-payload-limits.

[54] Yeo Jun-suk, "Seoul Seeks to Develop 'Frankenmissile' Targeting North Korea: Sources," *Korea Herald*, September 5, 2017, http://www.koreaherald.com/view.php?ud=20170905000841.

[55] "South Korea Conducts First Live Cruise Missile Drill amid North Korea Threats," *Irish Independent*, September 13, 2017, http://www.independent.ie/world-news/south-korea-conducts-first-live-cruise-missile-drill-amid-north-korea-threats-36127398.html.

preemptive attack or, at a minimum, simultaneous and massive counterattacks throughout North Korea.

As North Korea's asymmetrical capabilities have made major advances in the past several years, South Korea and the United States have to take into account the possibility of a North Korean nuclear strike. Or at a minimum, they must consider that the North might hold the ROK and Japan hostage with a possible nuclear attack in order to dissuade the United States from reinforcing troops and combat assets in the Korean theater. What has transformed the battle landscape on the Korean Peninsula is the need to mount a massive counterattack as soon as hostilities begin. There is no alternative but to pursue an aggressive forward-defense strategy while absorbing initial North Korean artillery, ballistic missiles, and possible biochemical weapon attacks.

In this context, where the ROK military spends its defense resources over the duration of the Moon administration is crucial. The new government has emphasized the need for South Korean nuclear-powered attack submarines (SSN) to undertake more robust antisubmarine warfare, especially since North Korea has attained SLBM capabilities.[56] Advocates argue that South Korea needs at least six SSNs, with deployment from 2026 to 2035.[57] But the more urgent need must be focused on accelerating South Korea's ballistic and cruise missile capabilities, missile defense, and other counterstrike assets. Assuring that the ROK can have an effective "kill chain" is far more important at this time than spending billions in developing SSNs. Taking the war deep into North Korea is the central strategic capability that needs the full attention of the MND and the National Security Council.

Alternative military strategies could be considered such as defense-in-depth (as was the case until the 1980s when the KPA had a numerical advantage over the ROK armed forces) or the repositioning of U.S. tactical weapons. However, nuclear artillery and landmines were withdrawn in the late 1950s, and all U.S. tactical nuclear weapons were withdrawn in 1991. The main rationale for a robust defense-in-depth strategy was to augment U.S. forces based in the Pacific or the continental United States so that the ROK forces and USFK could buy time. However, with North Korea's deployment of long-range artillery across the DMZ, ballistic missiles and biochemical weapons aimed at key counterforce and countervalue targets, and nuclear

---

[56] Wi Moon-hee and Ahn Hyo-seong, "Dandok, Hanmi, Hankuk hekchujin jamsuham boyu habeui" [Breaking News: South Korea and the United States Agree on Korea's Development of SSN], *Joongang Ilbo*, September 20, 2017, http://news.joins.com/article/21952147.

[57] "Jeonmunka 'Hankuk, 8 nyunnae hek jamsuham keonjo kaneung…6cheok hwakbo haeya'" [According to an Expert, "South Korea Can Deploy an SSN and Needs a Total of Six"], Yonhap, September 27, 2016, http://www.yonhapnews.co.kr/bulletin/2016/09/27/0200000000A KR20160927044200014.HTML.

capabilities, the ROK now has no choice but to mount an aggressive and immediate counterstrike or even a preemptive attack against North Korean forces. Seoul cannot be held hostage as a bargaining chip; North Korea must understand that the moment deterrence fails for South Korea, it can only lead to massive retaliation.

The Credibility of U.S. Extended Deterrence

A critical aspect of South Korea's military strategy toward North Korea is the degree to which the United States is willing to protect the ROK with nuclear weapons. Ever since North Korea conducted its first nuclear test in 2006, the United States has publicly reaffirmed its nuclear commitment to South Korea. The joint communiqué released after the 48th U.S.-ROK Security Consultative Meeting in October 2016 strongly stated the U.S. commitment to the ROK's defense by noting that "any North Korean aggression or military provocation is not to be tolerated and that the United States and the ROK would work shoulder-to-shoulder to demonstrate our combined resolve." The two sides asserted "that the U.S.-ROK alliance remains vital to the future interests of both nations in securing peace and stability on the Korean Peninsula and in Northeast Asia."[58] The communiqué also confirmed the credibility of U.S. extended deterrence, including the nuclear umbrella.

> The secretary reaffirmed the continued U.S. commitment to provide extended deterrence for the ROK using the full range of military capabilities, including the U.S. nuclear umbrella, conventional strike, and missile defense capabilities. The secretary also reiterated the longstanding U.S. policy that any attack on the United States or its allies will be defeated, and any use of nuclear weapons will be met with an effective and overwhelming response. The secretary and the minister committed to ensuring that extended deterrence for the ROK remains credible, capable, and enduring by continuing to enhance alliance deterrence measures and capabilities in response to the increasing North Korean nuclear, WMD, and ballistic missile threat and continuing to promote information-sharing and interoperability.[59]

Given the growing North Korean threat, and notwithstanding deeply rooted historical differences between South Korea and Japan, Seoul, Tokyo, and Washington have no choice but to cooperate on enhancing their joint responses. The three countries have also expressed their concern over China's increasingly robust military presence in the region, although their statements on this issue have not been nearly as explicit as those on North Korea. After the eighth trilateral U.S.-Japan-ROK defense ministers' meeting

---

[58] "Joint Communique of the 48th U.S.-ROK Security Consultative Meeting," Washington, D.C., October 20, 2016, 2.

[59] Ibid.

in Singapore on the margins of the Shangri-La Dialogue in June 2017, a joint press statement stressed the importance of trilateral security cooperation while stating that "the three ministers also discussed other regional security issues, including the importance of maritime security." In particular, the three ministers:

> lauded the progress in trilateral defense cooperation and praised collective efforts to enhance interoperability and exercise a variety of communication channels to share information and coordinate responses to North Korea's provocative actions. The three ministers applauded recent efforts to improve trilateral response capabilities, to include the execution of four missile warning exercises, an inaugural antisubmarine warfare exercise, a maritime interdiction operations exercise, and combined flight training events with U.S. bomber aircraft....The three ministers reaffirmed that freedom of navigation and overflight must be ensured, and that disputes should be resolved in a peaceful manner.[60]

Another important component of the U.S. defense posture in the Asia-Pacific is the increasing defense cooperation between the United States, Japan, and Australia. Such cooperation is perceived by key U.S. allies in the region, including South Korea, as an indispensable demonstration of U.S. military assurance.

Yet while Seoul continues to believe in the credibility of U.S. extended deterrence, South Korea is also much more focused on building up its offensive capabilities. What has changed during the so-called second nuclear age, defined by the rise of new nuclear powers such as India, Pakistan, and North Korea, is that the calculus of deterrence has become much more complex due to Pyongyang's rapid progress in developing a direct nuclear threat against the United States that has added a new layer of uncertainty. David Santoro and John Warden have written that "as the Northeast Asian security environment deteriorates—with continued North Korean nuclear threats and increased Chinese assertiveness—experts in Japan and South Korea more frequently debate whether the U.S. nuclear umbrella in Asia should evolve toward an arrangement that more closely resembles the NATO model."[61] A report published by the Center for Strategic and International Studies in 2016 also asserted that extended deterrence in the 21st century was less credible than during the Cold War:

> U.S. extended deterrence has lost much of its credibility and allies and friends are less dependent on the United States for their security. Real assurance, to the extent it exists, will depend on effective and demonstrated deterrence.

---

[60] "United States–Japan–Republic of Korea Defense Ministers Meeting," Joint Press Statement, June 3, 2017, 1.

[61] David Santoro and John K. Warden, "America's Delicate Dance between Deterrence and Assurance," *National Interest*, February 1, 2016, http://nationalinterest.org/feature/americas-delicate-dance-between-deterrence-assurance-15076.

> The degree to which extended deterrence has failed, or the degree to which states can be assured, will differ across and within regions throughout the hierarchy of nuclear powers.... In a world where positive security guarantees are less credible or desirable, major nuclear powers may seek to tip or balance the scales of deterrence through other means of support, such as with transfers of technology to their smaller nuclear-armed partners.[62]

Unlike NATO, in which a Nuclear Planning Group coordinates nuclear issues and policies, extended deterrence vis-à-vis South Korea is coordinated through bilateral consultations. Seoul and Washington have adopted a "tailored deterrence" approach to cope with the full spectrum of nuclear and ballistic missile threats. The Extended Deterrence Policy Committee and the Counter-Missile Capability Committee, which were established to foster greater coordination, merged into the Deterrence Strategy Committee in April 2015, and the Extended Deterrence Strategy and Consultation Group was set up in October 2016.[63] One key issue for reinforcing the credibility of the U.S. extended deterrence guarantee is where the United States should deploy nuclear weapons for maximum flexibility:

> As for the location of nuclear weapons, this also presents a dilemma. On the one hand, unless these weapons are forward-based in or near the theater, they might not be particularly useful in a crisis or credible as deterrent—especially air-delivered weapons that are carried by relatively short-range platforms. On the other hand, forward-based weapons can be particularly vulnerable to attack, and the political complications of stationing them abroad could create even bigger problems.[64]

Should Seoul Develop Independent Nuclear Weapons?

In the aftermath of successively more powerful North Korean nuclear tests, many South Koreans believe that the ROK's military strategy should include an indigenous nuclear deterrent. In a survey conducted by the *Joongang Ilbo* in February 2016, 67.7% supported South Korea's development of its own nuclear weapons (32.8% very strongly and 34.9% somewhat), while only 30.5% rejected the idea (20.9% opposed and 9.6% strongly opposed).[65]

---

[62] Clark Murdock et al., *Thinking about the Unthinkable in a Highly Proliferated World* (Washington, D.C.: Center for Strategic and International Studies, 2016), 39–40.

[63] Ministry of National Defense (ROK), *2016 Defense White Paper*, 67.

[64] Evan Braden Montgomery, "Extended Deterrence in the Second Nuclear Age: Geopolitics, Proliferation, and the Future of U.S. Security Commitments," Center for Strategic and Budgetary Assessments, 2016, 34.

[65] Kim Seong-tak, "Dandok, Kaesong Gongdan jungdan, chan 55%...ban 42% kukne THAAD baechi, chan 68% ban 27%"[Special, 55% Support Closing of Kaesong Industrial Complex, 42% Opposed and 68% Support THAAD Deployment while 27% Are Against], *Joongang Ilbo*, February 15, 2016, http://news.joins.com/article/19566209.

As expected, those on the right are much more supportive of an indigenous nuclear program, while those on the left are almost uniformly against it, given that such a move would considerably worsen the security environment on the Korean Peninsula.

Public sentiments, however, do not reflect official positions, although the nuclear taboo has been broken by an incessantly aggressive North Korea. President Moon stated in an interview with CNN in September 2017 that "I do not agree that South Korea needs to develop our own nuclear weapons or relocate tactical nuclear weapons in the face of North Korea's nuclear threat." He explained that "to respond to North Korea by having our own nuclear weapons will not maintain peace on the Korean Peninsula and could lead to a nuclear arms race in northeast Asia."[66] At the same time, Moon emphasized that it is imperative to strengthen South Korea's deterrence capabilities.

Those who argue that it is time for South Korea to at least consider some type of a nuclear option focus on five main points. First, they assert that de facto acceptance of North Korea's nuclear weapons does not make sense while South Korea has to rely exclusively on the U.S. nuclear umbrella for protection. Second, the 1991 Agreement on Reconciliation, Non-Aggression, and Exchanges and Cooperation between South and North Korea (known as the South-North Basic Agreement) and the 1992 Denuclearization Accord, in which the two Koreas agreed not to develop, test, or deploy nuclear weapons, were voided by the North's nuclear test in 2006. While South Korea might continue to adhere to its non-nuclear principle, it should at least announce that it will no longer recognize the validity of the denuclearization agreement. Third, South Korea is already surrounded by nuclear weapon states such as China and Russia, in addition to North Korea, so that concerns about creating an Asian domino effect make little sense. Fourth, India's and Israel's nuclear weapons programs show that when a country's fundamental interests are at stake, a sovereign state should have the right to choose whether it wishes to pursue the nuclear path. Fifth, proponents of the nuclear option argue that, at a minimum, the United States should reintroduce tactical nuclear weapons into South Korea.

In the United States, there has always been a strong aversion to either South Korea or Japan pursuing its own nuclear weapons, which would deal a major blow to the Nuclear Non-Proliferation Treaty and have global repercussions. Advocates of nuclear nonproliferation have always been suspicious of South Korea's potential tilt toward developing its own nuclear

---

66 Paula Hancocks and James Griffiths, "No Nuclear Weapons in South Korea, Says President Moon," CNN, September 14, 2017, http://edition.cnn.com/2017/09/14/asia/south-korea-moon-nuclear/index.html.

weapons ever since former president Park Chung-hee tried to pursue an indigenous nuclear program.

The costs of South Korea going nuclear would be considerable, including Chinese and Russian responses, the need to consistently finance both conventional and nuclear deterrent capabilities, major damage to its alliance with the United States, and international sanctions. Thus, since the North's first nuclear test, all South Korean governments have maintained that Seoul would retain its non-nuclear posture. As noted above, President Moon has made it clear that he is opposed to the reintroduction of U.S. tactical nuclear weapons or South Korea's own development of a nuclear weapons program. But if South Korea is to retain this position, policymakers should consider establishing a policy coordination mechanism akin to NATO's Nuclear Planning Group. Moreover, as Seoul and Washington have agreed in principle, the bilateral missile agreement should be revised in order to formally lift all ceilings on South Korea's development of ballistic and cruise missiles, and the agreement should be terminated.

Regaining Wartime Operational Control and Modernizing the ROK's Military Capabilities

For more than a decade, South Korea has been working toward regaining wartime OPCON of its military, which is currently in the hands of the USFK commander. If war breaks out on the peninsula, the National Command Authorities of South Korea and the United States will transmit their own orders through their defense ministers to their respective forces. The U.S.-ROK Combined Forces Command (headed by the USFK commander) will then execute the binational orders. During the Roh Moo-hyun government, an initial agreement was reached with the United States to revert wartime OPCON to South Korea by 2012 provided that the ROK military acquired the requisite capabilities. Roh advocated wartime OPCON transfer as a means of lessening South Korea's dependence on its alliance with the United States.

When Lee Myung-bak came into office in February 2008, the decision to pursue wartime OPCON transfer was postponed, and Park Geun-hye also decided that the ROK military was not ready to assume this responsibility. The dilemma that Seoul faces is that the transfer of wartime OPCON could weaken jointness between the ROK and the USFK, which are currently integrated at all levels of operation. The OPCON transfer would abolish the Combined Forces Command and replace it with "'independent, parallel national commands' acting in close liaison." Although this structure is effective for both NATO and the U.S.-Japan alliance, "none of those commands seriously envision a massive ground war in traditional fashion, potentially involving hundreds of thousands of casualties."[67]

It remains uncertain how strongly the Moon administration will pursue the transfer of wartime OPCON. President Moon served as the chief of staff to the late president Roh but has given no indication that he will prioritize this issue over more urgent military concerns. One of his major campaign pledges was to initiate long-overdue structural reforms of the ROK military, overhaul the defense procurement process, and increase the defense budget. In December 2005 the MND created its first Defense Reform Basic Plan (2006–20) to adapt more adroitly to network-centric warfare and create a more advanced military. This plan was revised in 2009, 2012, and most recently 2016 to reflect the growing nuclear threat from North Korea.

The ROK's proposed military reforms consist of the following core components: reducing total forces from 625,000 to 522,000 by 2020 by downsizing the army from 490,000 to 387,000 troops, while air force, navy, and marine corps personnel numbers will remain unchanged; reinforcing ground forces with 230-mm multiple launch rocket systems, attack helicopters, upgraded K2 main battle tanks, and K9 self-propelled howitzers; acquiring KDDX destroyers, FFX frigates, and KSS-III submarines (with added plans to develop the navy's own SSNs); operationalizing the KF-35s and developing South Korea's indigenous KF-X fighter aircraft; and allocating sufficient resources to expedite the military's Kill Chain capabilities by 2020.[68]

If the defense budget grows from 2.4% to 2.9% of GDP by the end of Moon's term, it will be the biggest net increase since the 1980s, and the ROK military will be able to implement key elements of its Kill Chain program. But as outlined earlier in this chapter, the ROK has to confront four highly challenging simultaneous missions: (1) enhancing its deterrence and defense capabilities against a widening and deepening North Korean threat, (2) ensuring the highest level of coordination in the U.S.-ROK alliance, (3) coping with an increasingly aggressive China that is determined to overtake the United States as the supreme military power in East Asia, and (4) preparing for very hostile nonlinear scenarios, such as regime collapse in North Korea or PLA intervention in an acute military crisis.

The ROK and the USFK should concentrate their efforts on responding to North Korea's expanding nuclear threat and preparing for extremely volatile nonlinear situations. The most difficult choice that ROK and U.S. political leaders will confront is how to respond in the event of a lethal but limited strike against the ROK, such as the launching of Nodong missiles at ROK

---

[67] Robert E. Kelly, "South Korea: Who Should Have Wartime Command?" *Diplomat*, August 12, 2013, http://thediplomat.com/2013/08/south-korea-who-should-have-wartime-command.

[68] Ministry of National Defense (ROK), *2016 Defense White Paper*, 104–6.

military targets, guerilla raids in key urban centers, or the use of chemical and biological weapons. South Korea not only will need to respond with active counterattacks but also must be prepared for rapid escalation. At the same time, China's reaction and potential military response, including active countermeasures against U.S.-ROK joint operations, will become an increasingly important factor.

If North Korea threatens to detonate a nuclear warhead in South Korean waters or in a rural area to demonstrate its nuclear capability, the United States will face the critical dilemma of whether it should respond with a nuclear strike. A 2013 U.S. Department of Defense report to Congress on the United States' nuclear employment strategy noted that the "fundamental role of U.S. nuclear weapons remains to deter nuclear attack on the United States and its Allies and partners [and] *the United States will only consider the use of nuclear weapons in extreme circumstances to defend the vital interests of the United States, or its Allies and partners*" (emphasis added).[69] The National Military Strategy issued by the Joint Chiefs of Staff in 2015 emphasized meeting the full spectrum of threats facing the United States and its key allies and partners. Specifically, the report stressed the importance of defeating violent extremist organizations, while also preparing for state conflict, hybrid conflict, and nonstate conflict in order to deter, deny, and defeat both state and nonstate adversaries.[70]

It is critical for the ROK and the United States to understand that they will confront pernicious, long-term uncertainty on the Korean Peninsula. There is little doubt that the United States has a critical technological edge over the KPA, and the ROK Armed Forces are likewise more advanced than North Korea's. But superior military technology has limits, as evinced by the Vietnam War and more recently by U.S. and coalition operations in Iraq and Afghanistan. Breaking the bureaucratic barrier within the ROK military to undertake structural reforms, inculcating the civilian leadership with realistic scenarios involving hybrid warfare scenarios, and ensuring that the ROK and the United States can coordinate their political and military strategies with unprecedented levels of jointness will determine whether the ROK emerges victorious in its counter-asymmetrical strategy.

If the ROK and the United States are to prevail in a future conflict, it is essential to ensure that both forces have the requisite ability to mount joint counterattacks on all critical North Korean targets in parallel with massive and relentless offensive operations to cut off North Korea's

---

[69] U.S. Department of Defense, "Report on Nuclear Employment Strategy of the United States Specified in Section 491 of 10 U.S.C.," 2013, 4.

[70] U.S. Department of Defense, *The National Military Strategy of the United States of America 2015* (Washington, D.C., June 2015), 4–6.

asymmetrical capabilities. High casualties are inevitable in another Korean War or even in a surgical strike against South Korean or U.S. forces. Making sure that allied forces will prevail with immediate, in-depth, and massive punitive strikes into North Korea lies at the heart of South Korea's "new strategic look."

Lessons for the U.S.-ROK Alliance and Policy Ramifications

Challenges Facing the U.S.-ROK Alliance

When the Korean War ended in July 1953, it would have been impossible to imagine that the ROK would ultimately emerge to become Asia's fourth-largest economy and the world's fifth-largest exporting power, possessing a modern, well-trained, and formidable military. That the U.S.-ROK alliance has grown and prospered through various domestic crises in South Korea and changes in government since the restoration of democracy in 1987 is a critical milestone. But it is important to remember that the cost for success in another Korean conflict or after a massive North Korean attack, such as a nuclear strike on Seoul, will go far beyond any war-gaming scenarios. Although the ROK and the USFK would eventually prevail and North Korea as we know it would cease to exist, the repercussions for South Korea would be truly horrific. Therefore, even as the ROK and the United States jointly prepare for a range of worst-case scenarios over the next decade, they must account for extremely difficult, volatile, and highly uncertain operations involving the KPA, as well as increasingly the PLA.

As a result, the real litmus test for the ROK's grand strategy and especially its dominant military strategy is the ability to conduct combined operations in the fullest sense of the term. The allies need to prepare for stacked military attacks from North Korea short of a major invasion but equally dangerous, such as long-range artillery and missile attacks on Seoul and key airports and sea ports. An additional priority will be controlling nuclear and other WMD sites in the event of violent regime change in Pyongyang with mass chaos in North Korea. Another possible scenario, as noted above, involves the PLA's military intervention in North Korea.

The second major variable is the response of the South Korean political leadership. Here, the ideological persuasion of the sitting president will significantly shape how the ROK chooses to respond. A left-wing administration might be inclined to reach an early and very disadvantageous political settlement with the North that is likely to lead ultimately to reunification under North Korean terms. This is only a hypothetical scenario, but one that cannot be discounted as pure fantasy. Hence, how President Moon copes with North Korean nuclear and missile threats, as well as intensifying pressures from China and to a far lesser degree Russia, will be an extremely important benchmark in forging a new national security paradigm premised on a bipartisan political consensus, depoliticized intelligence estimates about North Korea, and strong bipartisan support for sustaining the alliance with the United States.

Political forces will become as important as military campaigns and operations because of China's growing anti-access/area-denial capabilities in and around the Korean Peninsula. Chinese intervention in the Korean War saved Kim Il-sung from certain defeat. While the circumstances in 2017 are fundamentally different from those in 1950, the fact that China's military power, strategic and tactical intelligence, and ability to project power more accurately have never been greater means that the United States and the ROK, as well as Japan, must be prepared for varying degrees of Chinese intervention—political and military—in Korean contingencies. Regardless of the level of trade between South Korea and China and Beijing's greater linkages with the international system, China's growing military power and unilateral policies suggest that managing the China factor will become as important over the next decade as addressing North Korea's multiple threats.

Ever since North Korea acquired nuclear weapons, the prevailing view in South Korea, the United States, and Japan is that China is the only power that can exercise the leverage needed to convince North Korea to roll back and even give up its nuclear program. This is arguably the biggest fallacy in the North Korean nuclear saga. Even though Beijing pays lip service to UN-mandated sanctions and considers Pyongyang to be a major nuisance, such a perception misunderstands what North Korea really means to China: a nuclearized ally that constrains U.S. strategy and force postures in Northeast Asia and the East China Sea, while enabling the PLA to modernize its forces with greater resources, acumen, and technological prowess than ever before. It has become fashionable to characterize North Korea as a strategic liability for Beijing, but given the immense power gap between China and North Korea and the latter's critical economic, political, and even military dependence on China, North Korea is a strategic asset rather than a liability in the context of China's grand strategy in the early 21st century.

The most important dilemma confronting the United States' Asian allies, including South Korea, is how to preserve their growing and irreversible economic ties with China while maintaining robust military alliances with the United States. This dilemma will become increasingly prominent in the conduct of Seoul's, Tokyo's, and Canberra's balancing policies between the

United States and China. In the case of South Korea, Seoul's leverage vis-à-vis Beijing is very limited. ROK forces are geared almost wholly against North Korean threats, but as PLA capabilities continue to grow, South Korea must consider Chinese military operations either along the Sino–North Korean border or in South Korean waters to deter U.S. and ROK forces. Politically, Seoul's ability to influence Beijing's policies is constrained given China's much more aggressive political attacks on South Korea. The only way that South Korea can maintain leverage against China is by enhancing its alliance with the United States; deepening security cooperation with Japan; strengthening trilateral intelligence and military coordination among the United States, South Korea, and Japan; and jointly responding to North Korea's nuclear and WMD capabilities.

Policy Ramifications

There are numerous policy implications for the ROK and the United States from this analysis. For the first time since the two Koreas and the People's Republic of China were founded in 1948 and 1949, all armed forces on and around the peninsula—South and North Korea, China, Japan, and the United States—are modern, combat-ready, and technologically advanced, albeit with unique force structures. One of the key lessons that can be derived from such a configuration of military power in Northeast Asia is that political responses and operational tempos will face intense pressure under circumstances of limited and accurate real-time intelligence. In sum, five policy implications in particular should receive greater attention from South Korea and the United States.

First, the ROK government must narrow the gaps and inconsistencies between its overarching strategic objective of peaceful unification and the reality of a much more volatile path toward a unified Korea. A negotiated peace settlement leading to a unified Korean government is the most optimal outcome, but it is also the most unrealistic. Both sides have maintained totally different political systems for nearly seven decades, and given the depth of mistrust and North Korea's central goal of reunifying the peninsula under its own terms, South Korea cannot but prepare for nonlinear transitions on the path toward unification. Moreover, South Korea should reconfigure civil-military relations in order to maximize favorable outcomes during potential periods of unparalleled political uncertainties, simultaneous North Korean attacks, and Chinese military intervention.

Second, it is imperative that the South Korean National Assembly and the major political parties jointly create a "national security committee" that will help build a bipartisan foundation to address the threats confronting South Korea. The stakes are far too high for the country's political parties and their leaders to play political football over critical national security issues. Both the conservative and liberal parties must assume equal responsibility for the heretofore negative effects of putting their personal and party interests above existential national security interests. Although in any future scenario involving North Korea's employment of even "limited" nuclear attacks on South Korea, the government in power must assume primary responsibility, no major political party can run away from the legacy of decades of bitter internecine political battles that led to systematic politicization and weakened national security resolve. All major parties on the left and the right should agree on a joint defense modernization program to minimize budget battles in the National Assembly. It is also critical for the political parties to ensure that intelligence assessments are not politically biased.

Third, reverting wartime OPCON to the ROK, modernizing C4ISR and counter-asymmetrical assets, increasing the military budget, and implementing structural military reforms are important factors in augmenting the ROK military's warfighting capabilities. Yet greater attention must be paid to how civilian and military leaders will effectively respond to extremely volatile nonlinear operations. Otherwise, the ROK's ability to chart a path toward unification or respond effectively to simultaneous military crises will be denigrated, perhaps beyond repair.

Fourth, not only must the United States consider the North Korean nuclear threat as the most important security threat in the world, but it also must devote the requisite military, diplomatic, and political resources to ensuring the credibility of U.S. extended deterrence to South Korea and Japan. The worst possible outcome in the United States' East Asian alliances is if Seoul and Tokyo begin to believe that the U.S. security commitment is waning just as North Korea's nuclear threats cross new thresholds and China exercises its military muscle. Seoul and Tokyo are two of the most responsible allies in assuming common defense costs, and allegations of free riding from the highest levels of the U.S. government must stop. South Korea and Japan are critical linchpins that help shore up the U.S. military presence in East Asia, as well as being powerful economies with deep trade ties with the United States and democracies that share universal values. Denigrating these alliances will only deepen mistrust of the U.S. administration at a time when mutual trust is most needed.

Fifth, fostering greater trilateral security, defense, and intelligence cooperation among the United States, South Korea, and Japan will be an ongoing process. Deeply embedded historical memories in South Korea and just as strong historical perceptions in Japan have hindered Korean-Japanese relations and trilateral cooperation. There is unfortunately no silver bullet for resolving these outstanding issues. But Japan is not South Korea's major adversary, nor is South Korea (or a unified Korea under South Korean leadership) a major threat to Japan. South Koreans fear a remilitarized Japan based on their colonial experience, but they should understand that Japan has been a strong democracy in the post–World War II era and that Japanese support for the unification of the peninsula will be critical. Japan, for its part, must understand that outstanding historical wounds can only begin to truly heal if it assumes greater responsibility for its prewar atrocities. Domestic politics and public opinion play outsized roles in how South Korea and Japan deal with each other, but both countries now face existential security threats. Seoul and Tokyo need visionary and bold leadership to ameliorate and incrementally resolve their historical disputes and to strengthen bilateral security and defense ties.

EXECUTIVE SUMMARY

This chapter examines India's dominant military strategy, discusses how evolving requirements may induce changes in the country's thinking, and assesses the adequacy of this strategy in terms of its national ambitions.

MAIN ARGUMENT

India's security orientation has traditionally been continental, focused on internal unrest and external threats across contested land borders with Pakistan and China to the detriment of maritime concerns and expeditionary options. China's military expansionism, Sino-Pakistani cooperation, evolving regional nuclear dynamics, and other factors, however, are altering the strategic environment. Furthermore, India's ambitions to be a leading power on the global stage and the expectations of other international actors (not least the U.S.) for India to contribute as a regional "net security provider" impose substantial demands on Indian military capabilities. Despite its many strengths and significant potential, India will be challenged to respond to these new circumstances and objectives while still attending to its existing problems.

POLICY IMPLICATIONS

- The persistence of India's traditional internal and external security threats means that changes in its dominant military strategy will be slow and incremental. It will be difficult for India to serve as a net security provider without the ability to deploy at least a subset of world-class military formations with significant reach and endurance.

- While India's enhanced military capacity can benefit security in the Indian Ocean region, it will excite Pakistani concerns and could lead to increased Sino-Indian friction in the maritime domain as well as on land. The growing deployment of nuclear weapons at sea will be especially challenging.

- The U.S. will be in a position to support increases in India's capabilities through sustainment and expansion of military exercises, strategic exchanges, and defense sales, but this will be a long-term investment requiring continued strategic patience.

Challenges for India's Military Strategy: Matching Capabilities to Ambitions?

John H. Gill

India's rise will be one of the major factors shaping the world's geopolitical landscape in the near to medium term. The pace may vary, but barring war, a drastic economic downturn, or an environmental catastrophe, the elevation of India to the stature of a leading power, ongoing since the economic reforms of the early 1990s, seems inexorable and is already generating reverberations in South Asia, in the greater Indo-Pacific region, and across the globe.[1] This evolution is in accord with long-standing national ambitions for India to assume its "rightful place" in the world order with an essential voice as a permanent member of a revised UN Security Council and other institutions of global governance.[2] Furthermore, many features of modern India argue for its increased regional and global influence, specifically its location along some of the world's most important maritime trade routes, its position as one of China's largest neighbors, its large and youthful population

John H. Gill is an Adjunct Professor at the Near East South Asia Center for Strategic Studies in Washington, D.C. He can be reached at <gillnesa@gmail.com>.

The author wishes to thank Walter C. Ladwig III, Shashank Joshi, the editors, and an anonymous outside reviewer for insightful recommendations. The views expressed in this chapter are solely those of the author and do not represent the policy or position of the National Defense University, the Department of Defense, or the U.S. government.

[1] Shivshankar Menon, "India Will Not Become a Great Power by Loudly Proclaiming Its Intentions," *Wire* (India), November 22, 2015; and Ashley J. Tellis, "India as a Leading Power," Carnegie Endowment for International Peace, April 4, 2016, http://carnegieendowment.org/2016/04/04/india-as-leading-power-pub-63185.

[2] "PM's Statement to the Media with Japanese Prime Minister," Prime Minister of India and His Cabinet, December 12, 2015; and "UNSC Permanent Membership: India Offers to Temporarily Give Up Veto Power," *Indian Express*, March 8, 2017.

(predicted to surpass China's within a decade), its democratic political culture, and especially its impressive economic performance.

Particularly pertinent to this chapter is India's military potential. It has the world's third-largest military, behind only China and the United States, and possesses a demonstrated nuclear weapons capability. India, however, has traditionally approached questions of military force with reticence: its dominant strategy has been conservative, and its efforts have been hampered by governmental institutions unsuited to the task of managing "the acquisition of great-power capabilities."[3] If one adopts the view that countries aspiring to great-power status must "demonstrate mastery over the creation, deployment and use of military force in the service of national objectives,"[4] one must ask how India's considerable military potential relates to the promotion and protection of its national interests. This is not simply a case of India responding to its threat perceptions; rather, the country must cope with new circumstances that challenge its historically dominant strategy by translating its potential into usable military capacity in support of the role it envisages for itself in the Indo-Pacific and around the globe.

Previous *Strategic Asia* volumes examined India's national power, including military strength, and the strategic culture that informs the country's international behavior. In the 2015–16 volume, Rajesh Rajagopalan argued that India's potential power, despite numerous advantages, is "unrealized" because of political dysfunction and pervasive bureaucratic inefficiency.[5] Ian Hall's chapter in last year's volume on strategic culture stressed the persistence of Nehruvianism as the guiding tradition in Indian foreign policy, in particular shaping views on the utility of military force. Although other intellectual viewpoints now influence Indian behavior, Hall concluded that New Delhi's actions will be characterized by strategic restraint for the foreseeable future. "Status-seeking" and a desire for "recognition of civilizational greatness," however, will also continue to be important components of India's worldview.[6]

The current chapter builds on these assessments to analyze India's key strategic problems and consider the ways in which its national capabilities

---

[3] Ashley J. Tellis, "Future Fire: Challenges Facing Indian Defense Policy in the New Century" (speech presented at the India Today Conclave, New Delhi, March 13, 2004).

[4] Ibid.

[5] Rajesh Rajagopalan, "India's Unrealized Power," in *Strategic Asia 2015–16: Foundations of National Power*, ed. Ashley J. Tellis, Alison Szalwinski, and Michael Wills (Seattle: National Bureau of Asian Research [NBR], 2015), 160–89.

[6] Ian Hall, "The Persistence of Nehruvianism in India's Strategic Culture," in *Strategic Asia 2016–17: Understanding Strategic Cultures in the Asia-Pacific*, ed. Ashley J. Tellis, Alison Szalwinski, and Michael Wills (Seattle: NBR, 2016), 140–67. See also Teresita C. Schaffer and Howard B. Schaffer, *India at the Global High Table* (Washington, D.C.: Brookings Institution Press, 2016), chap. 4; and Manjari Chatterjee Miller and Kate Sullivan de Estrada, "Pragmatism in Indian Foreign Policy: How Ideas Constrain Modi," *International Affairs* 93, no. 1 (2017): 27–49.

and strategic culture combine to shape the military strategies it has adopted to address them. The chapter begins with an overview of India's strategic challenges and plausible military responses in the past before proceeding to an examination of why India chose manpower-intensive, continentally focused, conservative strategies with relatively low-technological content and minimal expeditionary capacity. India's situation, of course, is not static, and the analysis then proceeds to explore how the country's strategic environment is changing or could change and whether its military strategies and capabilities suffice to satisfy its ambitious geopolitical aims. The chapter concludes with a discussion of the implications that India's chosen strategies are likely to have for regional stability and U.S. policy interests.

Security Challenges: External and Internal

India has had to contend with significant security challenges in both the external and internal domains. China and Pakistan have been and remain the preeminent external threats, with Pakistan generally the most salient of the two. Though Pakistan is smaller and less militarily powerful, decisive elements of the state harbor a revisionist agenda that seeks to overturn the territorial status quo in the subcontinent by force or coercion through acquisition of all or a substantial portion of Indian Kashmir. At the same time, Pakistan also endeavors to retain a level of near-parity with its larger neighbor by retarding India's progress. These aims, especially the desire to take possession of Indian Kashmir, have led to three of the four India-Pakistan conflicts (1947–48, 1965, and 1999) and provide the rationale for creating numerous anti-India militant groups, which have employed terrorism and insurgency against the Indian state for 30 years.[7] Absent territorial change, Pakistan hopes, at a minimum, to mire India's large army in domestic conflicts, thereby staving off what it believes to be a standing Indian desire to destroy the Pakistani state.

The historical, linguistic, and cultural linkages between the two countries and Pakistan's support for jihadi organizations make the Pakistani threat both immediate and visceral. In contrast, since the 1980s, India has regarded China as a more theoretical and distant danger. This relative arrangement of threats has been changing over the past decade, however. The passion associated with Pakistan remains, but the prominence of China in New Delhi's threat perceptions has grown, owing to its increased international

---

[7] C. Christine Fair, *Fighting to the End: The Pakistan Army's Way of War* (Oxford: Oxford University Press, 2014); T.V. Paul, *The Warrior State: Pakistan in the Contemporary World* (Oxford: Oxford University Press, 2014); and Stephen P. Cohen, *Shooting for a Century: The India-Pakistan Conundrum* (Washington, D.C.: Brookings Institution Press, 2013).

assertiveness, its tightening ties with Pakistan, and material improvements in the transportation infrastructure in Tibet.[8]

Beyond the two rivals with which it shares land borders, India has had to include its maritime frontier and the possibility of more distant obligations in its calculations. Other than ad hoc responses to local situations and occasional rhetoric, however, India has suffered from "sea blindness," historically allocating only minimal resources and policy attention to maritime security.[9] Similarly, it has treated out-of-area operations (almost exclusively under the UN flag) as requirements that do not demand any particular strategic investment beyond the maintenance of routine army and navy capabilities.

On the domestic front, India has faced serious challenges combatting insurgency, terrorism, and communal violence. Many of these conflicts continue to simmer and flare today. Despite an enormous federal paramilitary establishment intended to supplement local police, these situations often demand the employment of the regular army. At present, the army's principal commitment is in the Indian-administered portions of Kashmir and in India's northeastern states, but it has been deployed in Punjab and elsewhere on many occasions, often for extended periods of time. These missions represent a significant distraction from the army's foundational task to "preserve national interests and safeguard sovereignty, territorial integrity and unity of India against any external threats by deterrence or by waging war."[10] Furthermore, Pakistan's support for militancy and terrorism in India greatly complicates New Delhi's responses to domestic security problems. China has also provided backing for Indian militants in the past and could do so again should bilateral tensions spike for a prolonged period. Although many of India's domestic security problems are homegrown, these cross-border connections make the resolution of internal violence significantly more difficult and create tinderboxes where insurgency or terrorist incidents could escalate to the level of interstate conflict on short notice.

The Evolution of a Dominant Strategy

India's colonial history and choices made in its earliest independent years continue to exert a powerful influence on New Delhi's strategic thinking in addressing security challenges. Upon gaining independence from Great Britain in 1947, India had three broad options in formulating a grand

---

[8] Shivshankar Menon, "As China's Ties with Pakistan Deepen, India Needs a Strategy to Mitigate the Fallout," *Wire* (India), July 11, 2016.

[9] C. Raja Mohan, "Choppy Waters, Unsure Navigator," *Indian Express*, March 7, 2017.

[10] Headquarters Army Training Command, "Indian Army Doctrine," 2004, part 1, 9.

strategy as it adjusted to its position as a sovereign state in a world system overshadowed by the nascent Cold War. The first option would have been to align itself with either the Communist bloc dominated by the Soviet Union or the anti-Communist Western powers led by the United States. Having just emerged from two centuries of foreign rule under a "Western" empire and determined to assert its autonomy, India, led by its first prime minister Jawaharlal Nehru, consciously rejected the alignment option as inconsistent with its cultural heritage, moral outlook, and future potential. Neutralism, the second option, was likewise spurned as inappropriate, given India's historical greatness and the global role its leaders expected the country to play in the post–World War II era. Wending a path between these two poles, Nehru crafted a policy of "nonalignment" intended to grant India an active role in the international system. He then employed that system to advance Indian interests and over time placed India in a leadership position among developing states in the Non-Aligned Movement.[11] The nonalignment concept, combined with India's colonial past, Nehru's Fabian socialist proclivities, and pragmatic policy concerns, frequently led to India tilting toward the Soviet Union or at least tolerating aggressive Soviet behavior. But New Delhi always kept some distance from the Kremlin; the Indian military, for instance, was never a Soviet clone, as some Arab states were, even though it was largely equipped with Soviet weaponry. Although the Cold War ended a quarter of a century ago, the allure of nonalignment lingers in India, now manifesting itself as the determination to maintain "strategic autonomy" in a multipolar world order.[12]

Having opted for nonalignment as a grand strategy, India had to adopt a national military strategy to account for the internal and external threats outlined above. The internal threats were multifarious and pernicious, ranging from law-and-order challenges associated with communal violence among India's multiethnic population to outright rebellion, especially in the northeast. Despite a growing profusion of police and paramilitary organizations, the army remained the state's ultimate resort in many situations. Externally, India had to contend with threats from Pakistan and China along lengthy and unsettled borders, giving its security strategy a decidedly continental focus. Although maritime security received frequent rhetorical attention, the navy was not a priority, and India's brief ground force forays to Sri Lanka (1987–90)

---

[11] Schaffer and Schaffer, *India at the Global High Table*, 14–30, 65–68.

[12] Nonalignment's most recent incarnation is a policy monograph prepared by respected scholars and former senior government officials. See Sunil Khilnani et al., *Nonalignment 2.0* (New Delhi: Center for Policy Research, 2012). For a critique, see Ashley J. Tellis, "Nonalignment Redux: The Perils of Old Wine in New Skins," Carnegie Endowment for International Peace, July 10, 2012. Foreign Secretary Subrahmanyam Jaishankar has been using the term "plurilateral" to characterize Indian thinking. See Subrahmanyam Jaishankar, "Indian Foreign Secretary Subrahmanyam Jaishankar's Remarks," Carnegie India, April 6, 2016.

and Maldives (1988) were "lesser included" missions, not core tasks. On the other hand, Nehru and his successors regarded support for UN peacekeeping as essential to their visions of India's place in the world, and India became one of the largest and most frequent contributors to blue-helmet missions. These, too, were within the general compass of the Indian Army's capabilities, requiring only some specialized pre-deployment training, not a major reorientation of strategy.

Given these broad military requirements, New Delhi could select from a spectrum of national military strategies to protect and promote its interests. On the low end was a "people's war" philosophy based on absorbing enemy invasions and fighting back with guerrillas, stay-behind parties, and regular formations largely composed of light infantry. At the other end of the spectrum was the option of constructing almost from scratch a smaller but much more mobile, mechanized army reliant on agile organizations combined with heavy injections of technology and modern hardware. India, however, developed a compromise strategy between these two extremes. This was founded on static frontier defense by large infantry formations backed up by limited mobile reserves to regain any terrain lost to an invader and to seize pieces of the enemy's territory for use as bargaining chips in the negotiations that were expected to ensue at the end of conflict. Notably, all these options privileged the ground forces. The air force was treated as an adjunct to the army's operations and the navy as an ancillary holding and harassing force. Both of the latter services certainly envisaged wider roles for themselves and endeavored to develop their own capabilities, but budget, manpower, and equipment allocations historically favored the army, a situation that remains true today.

Consciously or by default, India ended up on this middle path for several reasons. In the first place, the people's war option was anathema in a strategic culture that evinced extreme sensitivities about sovereignty and thus could not abide losing an inch of Indian soil. Moreover, this strategy seemed unworthy of a state that aspired to great-power status and might leave India vulnerable to fracturing along ethnic lines, given its diverse population, particularly in some of the more vulnerable border states. The mechanized, technology-heavy option, on the other hand, was unrealizable until recently. India possessed neither the financial resources to import sufficient high-end systems nor the technical-industrial base to develop, field, and sustain such a force indigenously. Evanescent forays toward increasingly mechanized and mobile forces in the 1980s generated some new thinking but proved overly ambitious and unsupportable. In contrast, the foot-mobile, infantry-dominant army that evolved during and after World War II exploited the comparative advantage of a large pool of potential soldiers who, provided with adequate if pedestrian doctrine, training, and equipment, could substitute numbers for technology. This sort of low-technology force also alleviated the suspicions that India's early political leaders harbored toward the military. For many key national figures, the armed forces represented a drag on national development and a potential political threat. They regarded the military as a necessary evil to be funded at the minimum level and restricted to a subservient status in the governmental hierarchy. In this manner, the armed forces would neither divert resources from essential developmental needs nor pose the danger of the sort of military takeover that plagued so many other newly independent nations. An unintended negative consequence of this attitude, however, was the distinct division of military and civilian security responsibilities. Cocooned in almost hermetically sealed compartments, military officers were excluded from the formulation of national security policy, while civilian bureaucrats and political leaders seldom perceived any need to inform themselves about military capabilities or involve themselves in the details of military operations.[13]

Beyond the appealing but misleading notion that supposedly inexpensive infantry units could replace costly hardware, this middle path also fit India's history and its conception of possible war aims. As far as a potential conflict with China or Pakistan was concerned, India harbored no serious dreams of conquest; its political objectives were conservative and defensive, aiming to deter any attack in the first instance and, should war eventuate, to preserve its own territorial integrity. Against Pakistan, a large army was expected to be able to hold its ground initially and then transition to a powerful counteroffensive that would defeat the Pakistan Army in the field and dominate enough of the enemy's territory to provide an advantage in postwar negotiations. Given the daunting terrain and dismal infrastructure in the Himalayas, India did not foresee significant offensive operations in the event of an attack by China. Rather, the Indian Army would hold its ground and seek to avoid a repeat of the humiliating debacle that the People's Liberation Army (PLA) had inflicted on it in the 1962 war. In short, India's strategy was to deter both adversaries, but if deterrence failed, its aims would be defeating Pakistan and defending against China.

India's colonial history and the legacy of the British Indian Army were also crucial factors in shaping its armed forces after independence. As a colony under the British Raj, India's strategic orientation had been principally concerned with thwarting any Russian thrusts from Central

---

[13] One former army chief laments what he calls "bureaucratic control instead of civilian control over the military." Ved Prakash Malik, "Introduction: Defence Policy and Management of National Security," in *The New Arthashastra: A Security Strategy for India*, ed. Gurmeet Kanwal (New Delhi: HarperCollins India, 2016), 12.

Asia and maintaining control over the native population. The Raj, of course, also supplied hundreds of thousands of troops for the empire's foreign wars. With the Royal Navy responsible for securing the seas and British authorities wary of arming a potentially restive colonial population, however, the forces drawn from India were almost exclusively light infantry. Though some two million Indian volunteers enlisted during World War II, for example, the vast majority served in foot infantry units. Indian mechanized formations, air force squadrons, and naval units were miniscule, and very few saw any real combat.

Independent India inherited this force largely intact, and the military legacy of its history as a British colony remains evident today in the dominance of the army, the limited mobility of the ground forces, and the military's residual continental orientation. Embodied in army regiments that trace their origins back to the 1780s, this legacy also helps explain the institutional inertia and conservative culture so prevalent in India's modern military.[14] Complacency after 1947 has also dampened urges to alter the dominant strategy.[15] Other than the ignominious loss to China in 1962 and the controversial counterinsurgency operations in Sri Lanka from 1987 to 1990, India's military performance in war has arguably been adequate to New Delhi's needs. The dramatic victory in the 1971 war that led to the creation of Bangladesh, for example, dampened future movement toward reform as the success seemed to validate existing arrangements. For independent India, therefore, the middle-path strategy was the path of least resistance—the one requiring the least change on the part of the country's governing institutions or its armed services and posing the lowest threat to the priorities of the civilian leadership. Moreover, this sort of force structure also provided other benefits. On the domestic front, large numbers of infantry would have utility *in extremis* in counterinsurgency situations and in quelling civil unrest. Likewise, UN missions seldom demanded mobile mechanized forces. A professional, but relatively simple, infantry-based army could supply reliable units to meet India's international duties.

Finally, in terms of strategic culture, the middle path India chose to tread matched well with its "conflicted attitude to power" and the unquestioned primacy of developmental goals in national policy. Moral imperatives favored strategic restraint and made the pursuit of maximized military power unpalatable, while considerations of realpolitik militated against these ethically inspired urges, painting them as naive in the context of a harsh and threatening world. A large, inwardly focused, relatively low-technology military thus

---

[14] Mrinal Suman, "Jointmanship and Attitudinal Issues," *Journal of Defence Studies* 1, no. 1 (2007): 71–87.

[15] Arzan Tarapore, "India's Use of Force: The Missing Indirect Approach," Observer Research Foundation, Issue Brief, no. 106, September 27, 2015.

seemed to achieve a practical balance consistent with the preferences of India's early leaders. It was sufficient to satisfy India's principal internal and external defense needs without violating foundational moral tenets or imposing costs that might impinge on the state's economic and developmental priorities. As Hall asserts, India's ambivalence toward power and its predisposition for strategic restraint are likely to remain important, if not always decisive, elements in policy formulation, despite the assertive nationalism embedded in much of the Narendra Modi government's rhetoric.[16]

Changing Circumstances Prompt Strategic Reconsideration

This dominant military strategy is now under reconsideration for two broad reasons. First, for perhaps the first time in India's history, there is a real possibility for change. This is a consequence of the economic reforms instituted in the early 1990s and the subsequent dramatic growth of India's economy. Higher state revenues have in turn laid the foundation for substantial increases in the Indian defense budget. Economic reforms and greater integration with the world have also bolstered national confidence.[17] Although foreign and defense policy are seldom major factors in Indian elections, this heightened confidence offers political leaders more scope for taking the initiative in the international arena and assuming new roles in regional and global security affairs.[18] India's economic boom and its broader interaction with the world have also opened the door for enhanced access to defense technologies, especially from the United States. The current level of U.S.-India defense exchange is unprecedented and will increase further if the two sides can conclude negotiations on the two remaining "foundational agreements" required by Washington.[19] The combination of these factors thus

---

[16] Hall, "The Persistence of Nehruvianism," 164–66; and Ashley J. Tellis, "Overview," in Tellis, Szalwinski, and Wills, Strategic Asia 2016–17, 22.

[17] Daniel Twining, "India's Optimism Is a Welcome Antidote to Western Pessimism," Foreign Policy, March 13, 2017.

[18] Subrahmanyam Jaishankar (speech at the second Raisina Dialogue, New Delhi, January 18, 2017), http://www.mea.gov.in/Speeches-Statements.htm?dtl/27949/Speech_by_Foreign_Secretary_at_Second_Raisina_Dialogue_in_New_Delhi_January_18_201. See also Prashant Jha, "Mr. Indispensable: Why S. Jaishankar Got Another Year as Foreign Secretary," Hindustan Times, January 24, 2017.

[19] The remaining items are known by their U.S. designations: the Basic Exchange and Cooperation Agreement and the Communications Compatibility and Security Agreement. The latter, renamed to be specific to India, is more commonly known as a communications and information security memorandum of agreement. India signed the General Security of Military Information Agreement with the United States in 2002 and the Logistics Exchange Memorandum of Agreement in 2016. See Mark Rosen and Douglas Jackson, "The U.S.-India Defense Relationship: Putting the Foundational Agreements in Perspective," CNA, February 2017.

positions India to explore previously unrealistic military strategies and back them up with hard capacity.

Second, India's strategic environment is shifting in ways that suggest the need for an Indian response. The most important factor here is the rapid rise of China. The size of its economy, the pace and scope of its military modernization, and its increasingly forceful, sometimes bellicose, international conduct have pushed India to shift its "strategic focus from Pakistan to China" over the past decade.[20] This is partly a structural outcome generated by the friction of two major states rising simultaneously, but it also derives from the manner in which Beijing is pursuing its growing prominence. From New Delhi's perspective, troubling aspects of China's aggressive behavior include claims on large swaths of Indian territory, persistent probes along the contested border, significant enhancements to force levels and logistical facilities in Tibet, and the almost routine presence of the PLA Navy in the Indian Ocean. The summer 2017 Sino-Indian confrontation at Doklam (where both countries border Bhutan) has accentuated India's perception of the trans-Himalayan threat. China's ties to India's neighbors are also a concern, especially the recent deployment of Chinese submarines to the region.[21] Above all, Beijing's seemingly uncritical military, economic, and diplomatic support for Pakistan has created fears in New Delhi about Sino-Pakistani collusion and the possibility of future two-front confrontations.[22] The inauguration of the ambitious China-Pakistan Economic Corridor (CPEC) in 2015 and its subsequent development have further heightened Indian concerns. Additionally, though actual conflict with China is unlikely, India is faced with the challenging prospect of coordinating ground and air forces along a 3,000-kilometer front in the Himalayas with naval operations in the Indian Ocean and integrating those conventional dimensions of warfare with its nuclear capacity.[23]

The situation vis-à-vis Pakistan has also altered since the early 2000s. Spurred by major incursions across the Line of Control (LOC) in Kashmir in 1999 that led to the Kargil conflict and by the December 2001 attack on the Indian parliament by terrorists based in Pakistan, India has

---

[20] Menon, "India Will Not Become a Great Power."

[21] C. Raja Mohan, "Neighborhood Defence," *Indian Express*, March 28, 2017; and Shaurya Karanbir Gurung, "New Threat in Indian Ocean: China to Build at Least Six Aircraft Carriers," *Economic Times*, April, 21 2017.

[22] Vinod Anand, "Review of the Indian Army Doctrine: Dealing with Two Fronts," *CLAWS Journal* (2010): 257–64; and Deepak Kapoor, "Challenge of a Two Front Threat," *Journal of the United Services Institution of India*, no. 603 (2016).

[23] For a recent overview of China's perspective on the land dimension of a potential conflict, see Larry M. Wortzel, "PLA Contingency Planning and the Case of India," in *The People's Liberation Army and Contingency Planning in China*, ed. Andrew Scobell et al. (Washington, D.C.: National Defense University Press, 2015).

sought conventional military responses that would deliver consequential punishment on short notice without crossing Pakistan's nuclear threshold. From consideration of "limited war" options, this thinking has evolved into the Indian Army's so-called Cold Start doctrine or "proactive strategy."[24] As several scholarly assessments have highlighted recently, however, New Delhi has no good options to achieve its desired result of curbing Pakistan's reliance on jihadi militants as an asymmetric tool against India. Not only is Cold Start problematic as a strategy, but India's conventional military superiority over Pakistan is not as substantial as is often assumed from simple bean-counting comparisons of hardware inventories or troop numbers.[25] Although the recently published "Joint Doctrine of the Indian Armed Forces" states that the "response to terror provocations could be in the form of 'surgical strikes'" (presumably similar to those conducted in September 2016), the strategic conundrum of effectively retaliating against terrorist attacks by groups based in Pakistan remains frustratingly intact with no viable military options at acceptable levels of risk.[26] Furthermore, the presence of Chinese personnel and investment in Pakistan complicates Indian military response options, especially in the Pakistani areas of Kashmir.

The evolving nuclear dynamic with China and Pakistan has also affected India's strategic situation. This is not an altogether new problem. India demonstrated an incipient atomic capability in 1974 and tested several warheads in 1998, as did Pakistan. Yet for many years, nuclear weapons were additive rather than transformative in strategic terms. That is, they were not weapons to be used but were intended solely to deter nuclear use by others. This "unusable weapons" paradigm is the foundation for India's no-first-use policy. Nuclear weapons thus have restricted India's conventional military options when considering reactions to terrorism originating from Pakistan, but have not fundamentally altered its overall strategic outlook nor been integrated into its military strategy against either Pakistan or China as warfighting instruments. As discussed below, however, technological

---

[24] Walter C. Ladwig III, "A Cold Start to Hot Wars? The Indian Army's New Limited War Doctrine," *International Security* 32, no. 3 (2008): 158–90; Vivek Chadha, *Even If It Ain't Broke Yet, Do Fix It: Enhancing Effectiveness through Military Change* (New Delhi: Pentagon Press, 2016), 54–58; Sandeep Unnithan, "'We Will Cross Again': Interview with Army Chief General Bipin Rawat," *India Today*, January 4, 2017; and Walter C. Ladwig III and Vipin Narang, "Taking 'Cold Start' Out of the Freezer?" *Hindu*, January 11, 2017.

[25] George Perkovich and Toby Dalton, *Not War, Not Peace? Motivating Pakistan to Prevent Cross-Border Terrorism* (Oxford: Oxford University Press, 2016); Walter C. Ladwig III, "Indian Military Modernization and Conventional Deterrence in South Asia," *Journal of Strategic Studies* 38, no. 5 (2015): 729–72; and Shashank Joshi, "India's Military Instrument: A Doctrine Stillborn," *Journal of Strategic Studies* 36, no. 4 (2013): 512–40. See also Shivshankar Menon, *Choices: Inside the Making of India's Foreign Policy* (Washington, D.C.: Brookings Institution Press, 2016), 62–64.

[26] Headquarters Integrated Defence Staff, "Joint Doctrine of the Indian Armed Forces," April 2017, 14.

developments are challenging this doctrinal foundation and opening new and potentially destabilizing possibilities on the nuclear front.

Other aspects of India's strategic environment are also changing, especially in the maritime realm and what may be termed India's "near abroad." Beyond the PLA Navy deployments across the Strait of Malacca into what India has traditionally seen as its neighborhood, the fact that the terrorists who attacked Mumbai in 2008 came from the sea has brought maritime border security into focus. Farther afield, Indian policymakers are devoting increased attention to Iran, the Gulf Cooperation Council (GCC) countries, and what India generally refers to as West Asia.[27] In addition to traditional interests in protecting seaborne commerce and access to oil and natural gas resources in the Persian Gulf, a key consideration is the large Indian diaspora population in the region.[28] The presence of over five million Indian citizens in the GCC countries alone imposes significant responsibilities on New Delhi. The evacuation of around five thousand civilians, including nearly one thousand non-Indians, from Yemen in spring 2015 was a successful but relatively small-scale example of what is certain to be a continuing requirement.[29] The evacuation of larger populations from less permissive environments, however, could seriously stress India's capacities.[30] The role of this vast diaspora in Indian foreign policy and security thinking is a concrete example of India's greater connectedness with the world at large in the context of the globalized 21st century. Combined with India's broad sense of confidence and the assertive nationalism exhibited by the Modi government, this expanding perception of national interests and security threats represents an ideational aspect of India's changing environment and is an additional motivation for greater engagement beyond the confines of South Asia.

Finally, the expectations of the international community, India's image of itself as a modern military power, and the interests of its military services are factors in the country's reconsideration of its military strategy. The United States has promoted the notion of India as a "net security provider" in the

---

[27] Recent examples include the May 2016 Indo-Iranian agreement on the development of Iran's Chabahar port and the attendance of Abu Dhabi's crown prince, Sheikh Mohammed bin Zayed Al Nahyan, as chief guest for India's annual Republic Day ceremonies in January 2017.

[28] Headquarters Integrated Defence Staff, "Joint Doctrine of the Indian Armed Forces," 9, 21; Kadira Pethiyagoda, "India-GCC Relations: Delhi's Strategic Opportunity," Brookings Doha Center, Analysis Paper, no. 18, February 2017; and W.P.S. Sidhu, "India in the Middle East," Brookings Institution, Interview, December 2015, https://www.brookings.edu/opinions/interview-india-in-the-middle-east.

[29] Ishaan Tharoor, "India Leads Rescue of Foreign Nationals, Including Americans, Trapped in Yemen," *Washington Post*, April 8, 2015; and Sahil Makkar, "The Dramatic Evacuation of Indians from Yemen," *Business Standard*, April 18, 2015.

[30] Sushant Singh, "The Poverty of Expectations: Likely but Unfamiliar Challenges," in *Defence Primer 2017: Today's Capabilities, Tomorrow's Conflicts*, ed. Sushant Singh and Pushan Das (New Delhi: Observer Research Foundation, 2017), 76–81.

Indian Ocean region since at least 2001. Indian leaders have deployed this term in international forums, and it is one of the key components in the Indian Navy's 2015 maritime strategy.[31] Additionally, as scholar Shashank Joshi notes, expansive military strategies can create "parochial pressures for service-specific prestige platforms" that "shape a country's force structure" and "generate incentives to find rationales for new capabilities" to suit specific branches of the military.[32] India's revived or rediscovered interest in the Indian Ocean also represents the beginning of a change from its traditional strategic posture. Over time, this attention to more distant interests will have an impact on international partnerships, military doctrine, and equipment acquisition, but this is still relatively new territory for India, and adaptation to accommodate this role will be gradual at best.

Challenges to the Reformulation of India's Military Strategy

India's defense establishment confronts significant challenges in attempting to adjust to these shifts in its strategic environment. The myriad interwoven problems may be grouped in four broad categories: hardware, institutional capacity, structural issues, and the emergence of new arenas of warfare.

The Hardware Challenge: Contending with Massive Obsolescence

The first of these challenges concerns hardware, both the massive obsolescence of key systems across all three services and the absence of essential enablers. The Indian Army, for instance, faces a crisis in key major weapon systems. Most of its tanks, armored fighting vehicles, and air defense missiles are Soviet-origin items initially inducted during the 1980s. Upgraded and rebuilt, its 1,950 T-72 models (constituting two-thirds of the tank fleet) and 2,500 BMP variants in the near term may suffice against Pakistan, which is more or less a peer competitor in terms of ground force technology, but they are reaching the end of their service lives.[33] Air defense systems such

---

[31] U.S. Senate Foreign Relations Committee, "Nomination of Colin L. Powell to Be Secretary of State," January 17, 2001, 34; "Speakers Praise Diplomatic Successes over Iran, Cuba-U.S., Address Long-Standing Africa Conflicts, as General Assembly Continues Annual Debate," United Nations, October 1, 2015, http://www.un.org/press/en/2015/ga11697.doc.htm; and Indian Navy, *Ensuring Secure Seas: Indian Maritime Security Strategy* (New Delhi, October 2015), 8.

[32] Shashank Joshi, *Indian Power Projection: Ambition, Arms and Influence*, Whitehall Paper 85 (London: Routledge, 2015), 10.

[33] Numbers drawn from International Institute for Strategic Studies (IISS), *The Military Balance 2017* (London: Routledge, 2017), 290.

as the SA-6 Gainful, SA-8 Gaskin, and SA-13 Gopher, on the other hand, are examples of what may be called "niche modernization" during the 1980s and 1990s: never acquired in numbers proportionate to an army the size of India's in the first place, they are now likely obsolete.[34] The army's artillery is in especially critical condition. India has not purchased any artillery since 1986 and has never possessed a self-propelled gun in sufficient numbers to equip even its modest number of mechanized formations. Some steps to address the artillery situation have been taken over the past two years with the issuance of contracts and the arrival of the initial batch of towed howitzers from the United States. But India still must replace some 3,000 artillery pieces and introduce self-propelled systems in numbers for the first time.[35] These major end items are only the tip of the army's equipment iceberg. Defense commentators consistently mention the lack of ammunition, spares, and essential gear such as assault rifles, body armor, and night vision devices when assessing the army's modernization needs.[36]

The situation is worse in the Indian Air Force. Described as a "crisis" by one outside observer, the air force faces "a growing force structure predicament as a result of its declining number of fighter squadrons" compared with the expanding capabilities of its potential Chinese and Pakistani adversaries.[37] The central problem in force size is the gap between the phasing out of obsolescent aircraft and the induction of new types in sufficient quantity. Authorized at 42 squadrons, the Indian Air Force maintains only 34 squadrons today, and that number could slip into the low twenties by 2022 as it retires its aging MiG-21s and MiG-27s.[38] The indigenous Tejas is not coming online fast enough, and the collapse of the 2012 deal to purchase and coproduce 126 French Dassault Rafale fighters has left the air force with an urgent requirement for 200 to 250 medium

---

[34] Gainful, Gaskin, and Gopher are the NATO designations for these former Soviet systems.

[35] "India—Army," *IHS Jane's World Armies*, January 10, 2017.

[36] Rahul Bedi, "Arrested Development: Indian Army Modernisation Falls Short," *Jane's Defence Weekly*, February 17, 2016; Manu Pubby, "Army Grappling with Arms Shortages, Delays in Acquisition of Weapons," *Economic Times*, September 28, 2016; and Rajat Panditl, "Urgent Arms Deals of Rs 20,00 Crore Inked to Keep Forces Ready," *Times of India*, February 6, 2017.

[37] Ashley J. Tellis, *Troubles, They Come in Battalions: The Manifold Travails of the Indian Air Force* (Washington, D.C.: Carnegie Endowment for International Peace, 2016), 1; Benjamin S. Lambeth, "India's Air Force at a Pivotal Crossroads: Challenges and Choices Looking to 2032," in Singh and Das, *Defence Primer 2017*, 35–51; and Justin Bronk, "Future Challenges for the Indian Air Force: Innovations and Capability Enhancements," in ibid.

[38] The number of active squadrons is estimated at between 33 and 35. See Lambeth, "India's Air Force at a Pivotal Crossroads," 35–36; "India—Air Force," *IHS Jane's*, January 2017; and Ajai Shukla, "Shrinking Fleet Poses Tough Choices for IAF: Light, Medium or Heavy Fighters?" *Business Standard*, January 4, 2017. Other analysts suggest that some of the legacy aircraft could continue in service even longer. See Abhijit Iyer-Mitra and Pushan Das, "The Advanced Medium Combat Aircraft: A Technical Analysis," Observer Research Foundation, Issue Brief, no. 105, September 2015.

combat aircraft, according to a recently retired air chief.[39] The quantity issue is compounded by the "staggering diversity" of fighter types at various levels of sophistication and imported from different foreign manufacturers, which creates enormous complications in logistics and maintenance.[40] Although the larger Rafale deal fell through, for example, India has decided to purchase 36 of these airframes from France under a one-time arrangement announced in 2015. As one analyst notes, the Indian Air Force will likely be "technologically adequate" but "short on mass" vis-à-vis Pakistan over the medium term. On the other hand, it could find itself numerically inferior and technologically outclassed by the PLA Air Force, particularly when it comes to fifth-generation fighters.[41] The acquisition of U.S. C-17s and C-130Js has modestly improved India's airlift and special operations capabilities, but their numbers remain small. Similarly, air-power enablers such as air-to-air refuelers, airborne early-warning platforms, search-and-rescue assets, and intelligence collectors are also in short supply. These represent especially significant gaps in the capacity to project power by air, as called for in the Indian Air Force's 2012 doctrine.[42]

The Indian Navy shares the hardware woes of the other services. An estimated 60% of its ships are approaching obsolescence, while procurement and construction delays retard the induction of replacements.[43] The decommissioning of India's two older aircraft carriers, for example, has left the navy with only one carrier, the *Vikramaditya*, commissioned in 2013 after a multiyear odyssey and a fourfold increase in the initial cost of transforming it from the former Russian *Admiral Gorshkov*. An indigenous carrier is under construction, and another is in the planning stages, but the former may not be ready until 2023, while the completion of the latter, a much larger vessel, may be even further in the future. In the interim, India will have to make do with a lone carrier rather than the preferred suite of three.[44] The submarine

[39] Manu Pubby, "India Needs About 200–250 Medium Fighter Aircraft: IAF Chief Raha," *Economic Times*, December 29, 2016. The new air chief recently estimated that induction of the Rafale fighters would be accomplished between 2019 and 2022, while the Tejas, a program that began in the mid-1980s, would not be complete until 2025–26. See Nitin Gokhale, "IAF Has a Two-Pronged Plan for Force Accretion, Reveals Air Chief," *Bharat Shakti*, February 12, 2017.

[40] Bronk, "Future Challenges for the Indian Air Force," 46.

[41] Joshi, *Indian Power Projection*, 96–118. The prospects for the Indian acquisition of a Russian fifth-generation fighter remain cloudy. See Rajat Pandit, "To Avoid Sukhoi 'Mistake,' India to Go for Russian 5th-Generation Fighter Only on Complete-Tech Transfer," *Economic Times*, March 9, 2017.

[42] Indian Air Force, *Basic Doctrine of the Indian Air Force* (New Delhi, 2012), 1.

[43] IISS, "Challenges for India's New Naval Chief," *Strategic Comments* 20, no. 4 (2014); and Pradeep Chauhan, "Ships and Shipbuilding in India through a Sino-Indian Prism," *Bharat Shakti*, April 7, 2016.

[44] Comptroller and Auditor General of India, "Report No. 17 of 2016—Union Defence Services Navy and Coast Guard," July 26, 2016, 37; and Rajat Pandit, "India without Aircraft Carrier for 8 Months," *Times of India*, July 27, 2016. The navy believes the ship can be commissioned as early as 2018.

force has likewise suffered degradation. At more than 25 years old, many of its diesel boats have exceeded their service lives and only two of the projected six Kalvari-class (India-built French Scorpène-class) replacements have been launched.[45] Moreover, subsystem and supply problems abound. In two prominent examples, the Kalvaris lack torpedoes, and the MiG-29Ks, which are slated to be the mainstays of the carrier air wings, are experiencing multiple problems.[46] Mundane but crucial enabling assets, such as mine countermeasures ships and naval helicopters, are also a problem.[47] With more than 40 hulls under construction in various dockyards, the navy's desire to expand from 135 to 200 ships by 2027 may be attainable, but equipment deficiencies and manpower shortfalls may leave them ineffective when they take to sea.[48]

The hardware obsolescence issues outlined above should not mask India's new equipment acquisitions: the army has initiated two new howitzer programs, the air force is slated to purchase U.S. Apache attack helicopters, and the navy now operates an indigenous nuclear-powered ballistic missile submarine as well as a nuclear-powered attack boat leased from Russia. However, the pricey proposition of replacing large numbers of aging systems across the three services will impose a serious drag on Indian military modernization efforts for the foreseeable future. It also highlights the importance of a nuanced review of India's defense budgets and stated modernization goals. That is, much of the relatively small capital portions of the defense budget will be consumed simply through replacing the many outdated items in India's inventory rather than acquiring adequate quantities of new systems. Similarly, the introduction of more technically advanced, but also more costly, weaponry in small numbers (niche modernization) can create a misleading impression of modernization without significantly improving national military capability.

Issues of Institutional Capacity

The second broad category of challenges for India's defense establishment concerns institutional capacity. A culture of strategic restraint, the continental legacy of the British Raj, civilian suspicions toward the employment of armed

---

[45] "Make the Weight Count: Interview with Former Chief of Naval Staff Admiral Suresh Mehta," *FORCE*, December 2016.

[46] Vivek Raghuvanshi, "No Torpedoes for India's Second Scorpene Submarine," *Defense News*, January 12, 2017; and Manu Pubby, "MiG-29K Fighter Planes Face Operational Deficiencies: CAG Report," *Economic Times*, July 27, 2016.

[47] Arun K. Singh, "Periscope: Indian Navy's 4 Critical Needs," *Deccan Chronicle*, March 14, 2017.

[48] "Indian Navy Aiming at 200-Ship Fleet by 2027," *Economic Times*, July 14, 2015. For comparison, see S. Vijay Kumar, "Navy Displays Marine Power," *Hindu*, November 14, 2013.

force, and decades of financial constraints have combined to produce a national political elite that seldom focuses on military power. Adapting to evolving strategic circumstances and achieving its bold national aspirations will require New Delhi to reassess many of these features of its extant military strategy and institutional culture. At the top level, this implies the need for "appropriate institutions to manage acquisition of leading power capabilities."[49] Whether this process results in the redesign of existing government agencies or the construction of new ones, the aim would be stating political goals clearly, mobilizing resources, and transforming those resources into the instruments that appertain to a great power capable of functioning as a net security provider. Such an approach places a burden on the central government to perform integrative functions to an extent perhaps unprecedented in India's independent history. That is, federal agencies in New Delhi will have to weave military capabilities into national policymaking in a conscious and deliberate fashion to overcome the "ad hoc defense planning" of the past.[50] Stated another way, India must decide on the role of military force in its grand strategy and thus the types of missions it expects its armed forces to perform, with the attendant requirements for equipment, manpower, doctrine, education, and training.

This process would have at least three immediate consequences for civil-military interaction. First, more purposive integration requires the civilian political leadership to provide clear guidance on national priorities to the armed services and to oversee implementation of that guidance in the pursuit of national objectives. India at present has no "apex" security strategy that might set broad national priorities for the missions, deployments, acquisitions, and integration of the three services in concert with the diplomatic corps, the vast paramilitary forces, and other arms of the state.[51] Second, it means involving the uniformed military in the formulation of policy, strategy, and decision-making at senior levels on a routine basis rather than solely during crises (as occurred during the Kargil War in 1999). Third, it suggests that significant benefits would accrue from incorporating serving officers into the Ministry of Defence and from creating a civilian cadre in the ministry that would specialize in national security affairs. The current practice of appointing generalist bureaucrats to defense postings may have

---

[49] This section draws heavily on Tellis, "Future Fire."

[50] Malik, "Introduction," in Kanwal, *The New Arthashastra*, 13. Close civil-military integration seems to have been a feature of the September 2016 "surgical strikes" along the Kashmir LOC.

[51] "Need National Military Strategy, Army Spending Considered a 'Burden': Rawat," *Asian Age*, May 4, 2017; Nitin Gadkari, "India's Defence Policy: Issues and Perspectives," *Bharat Shakti*, March 11, 2017; Pravin Sawhney and Ghazzala Wahab, *Dragon on Our Doorstep: Managing China through Military Power* (New Delhi: Aleph, 2016), 156–57; and Aditya Singh, "National Security Objectives," in Kanwal, *The New Arthashastra*, 77–91.

sufficed for the ruling authorities in British India, but it seems inconsistent with the goals that Indian leaders have set for the country in the 21st century.

The defense budget is a key manifestation of India's institutional challenges. The budget could be reasonably expected to underwrite the national military strategy, balancing the comprehensive requirements of the three services in support of the country's larger internal and external objectives. Instead, it often represents, in the evocative title of a recent book, a case of "arming without aiming"; that is, defense acquisitions as part of India's military modernization may not be organized around a "strategic intent," are seldom coordinated across the three services, and may not be consistent even within a single service.[52] A byzantine procurement process overseen by a risk-averse "itinerant generalist bureaucracy" has seldom been able to reconcile the competing—and frequently shifting—demands of the services or to assess them within the context of a broader national strategy.[53]

Compounding these institutional challenges is the presence of a large public-sector defense industrial establishment that has a long record of underdelivering on promises and has impeded rather than contributed to the formation of a solid technical-industrial base for defense items. The privileged position of agencies such as the Defence Research and Development Organization and the government's ordnance factories not only has led to the exclusion of foreign firms under the mantra of promoting self-reliance and indigenization,[54] but Indian private corporations also have been prevented from engaging in major defense deals. Only recently has this structure begun to change in an effort to tap into commercial innovation and incorporate Indian as well as foreign expertise on a more regular basis. Thus far, however, the legacy of the autarkic past, the murkiness of the new regulations, and the continued institutional dominance of the various public-sector units have left Indian firms cautious and foreign corporations distant.[55]

The size of the defense budget is another aspect of this challenge. Although growing in absolute terms in recent years, the budget has declined both as a share of the central government's expenditure and as a percentage of GDP. Moreover, the steady increase in personnel costs, most of which are

---

[52] Stephen P. Cohen and Sunil Dasgupta, *Arming without Aiming: India's Military Modernization* (Washington, D.C.: Brookings Institution Press, 2013); and Sushant Singh and Pushan Das, "India's Defence Goals," in Singh and Das, *Defence Primer*, 2–5.

[53] Arun Prakash, "No More Committees," *Indian Express*, January 21, 2017.

[54] Ravi Sharma, "Failing to Deliver," *Frontline*, April 17, 2013; and Laxman Kumar Behera, "India's Ordnance Factories: A Performance Analysis," *Journal of Defence Studies* 6, no. 2 (2012): 63–77.

[55] Laxman Kumar Behera, "Making FDI Count in Defence," Institute for Defence Studies and Analyses, June 22, 2016; Anuj Srivas, "No Bucks for Bang? India Has Netted Only $1 Million in FDI for Defence Sector," *Wire* (India), December 30, 2016; and Sushant Singh, "No Model, Make in India Defence Projects Stuck," *Indian Express*, January 4, 2017.

consumed by the 1.3 million–person army, has had "a debilitating effect" on operations and maintenance funding for readiness and capital modernization for the future.[56] The air force and navy, as more capital-intensive services, thus lack the funds for many urgent and long-term upgrades, and the army itself is unable to meet even modest modernization needs. Yet a larger budget would not automatically translate into increased military capability and would require improved revenue generation or cuts to domestic programs.[57] So far, New Delhi has placed a higher priority on the latter. The 2017–18 budget "contains no hint" of any shift in defense policy.[58] In contrast to the historically freighted and seemingly immediate dangers across India's land borders that command a domestic political constituency, it is difficult to orchestrate public support for the longer-term investments required in naval and air capabilities to address security concerns in Southeast Asia, the Indian Ocean littoral, or the Persian Gulf.[59]

Structural Issues in Defense: Joint Service Cooperation and Civil-Military Readiness

The third broad category of challenges concerns the structure of the three services, especially their ability to work together as joint forces constituted to accomplish missions assigned by the political leadership.[60] A robust capacity for joint operations will be particularly important in any force-projection operations, whether benign or opposed. Furthermore, many potential overseas scenarios would have to be executed in close conjunction with local Indian embassies, host countries, and almost certainly other governments and militaries as well. As such contingencies are likely to arise with little warning, advance training and preparation is necessary to build familiarity and promote interoperability among Indian services and between Indian forces and those of potential international partners. Despite rhetorical advocacy of joint operations in Indian military writings, however,

---

[56] Laxman Kumar Behera, "India's Defence Budget 2017–18: An Analysis," Institute for Defence Studies and Analyses, February 3, 2017; C. Uday Bhaskar, "India's Defence Budget: Trapped in a Straitjacket," *Economic Times*, February 7, 2017. For a discussion of the difficulty of deciphering the size and content of the defense budget over time, see Amit Cowshish, "Defence Expenditure: A Challenge for Defence Economists," Institute for Defence Studies and Analyses, March 14, 2017.

[57] Nirupama Soundararajan and Dyanada Palkar, "Spending More on Defence Won't Automatically Mean New Tanks, Weapons for Indian Army," *Wire* (India), October 25, 2016.

[58] Amit Cowshish, "Defence Budget 2017–18: Chugging Along," Institute for Defence Studies and Analyses, February 2, 2017.

[59] Arzan Tarapore, "India's Slow Emergence as a Regional Security Actor," *Washington Quarterly* 40, no. 2 (2017): 163–78. Thanks to the author for sharing a draft version of this article.

[60] In the U.S. lexicon, "joint" is used for organizations or operations where more than one service is involved; "combined" is the term for activities with other countries.

the history of interservice collaboration is thin. This is another legacy of India's strategic culture, historical experience, and institutional inertia. India has traditionally relied on personal relations among senior officers rather than adherence to universally accepted doctrine or institutional norms. As a result, the three services seldom cooperate in peacetime—on defense procurement, for example—and in wartime, they tend to fight in parallel domains, simultaneously but separately.[61]

India's highest military body is the Chiefs of Staff Committee, which is composed of the three sitting service chiefs. The most senior officer presides over the committee on a rotational basis while retaining management of his own service. The arrangement has long been criticized as ineffectual, and the Modi government has entertained long-standing proposals for a new four-star position that would serve as a single point of military advice for the highest circles of political leadership. After decades of interservice rivalry and bureaucratic resistance, this change may be edging toward partial implementation. Although many have advocated a true chief of defense staff, with apposite staffing and authority, the most probable outcome would be the appointment of a permanent chairman for the Chiefs of Staff Committee, an alteration that may be more symbolic than substantive.[62] India's embryonic joint staff is therefore likely to persist as a marginal organization with little influence over the powerful service chiefs. Similarly, the fringe Andaman and Nicobar Command remains the lone joint theater headquarters. Suggestions to establish other joint service organizations beyond the unique and secretive Strategic Forces Command (for nuclear forces) seem to have foundered, and even the Andaman and Nicobar Command may revert to its status as a single-service preserve.[63]

An additional challenge in terms of institutional capacity is the degree to which strategic thinking is incorporated into officer education. As one retired officer laments, this deficiency "is essentially because of the tactical orientation of instruction during formal teaching [in military educational institutions] that focuses on rote learning rather than holistic understanding of issues and a very weak theoretical framework to enable understanding...beyond

---

[61] One recent study characterizes steps toward integration as "almost entirely superficial/cosmetic." See Vijai Singh Rana, *Status of Jointness in Indian Security Apparatus* (New Delhi: Institute for Defence Studies and Analyses, 2016), 12. The April 2017 "Joint Doctrine of the Indian Armed Forces" does little to address these gaps. See Anit Mukherjee, "Joint Doctrine for Armed Forces: The Single-Service Syndrome," *Hindu*, May 9, 2017.

[62] Sushant Singh, "After PM Modi Steps In, Consensus Builds on Combined Services Committee's Top Post," *Indian Express*, February 21, 2017.

[63] Sushant Singh, "Three Services Are Split on Forming Joint Theatre Commands," *Indian Express*, May 9, 2017; Deepak Kapoor, "Need for Integrated Theatre Commands," *CLAWS Journal* (2013): 46–60; and Gurmeet Kanwal, "CDS and Theatre Commands: An Idea Whose Time Has Come," *Defence and Security Alert*, May 2015, 66–69.

the limited scope of military experience."[64] Commenting on the continual delays in establishing a national defense university, another observer remarks that "very little effort is being [done] to educate Indian civilian and armed forces officers in strategic studies and international affairs."[65] Within the larger defense establishment, these deficiencies can result in serious gaps in the conception of strategy and the utility of military force between the officer cadre, the defense ministry bureaucracy, and the elected national policymakers. That is, no one may be attending to broader strategy if senior officers whose horizon is tactical or perhaps operational are disconnected from generalist bureaucrats who are principally concerned with management and administration rather than serving as a conduit for strategic guidance from the political leadership. The navy, especially in peacetime, is often a notable exception to this weakness because its missions demand a wide outlook and nurture an inclination to support India's foreign policy as the principal practitioner of "military diplomacy."

Nonetheless, there is a danger of civilian leaders having an inadequate understanding of the nation's military instrument and of military officers failing to situate their actions within the larger context of the government's political intentions. "It is not just a question of political ends," notes one of India's most respected defense analysts, "but the necessity of the political leader controlling every aspect of war—its intensity, its direction and length." It is thus "vital for the politicians to have a grasp of military affairs," and "military leaders, too, need to understand national policy."[66] These concerns are especially salient in India's situation, where nuclear weapons are present and tactical actions (e.g., on the LOC) could have significant strategic consequences.[67] The considerable operational latitude that the Indian armed forces currently enjoy—owing to the prevalent attitude among civilian politicians that military detail is a matter for the generals and admirals—thus could prove detrimental to India's national interests.

---

[64] Vivek Chadha, "An Assessment of Organisational Change in the Indian Army," *Journal of Defence Studies* 9, no. 5 (2015): 238; and Harsh V. Pant, "Bridging the Soldier-Scholar Divide," *Hindu*, June 4, 2013.

[65] Gurmeet Kanwal, "The Role of Think Tanks in National Security," Forum for Strategic Initiatives, January 12, 2015, http://www.fsidelhi.org/author/gurmeet-kanwal.

[66] Manoj Joshi, "'Dragon on Our Doorstep'—Why Politics and Military Should Go Hand-in-Hand," *Wire* (India), February 13, 2017. As the doyen of American scholars on South Asia writes, "there may be civilian control but there is no credible civilian direction." See Stephen P. Cohen, "India and the Region," in *The Oxford Handbook of Indian Foreign Policy*, ed. David M. Malone, C. Raja Mohan, and Srinath Raghavan (Oxford: Oxford University Press, 2015), 351.

[67] Yogesh Joshi, "Political Abstention in War and the Influence of Nuclear Weapons," *Journal of Defence Studies* 7, no. 3 (2013): 147–58; and Vijay Shankar, "Catechism of a Minister," Institute of Peace and Conflict Studies, November 28, 2016.

Beyond Conventional War: Cyber, Space, Special Operations, and Nuclear Dimensions

Finally, new arenas of warfare constitute a fourth category of institutional challenges. These include cybersecurity and cyberwarfare, the military utilization of space, and the widely expanded employment of special operations forces—what the recent "Joint Doctrine of the Indian Armed Forces" terms "the new triad."[68] The Chiefs of Staff Committee proposed joint service commands for all three of these areas in 2012, and press reporting in 2015 indicated plans for their imminent establishment.[69] At the time of writing, however, these remain two-star "agencies" rather than three-star commands. Moreover, in all three cases, Indian commentators express concerns about the adequacy of synchronized long-term planning, the domestic technology base, the recruitment of appropriately qualified personnel, and the integration of military, civilian, and intelligence establishments. In the cyber realm, for example, India issued a National Cyber Security Policy in 2013 and is slated to inaugurate a National Cyber Coordination Centre in 2017, but progress otherwise has been slow. Similarly, despite an established space program and serious concerns about China's anti-satellite capabilities, India has few military satellites of its own and lacks a comprehensive national space policy to incorporate military communication, navigation, and intelligence needs across the services in a holistic fashion.[70]

Most significant among these unconventional forms of warfare, however, is the problem of nuclear weapons. Although India's no-first-use doctrine remains in place, as indicated in the April 2017 joint forces doctrine, some Indian strategists are now advocating a reassessment.[71] Regardless of the fate of India's no-first-use pledge, technological changes over the next few years will alter the regional security environment. Pakistan's highly advertised development of tactical or battlefield nuclear weapons, progress by both

---

[68] Headquarters Integrated Defence Staff (India), "Joint Doctrine of the Indian Armed Forces," 48–50.

[69] Rajat Pandit, "Govt Gets Cracking on Three New Tri-Service Commands," *Times of India*, August 20, 2015; and P. C. Katoch, "Special Operations Command—An Imperative for India," *Journal of the United Services Institution of India*, no. 603 (2016).

[70] Davinder Kumar, "India's Space Programme: The Need for a Techno-Military Orientation," in Kanwal, *The New Arthashastra*, 255–86; Davinder Kumar, "Cyber Security: Status and Imperatives," in ibid.; and Rajeswari Rajagopalan, "India's Space Program: Challenges, Opportunities, and Strategic Concerns," NBR, Policy Q&A, February 2016, http://www.nbr.org/downloads/pdfs/outreach/NBR_IndiaCaucus_Feb2016.pdf.

[71] Headquarters Integrated Defence Staff (India), "Joint Doctrine of the Indian Armed Forces," 37; Vipin Narang, "Plenary: Beyond the Nuclear Threshold: Causes and Consequences of First Use" (presentation at the Carnegie International Nuclear Policy Conference, Washington, D.C., March 20, 2017), https://fbfy83yid9j1dqsev3zq0w8n-wpengine.netdna-ssl.com/wp-content/uploads/2013/08/Vipin-Narang-Remarks-Carnegie-Nukefest-2017.pdf; Shashank Joshi, "India's Nuclear Doctrine Should No Longer Be Taken for Granted," Lowy Institute, Interpreter, March 22, 2017; and Dhruva Jaishankar, "Decoding India's Nuclear Status," *Wire* (India), April 3, 2017.

India and Pakistan on the deployment of sea-based weapons, India's possible purchase of a limited missile defense system, and the mutual pursuit of multiple independently targetable reentry vehicle payload options all challenge the existing—albeit weak and ambiguous—network of nuclear norms. That is, as arsenal sizes, weapon types, and deployment options on both sides expand, the long-standing expectations associated with the India-Pakistan nuclear dynamic appear to be under stress, especially the notion that neither side needs anything beyond some unspecified "minimal" level of credible deterrence. India will thus not only have to address the complicated interrelationship of these components of its nuclear arsenal and the impact of missile defense. It will also have to determine how these evolving systems are integrated with conventional force planning. At the present time, it is not clear that this daunting set of strategic tasks is being approached comprehensively by the political leadership, the scientific community, the defense bureaucracy, and the armed services, or whether, as one Indian expert worries, "the bomb is in charge."[72]

Incremental Change in the Dominant Approach

Despite the changes in India's strategic circumstances and the institutional challenges outlined above, the dominant strategy remains doggedly durable. Pakistan remains the immediate and persistent threat, but India has few, if any, conventional military responses that would induce Pakistan to reduce its reliance on anti-Indian jihadi groups. So-called surgical strikes similar to the actions taken along the LOC in September 2016 may be the new first response to "terror provocations" as part of what the recent joint forces doctrine calls "the sub-conventional portion of the spectrum of conflict."[73] India's ability to conduct a series of shallow incursions with conventional ground forces in line with the Cold Start doctrine, however, remains largely aspirational, and it is not at all clear that such incursions or sub-conventional surgical strikes would bring the desired results even if successfully executed. Both options, of course, contain significant escalatory potential.

A renewed focus on China has certainly been evident since approximately 2009. India has raised two new mountain divisions, stationed additional air force assets in the northeast, and initiated a long-term program to improve the transportation infrastructure along the Himalayan frontier.[74] It is also

---

[72] Author's discussion with a retired senior Indian officer, November 2016.

[73] Headquarters Integrated Defence Staff (India), "Joint Doctrine of the Indian Armed Forces," 14.

[74] Rajat Pandit, "Army Reworks War Doctrine for Pakistan, China," *Times of India*, December 30, 2009; and Monika Chansoria, "China's Infrastructure Development in Tibet: Evaluating Trendlines," Centre for Land Warfare Studies, Manekshaw Paper, no. 32, 2011.

developing ballistic missiles capable of placing much of China under threat of nuclear retaliation. Progress on the road projects in the northern border areas is torpid, however, and the creation of an offensive mountain strike corps with two more divisions is also moving slowly owing to budgetary deficiencies.[75] Largely spurred by concerns over Chinese influence, New Delhi is complementing these changes in force structure by proposing a defense agreement with Bangladesh.[76]

There are signs that India is beginning to pay greater attention to maritime security, particularly by strengthening defense ties with its Indian Ocean neighbors through capacity-building measures. Over the past four years, India provided patrol vessels to Mauritius and Seychelles (and gifted a patrol plane to the latter), signed agreements to construct coastal surveillance radar installations and other facilities, sent its P-8I Poseidon maritime patrol aircraft on goodwill visits, and created a loose security association with Maldives and Sri Lanka, to which it wants to invite other Indian Ocean countries. It also hopes to involve many of these island states in what could be a significant maritime domain awareness structure with more than 50 sites across the region.[77] How many of these ambitious projects will come to fruition, of course, remains a question. The Indian Navy, the pivotal service for such developments, is still third in priority in the most recent defense budget.

These evolutionary changes notwithstanding, India's dominant strategy is still continentally oriented, conservative, and founded on large, infantry-heavy ground forces. Given that the dangers on India's immediate borders have not evaporated, this outlook is unlikely to change in the near term. In addition to this practical consideration, there is little fresh thinking on mitigating either the Pakistani or the Chinese threat. As Hall and Rajagopalan point out, this traditional approach is both deeply rooted in India's strategic culture and dictated by the challenges New Delhi confronts trying to mobilize national resources.[78] The Modi government came into office in 2014 pledging to launch major defense reforms, but progress has been modest thus far. Entrenched tradition, inertia, and vested interests (both among the services and within the bureaucracy) militate against major reforms or changes in strategy, and many of the recommended reforms are likely to encroach on

[75] "Expanding Forces Increase Risk of LAC Conflict," *IHS Jane's Daily*, September 29, 2016; and Sushant Singh, "Eye on China, India to Raise Second Division for Mountain Corps," *Indian Express*, March 17, 2017.

[76] Charu Sudan Kasturi, "Defence Pact with Bangladesh on Table," *Telegraph*, March 25, 2017.

[77] IISS, "India's New Maritime Strategies," *Strategic Comments* 21, no. 9–10 (2015); and Aditi Malhotra, "India Sees New Regional Role for Its Navy," *Foreign Policy*, June 10, 2016.

[78] Hall, "The Persistence of Nehruvianism"; and Rajagopalan, "India's Unrealized Power."

venerated aspects of institutional cultures and traditional practices. As such, India's military strategy may only be susceptible to modification over the long haul. Some incremental changes may be in the offing in the wake of a 2016 reform committee report, but these are unlikely to produce substantially greater jointness or lead to force reductions to pay for modernization, as some have urged.[79] Effective modernization across the services is an expensive proposition, one that may require significant rethinking of defense allocations and possible tradeoffs with domestic programs. Moreover, in India's historical experience, major defense reforms have only been introduced in the wake of embarrassing crises such as the defeat at the hands of the PLA in 1962 or the surprise Pakistani intrusions that led to the Kargil War in 1999.[80] Barring such shocks to the system, meaningful alterations in current strategy and practice are likely to evolve only at a very slow pace.

If the engrained durability of the existing system suggests at best evolutionary modernization, then the old dominant strategy is unlikely to match India's *desiderata* for its regional and global roles in a time frame consistent with its ambitions. It could be difficult, for example, for India to serve as a net security provider in the Indian Ocean, meet the growing security demands of its diaspora in West Asia, or have a more prominent voice in Asian affairs if it is not able to deploy at least a small subset of world-class formations with significant reach and endurance.[81] Likewise, New Delhi may find itself stressed to respond to "black swan" crises (such as drastic instability in a neighboring country) that might endanger its national interests or evoke pressure to intervene from elements of the Indian population.

Even absent major reforms and substantial new acquisitions, however, India will retain significant capabilities and will slowly enlarge those through the near to medium term. First, it will be able to defend itself against ground or air incursions by Pakistan or China, except in the improbable scenario of Beijing exerting itself in some truly extraordinary fashion. Second, if provoked, it will have a limited ability to conduct a conventional counteroffensive against Pakistan, though probably not the envisaged Cold Start or any other

---

[79] Sushant Singh, "Defence Reforms: Shekatkar Panel Recommends Four-Star Rank for Top Military Adviser," *Indian Express*, January 11, 2017; and Singh, "After PM Modi Steps In." For several of the many proposals recommending significant personnel cuts to fund a smaller but more agile force that leverages technology, see Bhartendu Kumar Singh, "Rightsizing the Armed Forces: Problems and Prospects," Institute of Peace and Conflict Studies, June 28, 2016, http://www.ipcs.org/article/india/rightsizing-the-armed-forces-problems-and-prospects-5069.html; and Sheru Thapliyal, "Men and Machines," *FORCE*, August 2016.

[80] Anit Mukherjee, "In Need of a Crisis? India's Higher Defence Organisation at 75," in Singh and Das, *Defence Primer*, 31–34.

[81] Tellis, "Future Fire"; Walter C. Ladwig III, "India and Military Power Projection: Will the Land of Gandhi Become a Conventional Great Power?" *Asian Survey* 50, no. 6 (2010): 1171; and Anit Mukherjee, *Net Security Provider: India's Out-of-Area Contingency Operations* (New Delhi: Institute for Defence Studies and Analyses, 2012).

operation sufficient to effect a change in Pakistan's behavior. In any such case, of course, India would be launching itself into unpredictable territory with the risk of nuclear escalation. It would also have some minimal capability for conventional counterattacks against China, but these would be constrained by the exigencies of the terrain and the minimal infrastructure on the Indian side of the border (technically the Line of Actual Control).[82] India might also possess some capacity to insert special operations forces into Tibet in the hopes of fomenting unrest or harassing Chinese logistics, but an operation along these lines would be extraordinarily difficult and would likely have severe repercussions.[83]

Third, as shown by its raid into northwestern Myanmar in June 2015 and its surgical strikes along the Kashmir LOC in September 2016, India has some ability to execute small special operations missions locally and, if pressed, could no doubt reprise the ad hoc mission that quashed the amateur coup in Maldives in 1988. It would hope to keep any such operations at the sub-conventional level. Fourth, India has also repeatedly demonstrated its ability to conduct effective humanitarian assistance and disaster relief (HADR) and noncombatant evacuation operations in a wide variety of circumstances.[84] These will remain core tasks, especially for the air force and navy. Other expeditionary missions beyond India's borders, however, are likely to remain outside its reach, especially in nonpermissive environments. Fifth, India's capacity for monitoring foreign naval activity in the Indian Ocean (especially by the PLA Navy) is likely to increase steadily, and it will continue to be a potential contributor to counterpiracy and other law-enforcement tasks along the Indian Ocean littoral. The navy will thus be an important component of India's military diplomacy, and its capacity for extended deployments outside the Indian Ocean (into the Pacific Ocean or the Red Sea, for example) may grow over time but will be severely constrained for the near term. These naval activities, of course, will be greatly enhanced by, and at times dependent on, collaboration with foreign navies and access to overseas support facilities in areas such as the Persian Gulf, Southeast Asia, and East Africa.

Sixth, India will continue to expand its nuclear capability at a measured pace, including the gradual deployment of submarine-based delivery systems and land-based ballistic missiles with sufficient range to hold major Chinese targets at risk. As indicated in the April 2017 joint forces doctrine, India's

---

[82] India has "no high-value target we could seize and hold" in China, according to one general. See Sandeep Unnithan, "The Mountain Is Now a Molehill," *India Today*, February 24, 2016.

[83] Iskander Rehman, "A Himalayan Challenge," *Naval War College Review* 70, no. 1 (2017): 104–42.

[84] For an excellent overview of India's experiences with noncombatant evacuation operations, see Constantino Xavier, "India's Expatriate Evacuation Operations: Bringing the Diaspora Home," Carnegie India, January 4, 2016.

commitment to a nuclear no-first-use policy will likely remain in place—lively debate notwithstanding—but Pakistan's pursuit of warheads and delivery systems at the lower, tactical end of the spectrum will make the bilateral nuclear dynamic more complex and dangerous.[85] Finally, India is likely to devote considerable attention to exploring the military uses of space, as well as to expanding its offensive and defensive cybercapabilities over the medium term. The country has a fairly robust launch capability and an existing array of satellites, but there are concerns that its limited number of space assets might be vulnerable to Chinese anti-satellite weapons. India also may be susceptible to cyberattack, especially from Chinese sources.

Implications for Regional Stability and U.S. Interests

Regional Implications

India's evolving military strategy and the growing but still constrained capabilities of its armed forces will have both beneficial and worrying implications for regional stability. On the favorable side, India's military assets will allow it to be a major player in countering piracy, terrorism, narcotics trafficking, and other criminal activities throughout the Indian Ocean littoral. Employing deft diplomacy, it could be a reassuring presence to its island neighbors and might engage more vigorously with Southeast Asian nations as well, in accordance with Modi's Act East policy.[86] Similarly, India can contribute to sea-lane security in East Africa, the Arabian Sea, the Persian Gulf, and the greater Middle East, where noncombatant evacuation is likely to be an ongoing possibility.[87] India's military will also continue to offer major resources for protecting the environment, monitoring fisheries, and responding to HADR situations throughout the region.

Many of the tasks associated with the assumption of this role of a net security provider will consist of actions under the broad rubric of "military diplomacy"—that is, ship and aircraft visits, presence patrols, capacity building (as in the recent initiatives with Seychelles and Mauritius), or training and exercises.[88] Such missions obviously will place a premium on the Indian Navy, underwritten in some cases by the air force and, to a lesser

---

[85] Headquarters Integrated Defence Staff (India), "Joint Doctrine of the Indian Armed Forces," 37.

[86] Anit Mukherjee, "India's Act East Policy: Embedding the Andamans," S. Rajaratnam School of International Studies, Commentary, May 31, 2016.

[87] Yogesh V. Athawale, "Towards Enhancing Maritime Capability in the Indian Ocean Rim," *Journal of the National Maritime Foundation of India* 11, no. 2 (2015): 81–98.

[88] This is a central component of the Indian Navy's doctrine. See Syed Ata Hasnain, "Joint Training—How It Enhances Value of India's Military Diplomacy," *Defence and Security Alert*, June 2016, 27–31.

degree, by the army. Moreover, they imply what one retired Indian admiral terms "a truly Indian tri-service expeditionary capability," preferably with the support of the United States.[89] They also call for close and sustained collaboration between the armed forces and the Ministry of External Affairs.[90] Modi's emphasis on the maritime frontier as "one of my foremost policy priorities" notwithstanding, it is not yet clear that India will make the requisite financial investments or dedicate sufficient sustained policy attention to these offshore opportunities.[91]

In addition to these potential benefits, India's evolving military activism also presents risks for regional stability. These risks are likely to be most apparent in the Indian Ocean. Although some regional countries will welcome increased Indian engagement in the maritime domain, others will perceive threats to their own interests. Pakistan already views India with deep suspicion, and the Indian Navy's expanded presence could alarm Islamabad, especially if Sino-Pakistani development of the port at Gwadar truly takes off as part of CPEC.[92] The danger of a mishap or misunderstanding between the two navies is acute because they do not have a protocol on the prevention of incidents at sea. Pursuit of such an agreement was part of the Lahore Declaration in 1999, but no formal progress has been made. An incidents-at-sea agreement and closer communication between the Indian and Pakistani navies and coast guards might also help reduce the threat of seaborne terrorism and avert episodes such as the controversial destruction of a Pakistani fishing vessel in 2015. In addition, frictions could arise between the Indian Navy and the PLA Navy as the latter extends its presence west of the Strait of Malacca. Such situations could involve other littoral and island states as well (such as Sri Lanka), increasing the importance of Indian diplomatic-military coordination. As the PLA Navy is likely to be a routine feature of the Indian Ocean strategic arena, the two sides might work to mitigate future problems by initiating discussions on risk-avoidance procedures, perhaps along the lines of the recent agreements between the United States and China.

---

[89] Raja Menon, "The Strategic Imperative," *Indian Express*, April 13, 2016.

[90] Satu Limaye argues that coordination is improving. See Satu Limaye, "Weighted West, Focused on the Indian Ocean and Cooperating across the Indo-Pacific: The Indian Navy's New Maritime Strategy, Capabilities, and Diplomacy," CNA, February 2017, 34–40. Others are skeptical of defense-diplomacy coordination. See C. Raja Mohan, "Beyond Non-Alignment: New Imperatives for Defence Diplomacy," in Kanwal, *The New Arthashastra*, 104.

[91] Narendra Modi, "SAGAR Stands for Security and Growth for All in the Region: PM Modi at International Fleet Review in Vishakhapatnam," web log, February 7, 2016, http://www.narendramodi.in/pm-modi-at-the-international-fleet-review-2016-in-visakhapatnam-andhra-pradesh-413019.

[92] Manpreet Singh Chawla, "CPEC Drives China-Pakistan Naval Cooperation," National Maritime Foundation, January 3, 2017.

The most challenging change in the Indian Ocean, however, will be the slow accretion of naval nuclear weapons platforms, both submarines and surface ships. With India having commissioned its first ballistic missile submarine in 2016 and Pakistan recently testing a nuclear-capable cruise missile intended for its Agosta-class diesel boats, the two sides are entering what one scholar terms the "murky waters" of what could be "a dangerously volatile maritime environment." By initiating bilateral discussions and perhaps applying relevant experiences from the Cold War, the rivals might be able "to shape, rather than be shaped by the emerging nuclear regime" in the region.[93]

India's land borders will remain sources of tension with both Pakistan and China. Although there have been several irritating Chinese incursions along the lengthy border in recent years (the summer 2017 standoff at Doklam being the latest), the slow increase in Indian force structure on the Himalayan frontier is unlikely to generate significant concern in Beijing. Political issues are fraught with far more potential for tension than Indian military deployments. These include the activities of the Tibetan exile community in India, the future of the Dalai Lama, and Indian apprehensions about China's Belt and Road Initiative projects (including CPEC). Most important from New Delhi's standpoint, however, are Chinese vocal and intrusive territorial claims to almost the entire Indian state of Arunachal Pradesh in the northeast, such as publicly protesting Prime Minister Modi's visit there in 2015 and the Dalai Lama's trip to an important lamasery in 2017.

With respect to the border with Pakistan, the large-scale transportation infrastructure work connected with CPEC accentuates Indian concerns about Sino-Pakistani collusion, exacerbating animosity along the Kashmir LOC. New Delhi especially objects to the fact that CPEC will pass through Pakistan's Gilgit-Baltistan territory (part of the disputed Kashmir region) and is bringing large numbers of Chinese workers and possibly security personnel into the area. Likewise, India's strategic conundrum regarding the threat of infiltration and terrorist attacks emanating from Pakistan remains. Despite the Indian Army's so-called surgical strikes across the LOC in September 2016, none of the options available in India's dominant or evolving military strategy proffer strategic results, and all of them carry significant risk of escalation. The risk will be especially high if intelligence and policy are not closely integrated, and if the political leadership and military commanders are not functioning in complete harmony. Here at the intersection of internal and external threats, New Delhi is challenged to reconcile domestic policy for managing unrest on its side of the LOC with its international diplomatic and military choices

---

[93] Iskander Rehman, "Murky Waters: Naval Nuclear Dynamics in the Indian Ocean," Carnegie Endowment for International Peace, March 2015, 1, 49; and Yogesh Joshi and Frank O'Donnell, "India's Submarine Deterrent and Asian Nuclear Proliferation," *Survival* 56, no. 4 (2014): 156–74.

vis-à-vis Pakistan. Rather than one focused on military means, a strategy combining outreach to the disaffected local population with diplomatic steps on the international front would seem to be the most propitious means of reducing threats to India's security.[94]

Implications for the United States

For the United States, the evolution of India's military strategy outlined above offers significant opportunities and several policy imperatives. In the first place, the two sides will want to ensure that they lose no ground in military-to-military relations. Washington and New Delhi have constructed an unprecedented level of cooperation among their armed forces and across other security sectors over the past quarter of a century, including India's designation as a "major defense partner" in December 2016.[95] This progress, however, could stall or ebb away if not nurtured by a robust and sustained program of exercises and exchanges within the framework of a bilateral strategic dialogue and the extant array of counterterrorism and intelligence interactions.

In addition to expanding and deepening the rich menu of bilateral training that the two sides have explored previously, India and the United States could consider two new topics. One of these might be collaboration in support of India's capacity-building programs with the Indian Ocean island countries. As New Delhi may be more open to multilateral cooperation than it has been in the past, regional capacity-building initiatives might be a good venue for working with countries such as Australia, France, and the United Kingdom that have important interests in the Indian Ocean. Second, both India and the United States have considerable experience in planning for and executing noncombatant evacuations and both would encounter significant challenges in the event of a crisis or unrest in the Persian Gulf or elsewhere. Moving beyond HADR to cooperative discussion of noncombatant evacuation operations in bilateral training exercises would thus build a foundation of mutual understanding for future emergencies.[96] Such interaction would also offer an opportunity to create mutually beneficial linkages between the

---

[94] Perkovich and Dalton, *Not War, Not Peace?* 266–80.

[95] "Joint India–United States Statement on the Visit of Secretary of Defense Carter to India," U.S. Department of Defense, Press Release, December 8, 2016, https://www.defense.gov/News/News-Releases/News-Release-View/Article/1024228/joint-india-united-states-statement-on-the-visit-of-secretary-of-defense-carter.

[96] Nilanthi Samaranayake, Catherine Lea, and Dmitry Gorenburg, "Improving U.S.-India HA/DR Coordination in the Indian Ocean," CNA, July 2014.

Indian military and U.S. forces in the Gulf region, currently a significant gap.[97] Given the division of responsibilities between U.S. Central Command, Pacific Command, and Africa Command, cooperation of this nature will require close management by overarching U.S. bureaucratic structures at the Departments of State and Defense in Washington, D.C. Defense sales and technology exchange are additional avenues for bilateral interaction that could strengthen Indian capabilities while enhancing interoperability and familiarity. The current level of U.S.-India defense trade (around $14 billion) would have been unimaginable when military-to-military interchanges began in the mid-1990s. U.S. participation in signature Indian programs such as helicopter sales and the provision of technology for a third aircraft carrier will be key components of the broader bilateral relationship.[98]

India's military responses to its shifting strategic environment will also present several imperatives to Washington. The two most prominent of these are mitigating nascent India-Pakistan nuclear competition in the maritime domain and reducing the potential for Sino-Indian tensions in the Indian Ocean. The United States' leverage in the first instance is very limited, but sharing some experiences from the Cold War era may help both sides achieve acceptable deterrence goals without falling into the trap of open-ended arms racing. Regarding China, Washington could provide New Delhi with a U.S. perspective on the long process that culminated in the United States and China signing two memoranda of understanding concerning air and maritime safety and major military activities in 2014. The three countries might even seek opportunities to discuss these issues together on the margins of multilateral gatherings such as meetings of the Indian Ocean Rim Association.

Finally, as in other parts of the world, Washington will have to address Indian concerns about the United States' credibility, suspicion that U.S. policy under President Donald Trump will tend toward transactional rather than strategic interactions, and anxieties that the United States "may be less

---

[97] Manoj Joshi, "India, U.S. and an Eastward Tilt," *Indian Express*, May 23, 2016. India does participate in Shared Awareness and Deconfliction (SHADE) conferences hosted by the Combined Maritime Forces in Bahrain. See P.K. Ghosh, "Shared Awareness and Deconfliction Initiative: Can the Success Be Applied to Southeast Asia?" *India-Asia-Pacific Defense Forum*, February 23, 2016; and Nilanthi Samaranayake, Michael Connell, and Satu Limaye, "The Future of U.S.-India Naval Relations," CNA, February 2017.

[98] Amaani Lyle, "Carter, Indian Counterpart Champion Growing Trade, Technology, Security Ties," U.S. Department of Defense, Defense Media Activity, December 8, 2016; and Ashley J. Tellis, "Making Waves: Aiding India's Next-Generation Aircraft Carrier," Carnegie Endowment for International Peace, April 2015.

engaged in the region."[99] Early government-to-government interactions are reported to have produced "a very strong sense of optimism about the relationship."[100] However, an undercurrent of concern about enduring U.S. presence is evident among many Indian strategic observers, even after the U.S. administration reaffirmed India's status as a major defense partner in April 2017 and Prime Minister Modi's successful June 2017 visit to Washington.[101] If not bolstered by strong U.S. commitments, these concerns could generate pressures for New Delhi to recalibrate its thinking toward a new form of nonalignment or various irreversible accommodations with China or Russia. The uncertainties attendant on the arrival of the Trump administration and the lingering legacy of suspicion toward the United States harbored by many members of the Indian political elite will continue to demand considerable strategic patience from Washington. It will not always be easy to maintain this posture given that India's developmental infirmities and difficulties mobilizing national resources will hobble its ability to reciprocate. As Ashley Tellis notes, however, the United States will benefit from "a calculated altruism whereby Washington continually seeks to bolster India's national capabilities without any expectation of direct recompense."[102] That is, the strategic interests of the United States are best served by a long-term investment in the U.S.-India bilateral relationship within the context of a broader Asia policy, even if the dividends of that investment are not realized in the short term. The most lucrative approach will be one that combines a steady expansion of ties and persistent but patient nudging of New Delhi with sustained tolerance for policy timelines longer than most Americans either expect or prefer.

---

[99] Sanjeev Miglani and Tommy Wilkes, "India's Navy Spurns Homemade Warplane in a Blow to Asia's Push for Self Reliance," *Wire* (India), February 13, 2017; Monika Chansoria, "America First May Become America Alone," *Sunday Guardian*, February 12, 2017; Raj Chengappa, "How to Deal with Trump," *India Today*, March 2, 2017; and Shyam Saran, "Geopolitical Impact of Trump's Presidency," *Business Standard*, March 8, 2017.

[100] "Trump Administration Has Very Positive View of Indo-U.S. Ties: Jaishankar," *Economic Times*, March 4, 2017.

[101] See, for example, Ajai Shukla, "In the Era of Donald Trump, India-U.S. Defence Ties Change Tack," *Business Standard*, April 25, 2017; and Shyam Saran, "Read between the Lines," *Indian Express*, June 29, 2017.

[102] Ashley J. Tellis, "Avoiding the Labors of Sisyphus: Strengthening U.S.-India Relations in a Trump Administration," *Asia Policy*, no. 23 (2017): 43–48.

EXECUTIVE SUMMARY

This chapter analyzes Indonesia's security threats, material capacity, and strategic culture and assesses how these factors interact to produce the country's military strategies.

MAIN ARGUMENT

Indonesia lacks a coherent military strategy and as a result is currently under-balancing against the country's key external threat, China's maritime assertiveness. The adoption of a suboptimal strategy is a function of limited material capabilities as well as a strategic culture that emphasizes a defensive orientation and rejects military alliances as a threat to national autonomy. Indonesia has forgone investment in its power-projection capacity because it has traditionally viewed its primary security threats as internal ones, such as terrorism, separatism, and other challenges to social cohesion. Yet although Indonesia's military strategy is inadequate, it might be durable due to political contestation over the nature and severity of the China threat; divergent interests among military, economic, and political actors; and competition over resources within the military between the politically dominant army and the navy and air force, which would both benefit from the adoption of a new strategy.

POLICY IMPLICATIONS

- Indonesia's lack of a coherent maritime security strategy and power-projection capacity undermines its leadership position in ASEAN and its strategic position in the broader Asia-Pacific.

- Indonesia and the U.S. share common interests in a stable, rules-based maritime order in the Asia-Pacific, but Indonesia's lack of maritime capacity and aversion to military alliances limit the extent to which the two countries can cooperate in pursuit of these interests.

- Political debates over the severity of the maritime security threat from China, combined with Indonesia's staunch commitment to strategic autonomy, mean that the U.S. will find it difficult to convince Indonesia to join efforts to counter China's maritime assertiveness.

Power, Ideas, and Politics:
Obstacles to an Externally Oriented
Indonesian Military Strategy

Ann Marie Murphy

Over the past 50 years, Indonesia has faced a largely benign security environment that has permitted it to forgo an investment in military capacity. Indonesia has traditionally viewed its security threats as internal or transnational, such as terrorism, separatism, and other challenges to social cohesion. Rather than devote scarce resources to developing an outward-oriented military, Indonesia chose to promote economic and social development, which it believed would help mitigate security challenges. These social investments have paid off handsomely. Indonesia has joined the ranks of Asia's economic success stories, becoming a middle-income country with a per capita income of approximately $3,400 per annum and lifting millions out of poverty.[1] The country has witnessed dramatic rises in education, health, and social indicators. The Indonesian people have benefited immensely, if not equally, from this decision to prioritize domestic development over military buildup.

Indonesia's perception of a permissive security environment led the country to pursue nonmilitary mechanisms to promote regional and national

Ann Marie Murphy is an Associate Professor in the School of Diplomacy and International Relations at Seton Hall University and a Senior Research Scholar at the Weatherhead East Asian Institute at Columbia University. She can be reached at <annmarie.murphy@shu.edu>.

---

[1] See World Bank data sheet for gross national income per capita in 2016, available at http://databank.worldbank.org/data/download/GNIPC.pdf.

security. As Southeast Asia's largest state, Indonesia has traditionally defined its national interests broadly to include a region free from the hegemony of outside powers. To promote this interest, it helped create the Association of Southeast Asian Nations (ASEAN) in 1967. As the de facto leader of the organization, Indonesia has worked to bind outside actors to ASEAN's bedrock principles of noninterference in the domestic affairs of states and the peaceful resolution of disputes. It has pursued these interests by enmeshing great powers such as the United States and China in ASEAN-based institutions such as the East Asia Summit (EAS) and the ASEAN Regional Forum. For an archipelagic state, external security is maritime security. Indonesia has long harbored fears of China's irredentist claims to the South China Sea, but as long as great powers did not seek to revise the status quo, Indonesia had no reason to divert resources to external defense.

Indonesian fears were realized by China's 2009 submission to the UN Commission on the Limits of the Continental Shelf, which was accompanied by a nine-dash line map that includes virtually the entire South China Sea. Although China did not claim any Indonesian islands, the map appears to include parts of the Natuna Islands' exclusive economic zone (EEZ), home to one of the world's largest recoverable gas fields. China's claims threaten Indonesian territorial waters and the right to exploit the resources beneath them. At stake for Indonesia, however, is not only the Natuna Islands waters but also the sanctity of the United Nations Convention on the Law of the Sea (UNCLOS). Indonesia is the world's largest archipelagic state, but it lacks the naval capacity to defend itself. Its conception of its national territory encompasses not only the seventeen thousand islands that make up the archipelago but also the waters that connect them. Indeed, the Indonesian word for "country" is *tanah air*, literally "land and water." When UNCLOS came into force in 1994, it included the archipelagic principle, which grants island nations sovereignty over their internal waters. Because Indonesia does not possess sufficient power to protect itself, ensuring that larger states adhere to UNCLOS and ASEAN norms and ideas regarding the nonuse of force is a key Indonesian security interest.

Many Indonesian strategic thinkers, particularly civilians, have argued that Indonesia needs to change its strategic orientation from its traditional internal, land-based focus into an outward-looking maritime policy.[2] Since coming to power in 2014, President Joko Widodo (Jokowi) has declared his goal to transform Indonesia into a "global maritime fulcrum," capitalizing

---

[2] Ristian Atriandi Supriyanto, "The Superficiality of Indonesia's Defense Policy," *Jakarta Post*, June 15, 2016, http://www.thejakartapost.com/academia/2016/06/15/the-superficiality-of-indonesias-defense-policy.html; and Bob Lowry, "Indonesia's 2015 Defence White Paper," Australian Strategic Policy Institute (ASPI), Strategist, June 15, 2016, http://www.aspistrategist.org.au/indonesias-2015-defence-white-paper.

on Indonesia's status as an archipelago stretching over three thousand miles across some of the world's most strategic sea lines of communication. In contrast to Indonesia's traditional inward-looking strategic focus, this is clearly an outward-looking vision.

Indonesia does not have a coherent military strategy to respond to China and other external security challenges in part due to the country's lack of military capabilities and in part due to its inward-looking defense posture. As the Chinese threat to Indonesia increases, one would expect the country to mobilize national power in order to balance against China. To date, this has not occurred as a result of political contestation over the nature and severity of the China threat; the divergent interests of key military, economic, and political actors; and competition between the politically dominant army and both the navy and the air force, which would benefit from such a strategy. In theory, Indonesia could join a coalition against China, but a strategic culture that values autonomy and forswears military alliances mitigates against that choice.

The analysis presented in this chapter is the culmination of a three-year project to assess how material power and strategic culture interact to produce military strategies. In his contribution to *Strategic Asia 2015–16*, Vikram Nehru assessed Indonesia's national resource base and the country's ability to use these resources effectively in meeting its security challenges.[3] He concluded that despite rich resource endowments, Indonesia was unwilling—and perhaps unable—to translate those resources into national power and then project that power abroad to protect the country's interests. The following year, Yohanes Sulaiman analyzed Indonesia's strategic culture to illustrate how the ideational frames of references of Indonesian policymakers shaped their strategic choices.[4] He concluded that Indonesia's strategic culture is based on three principal elements: the need to protect national unity against the threat of foreign intervention, an inward focus that emphasizes maintaining an independent and resilient spirit, and the adoption of a completely free and active foreign policy that rejects military alliances. Building on the work of Nehru and Sulaiman, this chapter argues that Indonesia's paucity of material power and strategic culture produce an incoherent military strategy that under-balances against the maritime threat from China.

To support this argument, this chapter will proceed as follows. First, it outlines Indonesia's key strategic problems. The second section then provides

---

[3] Vikram Nehru, "Indonesia: The Reluctant Giant," *Strategic Asia 2015–16: Foundations of National Power*, ed. Ashley Tellis, Alison Szalwinski, and Michael Wills (Seattle: National Bureau of Asian Research [NBR], 2015), 190–222.

[4] Yohanes Sulaiman, "Indonesia's Strategic Culture: The Legacy of Independence," in *Strategic Asia 2016–17: Understanding Strategic Cultures in the Asia-Pacific*, ed. Ashley Tellis, Alison Szalwinski, and Michael Wills (Seattle: NBR, 2015), 168–93.

a rational reconstruction of the range of plausible strategies to respond to the country's external threats, while the third section specifically outlines Indonesia's response to China's maritime assertiveness. Fourth, the chapter explains the dominance of Indonesia's strategy of nonalignment without a concerted mobilization of national power and then provides an assessment of the durability of that strategy by discussing the obstacles to an effective maritime security strategy. The chapter concludes that although Indonesia's strategy is far from adequate to meet the China challenge, an inability to overcome differences means it may well be durable.

Indonesia's Key Strategic Problems

Indonesia has traditionally viewed its primary security challenges as internal or transnational ones. Its status as an archipelago of seventeen thousand islands stretching three thousand miles from east to west makes it difficult to maintain the territorial integrity of the state. Indonesia is also home to an extremely diverse population marked by ethnic, religious, class, and regional cleavages. Maintaining the social cohesion of its heterogeneous population and the territorial integrity of its archipelagic state have long been Indonesia's key security interests.

Indonesia continues to face a range of challenges to social and political cohesion. Religious intolerance is rising in Indonesia, home to the world's largest Muslim population with approximately 88% of its citizens professing the Islamic faith. Indonesian Islam has traditionally been characterized as tolerant, and the constitution guarantees freedom of religion to the six officially recognized religions (Islam, Catholicism, Protestantism, Buddhism, Hinduism, and Confucianism). In recent years, however, Indonesia's Muslim society has become more conservative, and some hard-line groups have been propagating a more militant brand of Islam and targeting religious minorities, sometimes violently. In addition, anti-Chinese sentiment against the country's economically privileged Sino-Indonesians, who make up approximately 3% of the total population, is also on the rise.[5] Both of these trends were successfully mobilized in Indonesia's largest street protests ever by opponents of the ethnically Chinese, Christian incumbent governor of Jakarta, Basuki Tjahaja Purnama (Ahok), who is now serving a two-year jail sentence for blasphemy after telling his Muslim constituents that Islam did not require them to vote for Muslims. Rising income inequality that often coincides with ethnic, regional, and religious cleavages is a further cause of social friction.

---

[5] See World Population Review, "Indonesia Population 2017," http://worldpopulationreview.com/countries/indonesia-population.

Like many postcolonial states, Indonesia legitimizes its claims to its current territorial borders not on the basis of an ancient civilization but as the successor to a European colony. Defending the territorial integrity of the state against secessionist challenges has always been the country's primary security interest. Indonesian leaders fear that if any part of the country were to separate, the state could unravel. Only East Timor, a former Portuguese rather than Dutch colony forcibly integrated into Indonesia in 1975, could become independent without threatening the fundamental justification of the Indonesian state. Since the resolution of the Aceh conflict in 2005, secessionist concerns have focused on Papua, where a small insurgency movement has simmered for years. Foreign human rights groups often argue that Papua should have the same option as East Timor: a referendum to determine whether Papuans want to remain a part of Indonesia or become independent. This is heretical to Indonesia, which views Papua strictly as an internal issue and external interference as a violation of Indonesian sovereignty.

Despite the prioritization of these challenges to social and political cohesion, in recent years the rise of transnational threats such as terrorism, climate change, and drug trafficking has attracted more attention in Indonesia. Transnational security challenges are magnified by the country's porous borders. Indonesia faces a terrorist threat that is both homegrown and inspired by foreign radical groups, as illustrated by a May 2016 attack in Jakarta for which the Islamic State of Iraq and Syria (ISIS) claimed responsibility. Indonesia is also suffering from a rise in drug addiction, which some believe is a foreign conspiracy to weaken the country. Further, Indonesia ranks as one of the countries that will be hardest hit by climate change. It has already lost some of its islands to rising sea levels, and experts predict Jakarta could be under water by the end of the century.[6] Indonesia sits on the ring of fire, making it susceptible to earthquakes, tsunamis, and other natural disasters that are predicted to increase as climate change triggers more extreme weather events.

Indonesia's external security threats are maritime threats given its geostrategic location as an island nation. The country faces piracy and kidnapping problems, particularly in the Malacca Strait and Sulawesi Sea, pitting Indonesian authorities against nonstate actors. Illegal, unregulated, and unreported (IUU) fishing by foreigners in its territorial waters costs Indonesia billions of dollars a year and harms Indonesian fisherman.[7] Only since China's

---

[6] Information on Indonesia and climate change can be accessed at the World Bank, http://projects.worldbank.org/P120313/indonesia-climate-change-development-policy-project?lang=en; and World Bank, "Jakarta Case Study Overview," https://siteresources.worldbank.org/INTURBANDEVELOPMENT/Resources/336387-1306291319853/CS_Jakarta.pdf.

[7] Johnny Langenheim, "Indonesia and U.S. Join Forces to Police the Seas," *Guardian*, February 3, 2016, https://www.theguardian.com/environment/the-coral-triangle/2016/feb/03/indonesia-and-us-join-forces-to-combat-illegal-fishing-protect-reefs.

recent assertive moves to promote its maritime claims in the South China Sea has Indonesia confronted a significant traditional external threat to its national security. To date, Indonesia has largely been spared the direct military coercion that China has directed at Vietnam and the Philippines, but this appears to be a matter of geography since the waters around the Natuna Islands lie at the southernmost tip of the South China Sea. The Natuna Islands are approximately 1,740 kilometers (km) from Hainan Island, home to Yulin Naval Base, China's most strategically important base for projecting power into the South China Sea.[8] If threats are a function of aggregate power, offensive capabilities, aggressive intentions, and geographic proximity, then China's demonstrated willingness to use its rapidly growing maritime power to seize the Scarborough Shoal from the Philippines, deploy and defend an oil rig in waters contested with Vietnam, and militarize reclaimed islands in the South China Sea clearly illustrates the country's intentions to assert its claims forcefully. This increasing power-projection capacity will erode the protection that Indonesia's geographic distance has hitherto provided. Today, therefore, China's claims to the South China Sea and its willingness to use military force to promote them directly threaten Indonesian national security and the stable, autonomous, rules-based regional order Jakarta has sought to create.

The Rational Reconstruction of Indonesian Military Strategies to Deal with Strategic Problems

Indonesia has never faced a clear and present danger from an external threat to its national security. Its key security challenges, as the previous section illustrated, have been internal and transnational ones. As a result, Indonesia's military strategy has traditionally been directed toward domestic threats, while it has adopted broader foreign affairs strategies to meet external challenges. It is therefore important to define these two strategies. Military strategy, according to the U.S. Joint Chiefs of Staff, is "the art and science of employing the armed forces of a nation to secure the objectives of national policy by the application of force or the threat of force."[9] This definition recognizes that military strategies include not only the direct application of organized violence, but also the threat of force as the basis for strategies of

---

[8] Damen Cook, "China's Most Important South China Sea Military Base," *Diplomat*, March 9, 2017, http://thediplomat.com/2017/03/chinas-most-important-south-china-sea-military-base.

[9] Terry L. Deibel, *Foreign Affairs Strategy: Logic for American Statecraft* (New York: Cambridge University Press, 2007), 5. This definition assumes that a nation's armed forces are the only actors that government officials will call on to help mobilize or threaten violence in the pursuit of national interests. As will be discussed below, Indonesia's armed forces have always been small, and its official doctrine calls on the Indonesian people to assist the military in defending the country.

coercive diplomacy to achieve national interests. This distinction is important in the Indonesian case because the only time that Indonesia has "successfully" achieved a national objective solely through the use of military force was its 1975 invasion and incorporation of East Timor, although the subsequent insurgency and vote for independence belie the notion of "success." Instead, Indonesia has achieved critical national interests such as independence and recovering Papua through a combination of military violence and diplomacy. Indonesian defense white papers have, therefore, often claimed that diplomacy is the first line of defense

When reconstructing Indonesia's strategy to meet external challenges, it is more appropriate to employ a broader conception of foreign affairs strategy, which one expert has defined as a "plan for the coordinated use of all of the instruments of state power to pursue objectives that protect and promote the national interest."[10] This section reviews Indonesia's strategic choices over time to illustrate how it has arrived at its current dominant strategy of nonalignment without a concerted mobilization of national power. In terms of the dichotomous choice between a nonaligned stance that safeguards a country's strategic independence and alignment with a foreign power that can provide security at the cost of dependence, Indonesia has long sought to retain its strategic autonomy. At the same time, the country has failed to mobilize national power domestically because it did not perceive an external threat, choosing to invest in economic development instead. These choices were rational at the time they were made. Indonesia has historically been fortunate that its benign security environment has allowed it to avoid the trade-off of investing in military capacity or forging military alliances to promote its security. The path-dependent nature of those choices, however, has left Indonesia today with a suboptimal strategy because it is unable to defend its maritime borders. Enhancing Indonesia's maritime security, therefore, requires either aligning with a country like the United States or embarking on a major build-up of naval capacity. Neither option seems likely, as subsequent sections of this chapter demonstrate.

Current Dominant Strategy: Nonalignment without a Concerted Mobilization of National Power

Vice President Mohammad Hatta promulgated Indonesia's *bebas dan aktif*, or "free and active," foreign policy doctrine in a 1948 speech entitled "Rowing between Two Reefs." Hatta likened Indonesia to a small boat that needed to steer free of the shoal of either Cold War bloc, lest it hit one and be damaged. The "free" component of this doctrine held that Indonesia should

---

[10] Deibel, *Foreign Affairs Strategy*, 10.

avoid Cold War alliances and chart its own course in international affairs, while the "active" component held that the country should seek to craft an international order that reflects its interests and values. The *bebas dan aktif* doctrine strongly influences current Indonesian strategic thinking, and many Indonesians perceive the United States and China as reefs between which Indonesia must navigate. This commitment to the idea of a "free" policy stance makes Indonesia wary of entering alliances as a means to enhance its military power, despite decades of underinvestment in military capacity. In short, its strategic culture and lack of hard power assets have left the country unable to defend its maritime security.

Indonesia's decision to forgo a concerted effort to mobilize national power in an external military strategy was a rational response to its perception that it faced no direct threat of military invasion in recent decades. In the absence of a military threat, Indonesia chose to eschew the costly investment in military power. External threats were subversive ones that sought to exploit social cleavages, such as the 1948 Communist uprising in Madiun. Indonesia's long-standing fears that its heterogeneous population, ideological differences, and porous borders made it ripe for subversion were realized in the Outer Island rebellions of 1957–58. The rebellions were triggered by economic grievances over the unfair distribution of revenue between the center and the outer island provinces, the resentment of local military commanders over the increasing centralization of the army, and opposition by the conservative Muslim population of these areas to President Sukarno's increasingly close ties to the Communist Party of Indonesia (Partai Komunis Indonesia, or PKI).[11] The roots of these rebellions had to do less with a desire to secede from Indonesia than to change the distribution of political and economic power within it. However, convinced that it was only a matter of time before Indonesia would succumb to PKI control, the United States and Britain provided money, arms, and air cover to the rebels. Even though the Indonesian military suppressed the rebellions, Western efforts to tear the fragile state apart only reinforced fears of external interference in domestic affairs.[12] Chinese intervention in the coup and countercoup of 1965 magnified this suspicion of outsiders, particularly on the part of the army.[13] The idea that outside actors harbor hostile intentions toward

---

[11] The seminal work on U.S. involvement in the Outer Island rebellions is Audrey R. Kahin and George McTurnan Kahin, *Subversion as Foreign Policy: The Secret Eisenhower and Dulles Debacle in Indonesia* (New York: New Press, 1995).

[12] For the seminal work on the role that Indonesian foreign policy played in domestic politics during this period, see Franklin B. Weinstein, "The Uses of Foreign Policy in Indonesia" (PhD diss., Cornell University, 1972). Weinstein's published works also make this argument, albeit with less detail. See Franklin B. Weinstein, *Indonesia Abandons Confrontation: An Inquiry into the Functions of Indonesian Foreign Policy* (Ithaca: Cornell Southeast Asia Program, 1969).

[13] Michael Leifer, "Indonesia and the Dilemmas of Engagement," in *Engaging Asia: The Management of an Emerging Power*, ed. Alastair Iain Johnston and Robert S. Ross (New York: Routledge, 1999), 91.

Indonesia and seek to weaken it is a key component of the country's strategic culture that continues to influence policy.

Nonalignment with the Mobilization of National Power

There is a historical precedent for Indonesia to mobilize power in pursuit of national interests. In the late 1950s and early 1960s, it mobilized to recover Irian Jaya, now termed Papua, the only part of the Dutch colony that the Netherlands had refused to transfer to Indonesia at independence in 1949. The Dutch had committed to resolve the issue through negotiations, but when they refused to do so and the United Nations rejected Indonesian requests for the appointment of a good-offices commission, Indonesia mobilized power domestically and externally. As the successor to the Dutch colonial states, it viewed any adjustments to those borders as an existential threat that could spur secessionist movements elsewhere.

Sukarno expropriated all Dutch enterprises in Indonesia, expelled thousands of Dutch citizens, and threatened military action in December 1961 if the Dutch refused to negotiate. His threat was made credible by the delivery of advanced weapons from the Soviet Union during the 1950s and Nikita Khruschev's offer of a $1 billion loan for military purchases during a 1960 visit to Jakarta. Sukarno's coercive diplomacy led the United States to pressure the Dutch to resolve the issue. An agreement was reached under which Irian was transferred temporarily to the United Nations, after which full control was transferred to Indonesia when it committed to give the people of Irian an opportunity to exercise self-determination at a later date.[14] As in its quest for independence, Indonesia achieved its objective in part by mobilization of hard power and in part through diplomatic means.

From 1963 to 1965, Indonesia engaged in a low-intensity war against Malaysia and Singapore after the British announcement of plans to create a new Malaysian state that would share the island of Borneo with Indonesia. Claiming that British bases in Malaysia would provide an avenue through which the West could subvert Indonesian sovereignty as the British had done in the Outer Island rebellions, Indonesia refused to extend diplomatic recognition when the new state was created in 1963, and Sukarno initiated a low-level war against Malaysia called Konfrontasi. Konfrontasi also served a domestic political function as a mechanism through which Sukarno could attempt to maintain his political authority atop an increasingly brittle triangle of the PKI and the conservative Indonesian military (Tentara Negara Indonesia, or TNI) and divert domestic attention away from Indonesia's

---

[14] In July and August 1969, Indonesia stage-managed an "act of free choice" in which 1,025 village leaders, handpicked by Indonesian authorities, unanimously agreed to become part of Indonesia.

economic and political problems.[15] Malaysia's Commonwealth allies deployed 40,000 troops to protect it from Indonesia. Konfrontasi increasingly isolated Indonesia from not only the West but also the Soviet Union, which feared becoming entrapped in an unwanted conflict with the West, and Indonesia's partners in the Non-Aligned Movement (NAM), which opposed the use of force against a smaller state.[16] Sukarno moved Indonesia closer to a revisionist China, quitting the United Nations when Malaysia was given a seat on the UN Security Council in 1965. Within months, the precarious balance of power that Sukarno had attempted to maintain between the TNI and the PKI erupted in violence. Konfrontasi represents the only time that Indonesia attempted to project power outside the archipelago, and the lesson Sukarno's successor would learn is that the projection of force is not effective; it only paves the way for great powers to intervene in regional affairs.

Alignment with a Foreign Power

During the Suharto era (1965–98), Indonesia formed a limited alignment with the United States based on their common perception of a threat from Communism.[17] For Indonesia, this threat was an internal one from the PKI that was magnified by Chinese support. The full circumstances of the October 1965 coup and counter-coup that resulted in the downfall of Sukarno, the decimation of the PKI, and the rise to power of General Suharto and the TNI remain unclear. According to the historiography of this period, a group of left-wing generals in league with the PKI and supported by China launched the coup with the aim of establishing a Communist regime. The TNI took harsh measures against the triple threat of the PKI, Indonesia's ethnic Chinese population, and China. In one of the worst massacres of the twentieth century, at least 500,000, and perhaps a million, Indonesians suspected of being Communists were killed and the PKI was banned. Viewing China as a source of subversion and its main external threat, Indonesia cut diplomatic ties with Beijing from 1967 to 1990.

Indonesia welcomed U.S. military training, assistance, and weapons to strengthen the TNI. Having been the largest recipient of Soviet aid outside of the socialist bloc under Sukarno, the country now became one of the top recipients of U.S. military aid. However, its commitment to strategic autonomy meant that Indonesia never joined a formal alliance

---

[15] John Mackie, *Konfrontasi: The Indonesia-Malaysia Dispute, 1963–1966* (London: Oxford University Press, 1974).

[16] Robert J. McMahon, *The Limits of Empire: The United States and Southeast Asia since World War II* (New York: Columbia University Press, 1999).

[17] John D. Ciorciari, *Limited Alignments: Southeast Asia and the Great Powers since 1975* (Washington, D.C.: Georgetown University Press, 2010).

nor permitted military bases on its territory. Jakarta also welcomed U.S. support for the 1975 invasion of East Timor, when Indonesian leaders feared that an independent East Timor would "go Communist" and become a "Cuba on its doorstep" or a base for foreign subversion of Indonesia.[18] After the Cold War, the loss of the shared interest in containing Communism significantly weakened Indonesia's alignment with the United States. The U.S. willingness to condition its military assistance on human rights and then cut military ties altogether after Indonesia's violent response to East Timor's 1999 vote for independence created a sense of abandonment and the impression that the United States is an unreliable strategic partner. It also reinforced Indonesia's belief in the value of an independent policy, which is a key element of its strategic culture.

Today, as Indonesian policymakers contemplate their military options in the face of China's maritime assertiveness, the memory of U.S. abandonment has discredited the idea of aligning with foreign powers—particularly the United States—as a means of securing military assets externally. As the next section discusses in depth, Indonesia's strategic culture, with its emphasis on autonomy and independence, and the lack of hard power have combined to produce a military strategy that is incapable of protecting the country's maritime domain.

Indonesia's Suboptimal Military Strategy in Response to External Threats

China's Maritime Assertiveness

Indonesia has adopted a series of legal, diplomatic, and military responses to China's maritime threat. In response to China's submission of its sovereignty claims and nine-dash line map in 2009, Jakarta filed a protest with UNCLOS in 2010 contending that China's claim "clearly lacks any international legal basis."[19] Indonesia has repeatedly requested that China clarify its claims—drawn freehand in 1947—by providing precise coordinates. It has also sought assurances that Chinese claims do not extend to the Natuna Islands EEZ. According to UNCLOS, rights to waters can only be derived from rights to land or islands. Because China claims no islands near Natuna, it cannot justify claims to surrounding waters through UNCLOS, which has

---

[18] Adam Schwarz, *A Nation in Waiting: Indonesia's Search for Stability* (Boulder: Westview Press, 2000), 201.

[19] Ann Marie Murphy, "Indonesia Responds to China's Rise," in *Middle Powers and the Rise of China*, ed. Bruce Gilley and Andrew O'Neill (Washington, D.C.: Georgetown University Press, 2014).

traditionally led Indonesia to contend that there is no conflict between the two countries. China, however, has failed to provide these assurances.

Indonesia has also continued its long-standing diplomatic efforts to manage tensions between its ASEAN partners and China to prevent escalation. Since Indonesian officials maintain that their country is not a party to the South China Sea disputes, it has traditionally sought to play the role of an honest broker. Indonesia has pressed China to join ASEAN in promulgating a binding code of conduct (CoC) on the South China Sea that would replace the nonbinding Declaration on the Conduct of Parties in the South China Sea (DoC) from 2002. The CoC would also create protocols for unplanned encounters between maritime forces to ensure that they do not escalate. Indonesia harbors no illusions that these disputes will be resolved, but it hopes that they can be managed. After making no progress for fifteen years, China and ASEAN agreed in May 2017 on a framework for how a CoC might be structured, but it still is unclear when the process might be concluded.[20] Critics contend that because China's island-building and militarization violate the core principles of the DoC, there is little reason to expect that the CoC will produce any meaningful change in China's behavior.

Following the arbitral ruling in July 2016 on the Philippines' UNCLOS case against China that overwhelmingly rejected the basis of the latter's claims to the South China Sea, there were expectations that Indonesia would mobilize ASEAN and other stakeholders to apply global pressure on China to abide by the UNCLOS ruling. Although the ruling was confined to the issues raised by the Philippines, the legal principles applied vindicated Indonesia's position. As an archipelago lacking the naval capacity to patrol and defend its waters, Indonesia regards ensuring the sanctity of UNLOS as a key interest. Moreover, using diplomatic means to raise the cost to China of violating the convention could have helped ensure Indonesia's maritime security. However, Philippine president Rodrigo Duterte's decision after the ruling to engage rather than pressure Beijing made it difficult for states like Indonesia to use the ruling to confront China. China's refusal to acknowledge and abide by the decision has the effect of weakening UNCLOS. Recently, Beijing has begun justifying its claims to the waters surrounding the Natuna Islands by using the argument that they are "historical fishing grounds." Indonesia has pushed back against this position, stating that there is no such thing as historical fishing grounds under UNCLOS.

Militarily, Indonesia has strengthened its forces in the Natuna Islands, where Indonesian and Chinese maritime vessels engaged in two direct confrontations over illegal fishing in 2016. Indonesia has deployed an army

---

[20] "China, ASEAN Agree on Framework for South China Sea Code of Conduct," Reuters, May 19, 2017, http://in.reuters.com/article/southchinasea-china-philippines-idINKCN18E1FW.

battalion, air force special units, three frigates, a new radar system, and F-16s. These forces, however, are woefully inadequate to survey, patrol, and secure the vast contested waterways. China does not claim the Natuna Islands, so their defense is not at issue.

Explanation for Indonesia's Suboptimal Military Strategy

As discussed above, the main reason that Indonesia has adopted a suboptimal policy toward protecting its maritime security is that the country has traditionally lacked an external threat. Until China published the nine-dash line map and began to defend it forcefully, Indonesia viewed its security environment as benign. Absent a perception of a traditional external military threat, Indonesia had no incentive to invest in external defense capacity. The country viewed its key threats as domestic ones. Outside separatist challenges to national integrity in Aceh, Papua, and East Timor, where military suppression predominated, economic, ideological, and political strategies were the primary ones adopted to meet internal challenges. An investment in military power would have diverted resources away from these strategies. Facing the dichotomous choice between defense and development, Indonesia chose development not only for its own sake but also for the security benefits it would provide.

The Suharto regime believed that economic underdevelopment and poverty were conditions that provided fertile ground for Communism, fostered secessionist movements, and exacerbated other social grievances against the state. It therefore viewed security in a comprehensive manner, as emphasized by its doctrine of *ketahan nasional* (national resilience). Resilience is conceived as the ability to withstand foreign pressures, and the promotion of nationalism, economic development, and military strength focused inwardly were means to achieve it. As Yohanes Sulaiman argued about Indonesian strategic culture in last year's *Strategic Asia* volume, promoting resilience had a strong ideological component, and the military played an important role in indoctrination through its thirteen territorial commands that parallel the civilian structure down to the village level.[21] This was particularly true with Pancasila, the vague nationalist doctrine that Sukarno had promulgated in an effort to unite his countrymen.

Due to its traditionally permissive security environment, Indonesia today retains its defense strategy of *hankamrata* (total people's war), which was first crafted in the fight for independence. People's warfare consists of three phases: a frontal attack opposing invaders using naval and air power before they reach Indonesian territory; second, containment of the enemy on land;

---

[21] Sulaiman, "Indonesia's Strategic Culture."

and third, a counteroffensive to force the enemy to withdraw or surrender. Indonesian military strategists sought to capitalize on the country's large population by having citizens participate in the defense of their country in phase two. An integral component of people's warfare is the army's territorial command, through which the military would mobilize Indonesian civilians. This doctrine leads the military to adopt an inward-looking, defensive orientation and prioritizes the army. The territorial command structure gives the army significant political power at the local level, and maintaining it has always been a key institutional interest.

Indonesia has survived with what many objective observers would contend is a suboptimal maritime strategy because the external threats that the country has traditionally faced, such as maritime piracy, could be met either collectively or through nonmilitary solutions. In the early 2000s, Indonesian waterways ranked among the most vulnerable to piracy, creating risks for ships transiting through the vital Malacca Strait, the world's busiest waterway. After al Qaeda's bombing of the USS *Cole* in 2000 and attack on the *Limburg* oil tanker off the coast of Yemen in 2002, Western, and particularly U.S., officials took the threat of seaborne terrorism in the Malacca Strait shipping lane seriously.[22] In March 2004, Admiral Thomas Fargo, then commander of the U.S. Pacific Command, discussed proposals for a regional maritime security initiative to address these threats, which, according to erroneous news reports, would include the deployment of U.S. forces on high-speed boats to interdict threats.[23] The proposal triggered a storm of protests from Indonesia, which rejected any military role for external powers in the Malacca Strait. Indonesian Foreign Ministry officials stated that the initiative was "not in Jakarta's interests," and Admiral Bernard Kent Sondakh, then chief of staff of the Indonesian Navy, stressed that the "Malacca Strait is not an international strait" and antiterrorism operations in Indonesia's territorial waters are challenges to its sovereignty.[24] Indonesia joined Malaysia and Singapore, the other littoral states, to form what is today the Malacca Straits Patrol, which has helped significantly reduce piracy. In this case, protecting Indonesia's sovereignty and the right of littoral states to an independent policy trumped a potentially more effective military strategy that would have involved dependence on outside actors like the United States.

---

[22] Lena Kay, "Indonesian Public Perceptions of the U.S. and Their Implications for U.S. Foreign Policy," Pacific Forum CSIS, Issues and Insights, Summer 2005, 4.

[23] Tim Huxley, "Piracy and Maritime Terror in Southeast Asia: Dire Straits," *Strategic Comments* 10, no. 6 (2004): 1–2.

[24] Bernard Kent Sondakh, "National Sovereignty and Security in the Strait of Malacca" (presentation at a conference at the Maritime Institute of Malaysia, Kuala Lumpur, October 11–14, 2004), http://www.mima.gov.my/mima/htmls/conferences/som04/papers/sondakh.pdf.

More importantly, consistent with its inward focus and comprehensive notion of security, Indonesia also believes that the roots of maritime piracy lie in secessionist, criminal, and other social problems that must be combatted on land. In this view, any successful maritime security policy must resolve the conflicts that produce maritime crime. Following the 2005 Aceh peace agreement that ended the long-running insurgency, piracy in the Malacca Strait declined dramatically.

Today, Indonesia and its neighbors Malaysia and the Philippines face a similar problem of maritime piracy in the Sulawesi Sea, often termed the "terrorist triangle." In recent years, the Abu Sayyaf Group has engaged in piracy and kidnapping for ransom from its base in Mindanao in the Philippines. Following the same pattern as in the Malacca Strait, the littoral states have adopted coordinated air and naval patrols to police the vast waters. Significantly, given that Indonesian ships and sailors are often targeted, Indonesia demanded and received the right to hot pursuit in Philippine waters. Jakarta has not been willing to cede this right to others, however, due to sovereignty concerns, which form a key component of its strategic culture.

Indonesia has largely addressed transnational threats such as drug trafficking, climate change, and terrorism through nonmilitary means. Since the separation of the police from the military in 1999, the police have taken the lead on counterterrorism. Indonesia has adopted a counterterrorism policy that focuses on the investigation, arrest, and legal prosecution of terrorists that has largely avoided the harsh military techniques that Indonesian officials believe would provide fuel for terrorist recruitment. It also cooperates with international law-enforcement agencies, and the country's elite counterterrorism unit, Densus 88, receives significant funding and capacity building from countries such as the United States and Australia. Given sovereignty concerns and the sensitivities related to the U.S. war on terrorism and invasions of Iraq and Afghanistan, which were universally opposed in Indonesia, this cooperation takes place under the radar.

A belief that diplomacy, not military strength, is the best means to ensure regional and national security also led Indonesia to forgo investment in power-projection capacity. The historical memory of Sukarno's failed Konfrontasi policy against Malaysia and Singapore convinced Indonesian officials that military aggression is not effective. According to this view, conflict between Southeast Asian states only creates opportunities for outside powers to intervene in the region's affairs, thereby threatening the regional autonomy from great-power competition that Indonesian officials view as critical for their country's security. As result, Indonesia pursued multilateral diplomatic strategies through ASEAN to promote regional order among the Southeast Asian states and bind outside actors like the United States and

China to norms of nonintervention and the peaceful resolution of disputes. The former minister of foreign affairs sought to create what he termed a "dynamic equilibrium" in the Asia-Pacific, which he stated was "marked by an absence of preponderant power not through the rigidity, rivalry and tensions common to the pursuit of a balance of power. Instead, through respect of certain principles and norms, reflecting common responsibility in maintaining the region's peace and stability."[25] By advancing the notion that principles and norms could shape the balance of material capabilities, Indonesia was attempting to use ideas to constrain the use of military force by more powerful states.

This belief in diplomacy extends beyond the Foreign Ministry. Indonesian defense white papers have traditionally stated that diplomacy is the first line of defense.[26] Given this traditional commitment to soft-power mechanisms, Indonesia has a tendency to downplay external threats that might require a radical rethinking of strategic priorities. The 2009 defense white paper did not mention the South China Sea issue. The 2015 white paper acknowledges that the policies of China and the United States, as well as instability in the South China Sea, will increasingly dominate Indonesia's strategic environment, but it does not discuss policies designed to address the issue. Instead, it states that "armed conflict will not happen" because ASEAN member states have committed to settle the conflict "without using armed violence."[27] This statement once again illustrates the influence of a strategic culture that has traditionally placed great faith in the power of norms and ideas to resolve problems while dismissing the need for hard power.

A Lack of Military Capacity

Indonesia's current strategy of under-balancing against China's maritime threats can be explained in part by the uncomfortable fact that Indonesia is woefully lacking in military projection capacity. The Indonesian military has been called "underfunded, undertrained, overpoliticized, and plagued by corruption."[28] Despite the prominent role that the TNI has traditionally

---

[25] Marty Natalegawa (address at Macquarie University, Sydney, July 15, 2013), http://kemlu.go.id/Documents/Remarks%20Menlu%20di%20Sydney/Remarks%20Dr.%20Marty%20Natalegawa.pdf.

[26] Rizal Sukma, "Indonesia's Security Outlook, Defense Policy and Regional Cooperation," in *Asia Pacific Countries' Security Outlook and Its Implications for the Defense Sector* (Tokyo: National Institute of Defense Studies, 2010), 21.

[27] Ministry of Defence (Indonesia), *Indonesian Defence White Paper 2015* (Jakarta, 2015), https://www.kemhan.go.id/wp-content/uploads/2016/05/2015-INDONESIA-DEFENCE-WHITE-PAPER-ENGLISH-VERSION.pdf.

[28] Sheldon Simon, "Southeast Asia Defense Needs: Change or Continuity?" in *Strategic Asia 2005–06: Military Modernization in an Era of Uncertainty*, ed. Ashley J. Tellis and Michael Wills (Seattle: NBR, 2005), 281.

played in Indonesian politics, it has always been a small force. In 2010, its 413,729 military personnel accounted for less than 0.05% of the country's population, which then numbered 240 million people.[29] Even during the Suharto era, Indonesia's military budget as a percentage of GDP peaked at 4.2% in 1983 before declining steadily. By 1990, it was only 1.5% of GDP. At $1.7 billion, the budget was almost unchanged from 1975.[30] This relatively low military allocation reflected Suharto's conviction that the country's primary security threats were internal and that investing in development would yield security payoffs. During the three decades of Suharto's rule, the economy grew at an average annual rate of 6%. The prioritization of development over defense was a distinct policy choice influenced by the goal of promoting national resilience.

Military spending was further slashed during the 1997–98 Asian financial crisis that led to Suharto's overthrow. Although it rose from $2.37 billion in 2005 to $4.47 billion in 2010, the military budget accounted for a paltry 0.78% of GDP.[31] During this time, therefore, resource constraints negatively affected Indonesia's military capacity. Yet efforts to strengthen the military have also been hampered by politics. In the early years of Indonesia's democratic era, reforming the military and bringing it under civilian control were key objectives. Enhancing its capacity was not. Since the Indonesian parliament has been given the power to authorize defense budgets, which compete for scarce resources with social spending, legislators have chosen to invest in nonmilitary priorities. In 2010 the Ministry of Defence submitted a budget request of $14.9 billion, but parliament allocated only $4.47 billion, which covered less than a third of the country's minimum needs.[32]

Convincing Indonesia's parliament to increase the military budget was tied to reform of the TNI's off–balance sheet financing. The TNI traditionally funded a significant portion of its budget from an empire of military-run businesses. Bringing these businesses under state control has been an aspect of security sector reform. A 2004 law required the TNI to inventory these businesses and transfer them to the state by 2009. The TNI, however, made many military cooperatives and foundations exempt from the law and sold

---

[29] Sukma, "Indonesia's Security Outlook," 12.

[30] Dewi Fortuna Anwar, quoted in Rizal Sukma, "Indonesia-China Relations: The Politics of Re-engagement," *Asian Survey* 49, no. 4 (2009): 591–608.

[31] Charles "Ken" Comer, "Leahy in Indonesia: Damned If You Do (and Even If You Don't)," *Asian Affairs: An American Review* 37, no. 2 (2010): 53–70.

[32] Leonard C. Sebastian and Iis Gindarsah, "Assessing 12-Year Military Reform in Indonesia: Major Strategic Gaps for the Next Stage of Reform," S. Rajaratnam School of International Studies (RSIS), Working Paper, no. 227, April 6, 2011, 17. See also Sukma, "Indonesia's Security Outlook," 34.

off many profitable businesses before the deadline.[33] Only since the TNI ostensibly complied with this law has parliament been willing to consider increasing the military budget.

Low military spending, combined with the suspension of military sales by the United States, severely degraded Indonesian military capacity. According to one analysis, operational levels of different Indonesian military platforms ranged from 30% to 80%.[34] Ironically, while the blanket U.S. embargo on the sale of military equipment and spare parts was a response to human rights abuses committed by the army, the sanctions had their greatest impact on the air force and navy, which were extremely dependent on U.S. military equipment.[35] As a result of Indonesia's efforts to diversify its sources of military equipment following the U.S. embargo, the country now has approximately 173 weapons systems supplied by 17 different countries, with Russia, South Korea, and Great Britain emerging as important arms suppliers.[36] This creates huge operational, coordination, and maintenance problems. Beefing up the navy is central to promoting Indonesia's maritime security, but this will entail a large and long-term commitment. The navy has only 171 vessels to patrol the archipelago's vast waterways.[37]

Recognizing the need to upgrade Indonesia's military capacity, the Ministry of Defence in 2010 released its Minimum Essential Force (MEF) document, which outlined the country's defense requirements based on an assessment of actual and potential threats. Significantly, a year after China's issuance of its nine-dash line map, the ministry identified terrorism, separatism, border disputes, outer island management, natural disasters, communal conflict, and energy security as actual threats. Climate change, violations of Indonesian waterways, environmental degradation, pandemics, foreign aggression, financial crises, cybercrime, and water and food crises were identified as potential threats. The MEF is a recognition that Indonesia's decision to forgo military investment over a long period of time, combined with the impact of the financial crisis and U.S. embargo, has left the country unable to meet its basic needs.

The MEF calls for a 274-ship green water navy, an air force consisting of 10 fighter squadrons, upgrades in air-combat capacity, a more mobile land force, and the development of a capable industrial base.[38] The 274-ship navy is

---

[33] Marcus Mietzner, *Military Politics, Islam and the State in Indonesia* (Singapore: Institute of Southeast Asian Studies, 2009).

[34] Sebastian and Gindarsah, "Assessing 12-Year Military Reform in Indonesia."

[35] Comer, "Leahy in Indonesia."

[36] Sebastian and Gindarsah, "Assessing 12-Year Military Reform in Indonesia," 22.

[37] "Modernized Weaponry Defense Needed, Says Jokowi," *Jakarta Post*, October 5, 2015.

[38] Nehru, "Indonesia: The Reluctant Giant."

to consist of 110 surface combatants, 66 patrol vessels, 98 support ships, and 12 new diesel-electric submarines. In addition, the Ministry of Defence has also called for the creation of three integrated regional defense commands, with an emphasis on force integration across the army, navy, and air force.

To achieve these goals, Indonesia began to increase its defense spending in the years after the 2010 release of the MEF. The military budget ranged between 0.8% and 0.9% of GDP between 2010 and 2015, but due to economic growth of approximately 6% per annum over this period, the defense budget has increased approximately 40% in real terms. Much of the increase has paid for raises in soldiers' salaries and benefits rather than acquisitions to enhance military capacity. While campaigning for the presidency, Jokowi pledged to raise the defense budget to 1.5% of GDP within five years, but the 2015 defense white paper only expects 1.0% of GDP within ten years.[39]

Despite the increase in the military budget, politics continue to influence Indonesia's internal balancing efforts. Given that the country's major external threats are maritime ones, enhancements to the naval and air forces should be prioritized. The politically powerful army, however, has won a demand that the increases in the procurement budget should be divided equally among the forces. Deference to the institutional interests of the army, as well as the pecuniary interests of its top officers, who traditionally have received kickbacks from procurement contracts, hinder Indonesia's efforts to balance efficiently.

Indonesia's 2015 defense white paper outlines a new defense strategy with three main priorities: transforming Indonesia into a global maritime fulcrum, meeting the MEF, and building up the state defense program over the next ten years.[40] Like its predecessor, the 2015 defense white paper also focuses significantly on nontraditional security issues, particularly terrorism. The investment in the local defense industry is meant to promote the local economy and make Indonesia "independent" of foreign military suppliers, which minimizes the risk of an arms embargo like the one the United States imposed after the East Timor crisis.[41] Relying on its indigenous defense industry, however, exposes Indonesia to the risk of poor equipment. The Indonesian defense industry has suffered quality-control issues, cost overruns, and delivery postponements, even when working on joint ventures with countries like South Korea. Although this policy makes for good domestic politics and is consistent with a strategic culture that values autonomy, it is unlikely to help enhance the country's military capacity.

---

[39] Supriyanto, "The Superficiality of Indonesia's Defense Policy."

[40] Nani Afida, "Indonesia Introduces New Defense Strategy," *Jakarta Post*, January 22, 2016, http://www.thejakartapost.com/news/2016/01/22/indonesia-introduces-new-defense-strategy.html.

[41] Ibid.

In summary, Indonesia's long-standing perception that its external environment is benign, that its primary threats are internal, and that transnational threats are best combatted by economic development, ideological indoctrination, and diplomacy has led the country to forgo investment in military capacity over a long period of time. Indonesia's assessment of both its threats and the appropriate ways to address them were arguably rational. In contrast to many developing countries under military governments that invested heavily in guns at the expense of butter, Indonesia's investment in economic development has produced social welfare gains that have in turn enhanced social and political stability.

Today, however, the country faces a more threatening external environment that it is inadequately prepared to meet as a result of its long-term lack of investment in hard power. Indonesia's limited military capacity makes it difficult to adopt a more robust maritime military strategy. In theory, Indonesia could seek to enhance its military capacity through a concerted effort to mobilize national power independently or join a coalition to balance against China. As the following section argues, political contestation and a fierce commitment to national autonomy make that unlikely. The current dominant strategy of nonalignment without a concerted mobilization of national power is therefore a product of the country's limited material capacity and a strategic culture that prioritizes independence.

Obstacles to Adopting an Externally Oriented Military Strategy

The reluctance of Indonesia to adopt a more externally oriented military strategy is somewhat surprising given President Jokowi's goal to transform Indonesia into a "global maritime fulcrum." Jokowi named this as the country's core national priority, an apparent shift to a more outward-looking strategic vision. To date, however, the domestically focused pillars of this strategy, such as building infrastructure, promoting maritime connectivity, and combatting illegal fishing, have been prioritized over the defense component. The concept also remains fuzzy; it was crafted without deliberation and input from the ministries involved in its execution, and was announced without clear guidelines. Indonesia's maritime governance structure is complex, involving twelve different agencies with overlapping and conflicting jurisdictions and duties. Indonesia established the Maritime Coordinating Agency (Bakamla) to help resolve coordination problems, but its efforts have met resistance from other agencies that are unwilling to relinquish their role to streamline maritime security governance.[42]

Competing Bureaucratic Interests

The main obstacle to the adoption of a more effective maritime strategy by Indonesia is the competing interests of the major actors, which create incentives to highlight or downplay the Chinese threat. The Indonesian Navy, Air Force, and Ministry of Marine Affairs and Fisheries all have an interest in highlighting the Chinese threat in order to secure greater budgetary resources and have been the leading proponents of an outward-looking maritime defense strategy. In contrast, the Ministry of Foreign Affairs and the politically powerful army have the opposite incentives. The Ministry of Foreign Affairs has an interest in maintaining good working relations with China across a wide range of issues and therefore downplays the China threat, while any increase in support for the navy and air force would come at the army's expense.

With respect to the latter issue, the Indonesian Army has long been the dominant military force due to the country's traditional preoccupation with internal threats and the political role that the army has played in domestic politics.[43] In contrast, the navy and air force have traditionally been relegated to subordinate positions. Since the army absorbs the majority of the military budget, the navy's ability to modernize its military platforms and operational readiness has been constrained.[44] The army consumes 70% of the total defense budget, leaving little for increased procurement for the navy and air force.[45]

The army also does not favor a maritime-oriented defense because it would divert Indonesia's focus from internal security.[46] The 2015 defense white paper illustrates the army's argument for preserving a land-oriented defense and inward-looking strategic orientation. The goal of becoming a global maritime fulcrum was mentioned fewer than twenty times, but the white

---

[42] Ristian Atriandi Supriyanto and Siswanto Rusdi, "Maritime Security Agencies in Indonesia: More Not Merrier," RSIS, Commentary, January 2, 2013, https://www.rsis.edu.sg/wp-content/uploads/2014/07/CO13001.pdf.

[43] Mietzner, *Military Politics, Islam and the State in Indonesia*.

[44] Koh Collin, "Tough Times Ahead for the Indonesian Navy?" *Diplomat*, August 18, 2015, http://thediplomat.com/2015/08/tough-times-ahead-for-the-indonesian-navy/.

[45] International Institute of Strategic Studies, *The Military Balance 2015* (London: Routledge, 2015), 253–56.

[46] See Defence Ministry (Indonesia), *Defence White Paper 2015* (Jakarta, November 2015), https://www.kemhan.go.id/wp-content/uploads/2016/05/2015-INDONESIA-DEFENCE-WHITE-PAPER-ENGLISH-VERSION.pdf. Please note that the latest version of Indonesia's defense white paper was published in November 2015, but released in English in April 2016. Some English-language analyses therefore refer to the document as the 2016 defense white paper, but since it is dated 2015 by the Indonesian Defense Ministry, this chapter will use that date.

paper devoted a whole chapter to Bela Negara, a program of compulsory state defense education. The program has two key components: a plan to bolster civilian reserves through military training, and an ideological indoctrination plan to instill values of "patriotism, national awareness, belief in Pancasila as the country's ideology, willingness to sacrifice for the nation [sic] and having the basic capability to defend the nation."[47]

To justify the Bela Negara program, Defense Minister Ryamizard Ryacudu, a former army general and Suharto-era throwback, and General Gatot Nurmantyo, the army chief of staff, have been raising the specter of "proxy wars" and engaging in a public campaign to argue that foreign proxies are behind many of the country's social ills.[48] General Nurmantyo has argued that foreign powers were furthering their own interests through Indonesian NGOs, media, and other social groups, and might be behind issues such as drug abuse, homosexuality, pornography, and demonstrations against palm oil plantations. In a 2015 booklet, he claimed that foreign powers sought to infiltrate Indonesian media, social groups, the education system, and Islamic organizations in order to weaken the country by seizing its strategic industries.[49] Bela Negara is fully consistent with Indonesia's people's war doctrine and would be carried out through the army's territorial defense structure. Some view the program as an attempt by the army to advance its parochial, institutional interest at the expense of a rational, threat-based military strategy that would call for an investment in naval and air power.[50]

The Ministry of Marine Resources and Fisheries has not traditionally been a major player in Indonesian foreign and defense policy. Jokowi's decision in his election campaign to highlight the plight of Indonesian fishermen, who have seen their catch fall and poverty rise as a result of IUU fishing, raised the political salience of the issue. Jokowi claims that Indonesia loses billions of dollars annually from IUU, making it imperative to protect Indonesian fishermen through a defense of the country's sovereignty and exclusive right to exploit resources in its EEZ.[51] His appointment of Susi Pudjiastuti,

---

[47] Dharma Agastia, "Bela Negara: Appreciating Both War and Peace," *Jakarta Post*, August 9, 2016, http://www.thejakartapost.com/academia/2016/08/09/bela-negara-appreciating-both-war-and-peace.html.

[48] Terry Russell, "'Proxyphobia' in Indonesia," New Mandala, November 17, 2016, http://www.newmandala.org/proxyphobia-indonesian-militarys-fear-campaign-trumps-trumps.

[49] Tom Allard and Kanupriya Kapoor, "Indonesia's President Moves to Rein In 'Out of Control' Military Chief," Reuters, January 9, 2017, https://Reuters.com/2017/01/09/indonesias-president-moves-to-rein-in-out-of-control-military-chief.

[50] For example, see the Institute for Policy Analysis of Conflict, "Update on the Indonesian Military's Influence," Report, no. 26, March 11, 2016, http://file.understandingconflict.org/file/2016/03/IPAC_Report_No._26_.pdf.

[51] Prashanth Parameswaran, "Indonesia Sinks 34 Ships in War against Illegal Fishing," *Diplomat*, August 19, 2015, http://thediplomat.com/2015/08/indonesia-sinks-34-foreign-vessels-in-its-war-on-illegal-fishing.

a tough-minded businesswoman, as minister of marine resources and fisheries and her adoption of a "sink the ships" policy has made the ministry a player in policy toward China.

Because Indonesia lacks the capacity to patrol its vast waterways, it has declared a ban on foreign fishing in its waters and adopted a policy of blowing up boats that are captured fishing illegally as a deterrent to foreign fishermen. Since 2014, Indonesia has sunk 236 boats, but only one of these boats has been from China compared to 98 from Vietnam, 58 from the Philippines, and 39 from Malaysia.[52] Minister Susi's policies, which also include compliance audits of foreign vessels and a ban on transshipment at sea, have generated opposition from other maritime agencies, some of which have traditionally profited from bribes from foreign fishermen engaged in IUU fishing.[53] The Ministry of Marine Resources and Fisheries thus has an interest in highlighting the China threat to enhance its own patrol capacity, increase naval capacity, and adopt a more outward strategic focus.[54]

The Ministry of Foreign Affairs, on the other hand, has an interest in ensuring that Indonesia's policy toward the South China Sea does not compromise its engagement with Beijing.[55] It therefore has a tendency to downplay the China threat.[56] The Ministry of Foreign Affairs advocates the legal position that because Indonesia and China have no territorial conflict over land, there is no dispute between the two countries in the South China Sea. Beyond the legal issue, the ministry argues that acknowledging a dispute only serves to justify China's claims, which Indonesia views as illegitimate under UNCLOS. Once a conflict is recognized, then it must be resolved through bargaining, which inevitably requires compromise. Given the Ministry of Foreign Affairs' privileged place in foreign policy decision-making, its position is the government's official position.

Economic Interests

Jokowi, as the ultimate authority, has the capacity to determine which interests prevail, and his own interest in securing Chinese economic benefits

---

[52] Presidential Task Force to Combat Illegal Fishing (Indonesia), "Indonesia's Experiences and Challenges in Combatting Fisheries Crime," February 2017, 19.

[53] Ministry of Marine Resources and Fisheries (Indonesia), "Implementasi visi kemaritiman Indonesia" [Implementing Indonesia's Maritime Vision], March 3, 2015, http://kkp.go.id/2015/03/18/implementasi-visi-kemaritiman-indonesia.

[54] Eka Permadi, "Menteri Susi menempati posisi pertama" [Minister Susi Is the Most Popular Minister], Viva News, October 21, 2015, http://politik.news.viva.co.id/news/read/689407-10-menteri-paling-populer-versi-lembaga-survei-life.

[55] René L. Pattiradjawane, "South China Sea Disputes: Sovereignty and Indonesian Foreign Policy," RSIS, Commentary, May 13, 2015.

[56] Murphy, "Indonesia Responds to China's Rise," 131.

has led him to downplay the threat from China. As Randall Schweller has argued, when elites fail to agree on the nature of an external threat and the appropriate measures to take in response, threats go unanswered.[57] As the following analysis illustrates, there is no consensus among key Indonesian actors on the nature and severity of the China threat. Indonesia, therefore, is currently under-balancing against the Chinese maritime threat and remains committed to its dominant strategy of nonalignment without mobilization of military power.

Jokowi came to power determined to revamp Indonesia's dire infrastructure, particularly maritime connectivity. As a former businessman, he fully understands that high transportation costs have a negative impact on Indonesia's business climate. Moreover, Indonesia's outer islands are much poorer than the main islands and enhancing connectivity would help alleviate poverty. Achieving this economic goal requires enormous capital investment, and China is the key source of assistance today. Indonesia reportedly needs $450 billion to realize its infrastructure development plan, consisting of building roads, railways, ports, and power plants, and is relying on investors and state-owned companies to fund 70% of its infrastructure needs.[58] China has not traditionally been a major source of FDI in Indonesia and only became one of the country's top-ten sources of FDI in 2015.[59] It has, however, "become a major financier to mega projects in Indonesia, the role played by the World Bank, Asian Development Bank, Europe, Japan and the United States in the past."[60] Indonesia is hoping that the recent $50 billion pledges from the China Development Bank and the Industrial and Commercial Bank of China are realized.[61] Indonesia also expects the new China-led Asian Infrastructure Investment Bank (AIIB) to be an important source for funding its projects; it is the eighth-largest shareholder in the AIIB and aims to finance a third of the cost of developing its ports and maritime highways through loans from the bank.[62]

---

[57] Randall L. Schweller, *Unanswered Threats: Political Constraints on the Balance of Power* (Princeton: Princeton University Press, 2006), 47–49.

[58] Satria Sambijantoro, "AIIB May Take Major Role in RI Projects," *Jakarta Post*, April 29, 2015, http://www.thejakartapost.com/news/2015/04/29/aiib-may-take-major-role-ri-projects.html; and Shannon Tiezzi, "Indonesia, China Seal 'Maritime Partnership,'" *Diplomat*, March 27, 2015, http://thediplomat.com/2015/03/indonesia-china-seal-maritime-partnership.

[59] Emirza Adi Syailendra, "A Non-balancing Act: Indonesia's Failure to Balance Against the Chinese Threat," *Asian Security* 13, no. 3 (forthcoming, 2017).

[60] "60 Years of Indonesia-China Relations," *Jakarta Post*, April 13, 2010, http://www.thejakartapost.com/news/2010/04/13/60-years-indonesiachina-relations.html.

[61] "China to Invest US$50 Billion in Indonesia's Infrastructure Projects," Global Indonesia Voices, April 27, 2015, http://www.globalindonesianvoices.com/20456/china-to-invest-us50-billion-in-indonesias-infrastructure-projects.

[62] Sambijantoro, "AIIB May Take Major Role in RI Projects."

Lack of Public Consensus

There have been clear public differences between Indonesian officials on their willingness to recognize the China theat. After then foreign minister Marty Natalegawa reaffirmed his position that Indonesia did not have any territorial disputes in the South China Sea in March 2014, Air Commodore Fahru Zaini stated that China had included parts of the Natuna island chain in its nine-dash line.[63] General Moeldoko, former commander-in-chief of the TNI, took the unusual step of writing an op-ed in the *Wall Street Journal* in which he expressed "dismay in discovering that China has included part of the Natuna Islands within its nine-dash line map as Chinese territory."[64] This directly contradicted the Ministry of Foreign Affairs' efforts to downplay the potential controversy, and from its legalistic perspective, gave credence to China's claim.[65] Similarly, in November 2015, Luhut Binsar Pandjaitan, the coordinating minister for maritime affairs, in a reference to the Philippines' decision to file a claim against China in the UNCLOS arbitral tribunal, stated that Indonesia would bring China to court if their dispute could not be resolved through dialogue.[66] Once again, the spokesperson of the Ministry of Foreign Affairs refuted this statement by stressing its long-standing position—that there is no territorial dispute between Indonesia and China.[67] When announcing the 2015 white paper, Defense Minister Ryamizard reinforced this position, stating that "Indonesia doesn't have any conflict with other countries, and we don't consider our neighbors as a threat. We are destined to be friends."[68]

Indonesia's Muddled Response to China's 2016 Incursions

These divergent bureaucratic interests, economic factors, and the lack of public consensus produced an incoherent response to two high-profile incursions of Chinese vessels in Indonesian waters in 2016. Similar incidents occurred under the Yudhoyono administration in 2010 and 2013, but in those

---

[63] "Indonesia Flexes Muscle as S. China Sea Dispute Looms," *Jakarta Globe*, March 13, 2014, http://www.thejakartaglobe.com/news/indonesia-military-flexes-muscle-s-china-sea-dispute-looms.

[64] Moeldoko, "China's Dismaying New Claims in the South China Sea," *Wall Street Journal*, April 24, 2014.

[65] Ibid.

[66] "Indonesia Says Could Also Take China to Court over South China Sea," Reuters, November 11, 2015, http://www.reuters.com/article/us-southchinasea-china-indonesia-idUSKCN0T00VC20151111.

[67] Randy Fabi and Ben Blanchard, "Indonesia Asks China to Clarify South China Sea Claims," Reuters, November 12, 2015, http://www.reuters.com/article/us-southchinasea-china-indonesia-idUSKCN0T10KK20151112#FpxvFikQ4V2vr8eB.97.

[68] Nani Afrida, "Indonesia Introduces New Defense Strategy," *Jakarta Post*, January 22, 2016, http://www.thejakartapost.com/news/2016/01/22/indonesia-introduces-new-defense-strategy.html.

cases the authorities attempted to sweep them under the rug.[69] Indonesia has traditionally preferred to exercise quiet diplomacy on such issues in an attempt to limit media exposure to reduce the chance of stoking tensions with China and raising nationalist sentiment at home.

On March 19, 2016, the Indonesian coast guard captured a Chinese fishing boat as it entered the Natuna Islands' EEZ. When the boat was being pulled in toward the islands, a Chinese coast guard vessel physically intervened, freed the boat, and towed it back to China. A spokesperson from China's Ministry of Foreign Affairs protested Indonesia's detention of the boat's crew, claiming that the boat had been "in Chinese traditional fishing grounds" doing "regular activities," and demanded the release of the crew members. Indonesia refused and insisted that there is no concept of traditional fishing grounds under UNCLOS.[70] On June 17, 2016, an Indonesian Navy ship was in another standoff with a Chinese coast guard vessel after capturing an illegal Chinese fishing trawler. The China Coast Guard demanded the release of the detained vessel and its crew, which was rejected by the Indonesian Navy.[71] China responded by filing a diplomatic note protesting Indonesia's action.[72]

Less than a week after the second incident, on June 23, Jokowi responded with a high-profile move. He visited Natuna and held a limited cabinet meeting aboard a naval ship in the disputed maritime area. This action garnered significant public attention and domestic approval for Jokowi.[73] The Indonesian military responded with plans to reinforce military deployments on the Natuna Islands.[74] On October 3, the Indonesian Air Force held a large

[69] Scott Bentley, "Mapping the Nine-Dash Line: Recent Incidents Involving Indonesia in the South China Sea," ASPI, Strategist, October 29, 2013, http://www.aspistrategist.org.au/mapping-the-nine-dash-line-recent-incidents-involving-indonesia-in-the-south-china-sea.

[70] Leo Suryadinata, "Did the Natuna Incident Shake Indonesia-China Relations?" ISEAS–Yusof Ishak Institute, Perspective, April 26, 2016, https://www.iseas.edu.sg/articles-commentaries/iseas-perspective/item/2980-did-the-natuna-incident-shake-indonesiachina-relations.

[71] "Ministry Narrates Chronology of Chinese Fishing Boat in Natuna Sea," Antara, June 21, 2016, http://www.antaranews.com/en/news/105317/ministry-narrates-chronology-of-chinese-fishing-boat-in-natuna-sea.

[72] Prima Gumilang, "Soal Natuna, RI tegaskan tak ada masalah politik dengan China" [With Regard to Natuna, Indonesia Stressed That It Has No Political Conflict with China], CNN (Indonesia), June, 22, 2016, http://www.cnnindonesia.com/nasional/20160622122353-20-140080/soal-natuna-ri-tegaskan-tak-ada-masalah-politik-dengan-china.

[73] Agus Trihartono, "Diplomasi (megafon) di Natuna: Langkah kuda Presiden Jokowi" [Strong Diplomacy in Natuna: President Jokowi's Maneuver], CNN (Indonesia), July 1, 2016, http://www.cnnindonesia.com/nasional/20160701102959-21-142315/diplomasi--megafon--di-natuna-langkah-kuda-presiden-jokowi.

[74] "TNI to Increase Its Forces around Natuna Waters," Antara, February 27, 2014, http://www.antaranews.com/en/news/92881/tni-to-increase-its-forces-around-natuna-waters; and "Natuna Islands Rightfully Belong to Indonesia: TNI Chief," Antara, September 27, 2016, http://www.antaranews.com/en/news/106915/natuna-islands-rightfully-belong-to-indonesia-tni-chief.

military exercise in a show of force over the Natuna waterways.[75] These actions all appeared to signal resolve to stand up to China.

These assertive responses to China's incursions, however, were offset by conciliatory statements toward Beijing. Jokowi himself stated that Indonesia was still hoping to build a strong diplomatic relationship. Minister Luhut issued a statement assuring China that Indonesia had no hostile intentions toward it.[76] Foreign Minister Retno Marsudi claimed that the military exercise was a regular activity and that Indonesia had no intention to confront China. Even the coordinating minister for political and security affairs, General Wiranto, made a series of statements denying that the military exercises were a "show of force" aimed at confronting a "perceived threat from a particular country."[77]

In short, Indonesia took a series actions to demonstrate resolve to a domestic audience and to deter Beijing, while also attempting to ensure that its actions did not jeopardize diplomatic ties. The mixed signals emanating from divergent actors clearly illustrate a lack of consensus on how to respond to China's maritime assertiveness. Returning to Schweller's arguments that a threat goes unanswered when elites fail to agree on its nature and the appropriate response, the divergent interests of key actors are preventing Indonesia from adopting a more coherent maritime defense strategy to balance against the Chinese threat.[78] To date, Chinese incursions into Indonesian waters have been limited. If threats are a function of intent and capability, however, China's actions clearly demonstrate that it does not recognize Indonesian rights to the waters around the Natuna Islands, that it intends to enforce its claims, and that it is developing the capacity to do so.

Indonesia's lack of military capacity means that it is incapable of responding to China's threat independently. Indonesia aspires to build a green water navy that would be oriented primarily to patrolling its EEZ, which totals 93,000 square km.[79] Even if Indonesia were to meet its MEF goal of developing a 274-ship navy by 2024, it is difficult to envision how a force of that size could defend its EEZ, as well as the country's 54,716 km of coastlines.

Allying with other states facing similar threats would be the policy prescription of realist balance-of-power theorists. This option, however, is

---

[75] "Indonesia Air Force Holds Its Largest Military Exercise in South China Sea," Reuters, October 4, 2016, http://www.reuters.com/article/us-southchinasea-indonesia-idUSKCN1240O9.

[76] Prima Gumilang, "Indonesia tegaskan tak berniat konfrontasi dengan China" [Indonesia Clarifies That It Has No Hostile Intents toward China], CNN (Indonesia), June 23, 2016, http://www.cnnindonesia.com/nasional/20160623044141-20-140280/indonesia-tegaskan-tak-berniat-konfrontasi-dengan-china.

[77] Suryadinata, "Did the Natuna Incident Shake Indonesia-China Relations?"

[78] Schweller, *Unanswered Threats.*

[79] Koh Swee Lean Collin, "What Next for the Indonesian Navy? Challenges and Prospects for Attaining the Minimum Essential Forces by 2014," *Contemporary Southeast Asia* 37, no. 3 (2015): 435–36.

inconsistent with Indonesia's strategic culture. Indonesia staunchly defends its strategic autonomy, and military alliances are viewed as antithetical to its free and active foreign policy doctrine. No coalition of regional actors can match China's power, and none have an interest in directly confronting China. The only Southeast Asian state to balance against China was the Philippines under Benigno Aquino III, a policy that has been reversed by his successor, Duterte. Indonesia has traditionally preferred to engage and confront China multilaterally in ASEAN.

The United States is viewed as an unreliable strategic partner as a result of the arms embargo. Indonesia welcomes U.S. military assistance, training, and intelligence sharing and participates in joint exercises, but its attachment to strategic autonomy limits the potential for cooperation. Moreover, Indonesia believes that many of the steps that the United States takes in Asia, such as conducting freedom of navigation operations and rotating troops out of Australia's Darwin air force base, only exacerbate tensions with China, thereby threatening the regional autonomy from great-power conflict that Indonesia seeks. Combined with Indonesia's staunch opposition to U.S. military action in the Middle East, these factors make it difficult to envision the country returning to a policy of alignment with the United States.

Assessment of Indonesia's Dominant Military Strategy

Durability

Indonesia's current dominant military strategy of nonalignment without concerted mobilization of national power is woefully inadequate to meet the country's security needs, but it may well be durable. If China restrains its fishery fleet and maritime vessels from incursions in Indonesian waters and confrontation with Indonesian forces, Indonesia's current under-balancing policy will likely endure because proponents of a more confrontational approach to China will lack a rationale to support a policy change.

Indonesia's nonalignment strategy clearly helps it maintain good relations with China. Indeed, President Jokowi's interest in securing economic benefits from China is a key reason that the strategy endures despite the rising maritime threat. Beijing punished the Philippines when President Aquino adopted a balancing policy by cutting some economic ties, advising Chinese tourists not to visit the Philippines, and refusing diplomatic meetings with Philippine officials. Since Duterte abandoned this policy, relations with China have improved. Other Southeast Asian states took notice of the risk of confronting China, and Indonesia under Jokowi has chosen not to jeopardize potential economic benefits by adopting a balancing strategy. As long as China continues to offer significant financial incentives and limits its maritime assertiveness in Indonesian waters, this policy will likely continue.

If China takes a more confrontational approach toward Indonesia that heightens anti-Chinese sentiment, some political elites might mobilize anti-Chinese nationalism to build support for a more confrontational approach. The defeat of the ethnically Chinese, Christian governor in the recent Jakarta election illustrates the potency of identity politics as a mobilization tool to win votes. Anti-Chinese sentiment is latent in Indonesia and could be used in upcoming elections by the same right-wing Islamic populists who influenced the outcome of the Jakarta elections. If this trend in domestic politics continues, it is possible to imagine the election of a populist strongman who would adopt a more confrontational approach to China. Whether this would be accompanied by a rational investment in maritime capacity and concerted national effort to mobilize power is unclear.

Nonetheless, it is difficult to imagine Indonesia's external military strategy changing as a result of growth in national power given the financial, technological, and labor constraints outlined in Vikram Nehru's chapter in the 2015–16 *Strategic Asia* volume.[80] Despite Indonesia's economic growth, 40% of Indonesian citizens still live on less than $2 a day, and in an open political system the government is accountable to their needs. Rising income inequality was a political issue in the 2014 presidential campaign when both Jokowi and his rival Prabowo Subianto ran on populist platforms. This is likely to be the case again in the 2019 presidential election. Absent assertive moves by China that provide politicians with a compelling argument to mobilize public support for investments in military power, it is difficult to envision from where the demand for a significant upgrade of maritime defense capacity would come.

Adequacy

As argued above, Indonesia's current military strategy is inadequate to meet its maritime security needs. Despite the rise in external maritime threats, the current defense strategy is inwardly focused and land-based, not externally oriented and maritime-based. Furthermore, the army's new Bela Negara program and proxy war rhetoric that hypes perceived threats to Indonesia's resilience—often by linking them to foreign influences—are not only inadequate for maintaining internal stability but downright dangerous. As one of Indonesia's most astute political observers argued, Islamist actors conflate "the issue of China's economic and political rise with the position of ethnic Chinese in Indonesia, producing a toxic mash that threatens to

---

[80] Nehru, "Indonesia: The Reluctant Giant."

undermine social stability in the country."[81] Heightening social divisions in Indonesia could lead to sectarian conflict that threatens national resilience and regional stability. Playing the Islamic card against the Chinese one also creates openings for a rise in Islamic radicalism, which in turn could lead to an increase in terrorism. A rise in terrorist activities would likely be used by the TNI and police as justification for greater investment in land-based rather than maritime security.

Impact

The continuation of Indonesia's current underinvestment in naval, coast guard, air force, and other maritime security assets undermines its national security. Indonesia's inability to defend its maritime borders makes it vulnerable not only to foreign countries like China but also to transnational security threats such as drug trafficking, human smuggling, and piracy. Furthermore, it renders Indonesia unable to project power abroad in pursuit of its strategic interests, the most important of which is a stable, autonomous Southeast Asia that is free from the hegemony of any outside power.

Indonesia's lack of military capacity increasingly undermines its authority in ASEAN. The country has traditionally portrayed itself as the leader of ASEAN, and this status is an important component of its international standing both in the broader Asia-Pacific and on the global stage. Diplomacy has always been the first line of defense for Indonesia. Multilateral diplomacy through ASEAN and the organizations built on it like the EAS has been an important mechanism through which Indonesia seeks to ensure that great powers abide by the commitment they made when signing ASEAN's Treaty of Amity and Cooperation, which includes pledges to renounce the use of force and resolve differences peacefully.[82] Indonesia's deficit of hard power means that it lacks leverage when negotiating with China, particularly over a CoC. Furthermore, the South China Sea disputes are increasingly dividing ASEAN into two camps: maritime countries like Indonesia and Vietnam that want to use the organization as a means to confront and constrain China over its assertiveness, and mainland countries with no stake in the disputes that want to avoid paying the costs of opposing China. In recent years, China has used its economic influence over small states like Cambodia and Laos to advance its interests in ASEAN deliberations, a tactic that completely undermines Indonesian leadership and ASEAN cohesion. If this pattern continues,

---

[81] Bhavan Jaipragas, "How Indonesia's Anti-Chinese Fake News Problem Spun Out of Control," *South China Morning Post*, December 22, 2016, http://www.scmp.com/week-asia/politics/article/2056627/how-indonesias-anti-chinese-fake-news-problem-spun-out-control.

[82] The text of ASEAN's Treaty of Amity and Cooperation, which all EAS members must sign, is available at http://asean.org/treaty-amity-cooperation-southeast-asia-indonesia-24-february-1976.

Indonesia's ability to pursue its interests in a peaceful, autonomous Southeast Asia diplomatically through ASEAN will decline.

The United States and Indonesia share common interests, but the combination of Indonesia's lack of material power and deeply ingrained commitment to an independent strategic posture limits cooperation to pursue them. The fundamental U.S. interest in Southeast Asia is freedom of navigation through the region's critical sea lines of communication, making Indonesia a key partner for the United States. The lack of a robust navy, however, limits the extent to which Indonesia can contribute to regional maritime security. Given the archipelago's geographic position astride some of the world's most strategic chokepoints, the capacity to patrol and defend these vast waterways would enable Indonesia to make a significant contribution to maritime security.

Indonesia values the U.S. role in providing international public goods such as freedom of the seas and understands that only the United States has the power-projection capacity to counter China militarily. Because of its strategic culture of autonomy, however, it does not want to be drawn into a coalition to counter China, and the United States should not attempt to do this. Instead, the United States should continue to expand Indonesia's current efforts to build up its own maritime capacity. Indonesia welcomes U.S. support for capacity building, training, and enhanced maritime surveillance. These are necessary actions to enhance Indonesia's national defense and build its capacity to maintain the sovereign integrity of its archipelago and surrounding waters, and they should be portrayed that way. In addition, since the restoration of bilateral military-to-military ties over a decade ago, Indonesia and the United States have expanded naval exercises such as CARAT (Cooperation Afloat Readiness and Training). These exercises could be further enhanced and expanded.

Anti-American sentiment is also latent in Indonesia and easily mobilized, making it imperative that cooperation be viewed as serving Indonesian rather than U.S. interests. As it works with Jakarta, Washington must be cognizant of the domestic debates over the China threat and be careful not to become embroiled in them. Given Indonesia's suspicion of outside intervention in domestic affairs, any perception that the United States is attempting to sway Indonesia's own strategic debates to suit its interests would only backfire and undermine the efforts of those Indonesian actors most amenable to U.S. interests.

EXECUTIVE SUMMARY

This chapter explores the continuities in U.S. grand strategy and national military strategy, assesses how U.S. military strategy is produced through the interaction of material capabilities and strategic culture, describes threats to the strategy of power projection, and outlines the need to develop a long-term strategy to defend U.S. interests in an increasingly contested security environment.

MAIN ARGUMENT

Since the end of World War II, the U.S. has pursued a grand strategy of global primacy supported by efforts to achieve and maintain favorable regional balances of power. In the service of that grand strategy, the U.S. has pursued a military strategy based on forward-stationed forces backed by power projection. Across the decades, this approach has periodically been questioned from the left and the right of the political spectrum. The renewed debate over a strategy of primacy coincides with the rise of great-power competitors such as China and Russia and the spread of precision-strike capabilities, which are calling into question the military strategy of power projection. As a result, the U.S. finds itself in an increasingly unfavorable position in a series of regional military balances, which could ultimately threaten its global primacy.

POLICY IMPLICATIONS

- Those who favor an engaged, internationalist strategy backed by military power will increasingly need to elucidate their arguments both at home and abroad. The logic underpinning those strategies is no longer self-evident to many.

- The U.S. needs to prepare seriously for the reality of great-power competition and the rising possibility of great-power war, something it has not had to do in more than a quarter century.

- The U.S. must develop a long-term strategy to compete with China, one that allows it to defend its interests at an acceptable price while increasing the costs of Chinese expansion and rechanneling Beijing's efforts in less threatening directions.

U.S. Strategy: Confronting Challenges Abroad and Constraints at Home

Thomas G. Mahnken

This chapter builds on the previous two volumes of *Strategic Asia* to explain how U.S. national power and strategic culture have combined to produce a characteristically American approach to grand strategy and military strategy.[1] Specifically, since the end of World War II, the United States has pursued a grand strategy of global primacy supported by efforts to achieve and maintain favorable regional balances of power. In the service of that grand strategy, it has pursued a national military strategy based on forward-stationed forces backed by power projection. Across the decades, this approach has periodically been questioned from the left and the right of the American political spectrum. As Colin Dueck noted in last year's *Strategic Asia* volume, the progressivism and nationalism that manifested themselves in the 2016 presidential election are the most recent example of a pattern that has recurred throughout U.S. history. The renewed debate over a strategy of primacy coincides with the rise of great-power competitors such as China and Russia and the spread of precision-strike capabilities, which are calling into question the national military strategy of power projection. As a result, the

Thomas G. Mahnken is the President and Chief Executive Officer of the Center for Strategic and Budgetary Assessments and Senior Research Professor at the Johns Hopkins School of Advanced International Studies. He can be reached at <mahnken@csbaonline.org>.

[1] See Dennis C. Blair, "The United States: A Strong Foundation but Weak Blueprint for National Security," in *Strategic Asia 2015–16: Foundations of National Power*, ed. Ashley J. Tellis, Alison Szalwinski, and Michael Wills (Seattle: National Bureau of Asian Research [NBR], 2015), 223–58; and Colin Dueck, "U.S. Strategic Culture: Liberalism with Limited Liability," in *Strategic Asia 2016–17: Understanding Strategic Cultures in the Asia-Pacific*, ed. Ashley J. Tellis, Alison Szalwinski, and Michael Wills (Seattle: NBR, 2016), 194–218.

United States finds itself in an increasingly unfavorable position in a series of regional military balances, which could ultimately threaten its global primacy.

The United States today faces arguably the most challenging security environment since the end of the Cold War and the collapse of the Soviet Union more than a quarter century ago. U.S. leaders not only must think about great-power competition and contemplate seriously the possibility of great-power conflict for the first time in a generation; at the same time, they are also confronted by challenges posed by regional powers, including those possessing or seeking nuclear weapons and the ability to deliver them against U.S. allies and even the U.S. homeland.

The most consequential challenge that the United States faces is the re-emergence of great-power competition and the growing possibility of great-power conflict. Specifically, the United States faces challenges from China and Russia, both in their respective regions and beyond.

China's economic growth has given Beijing greater interest and weight in international affairs. Under Xi Jinping, the government is more externally focused than it has been in the past. As Chinese leaders look abroad, they are increasingly dissatisfied with the international status quo and seek to reshape it to be more to their liking. In particular, China's multi-decade program of military modernization is yielding an increasing family of options for remedying the sources of that dissatisfaction. The Chinese government has pressed its territorial claims against Japan in the East China Sea and has undertaken a massive construction project to create and then militarize new geographic features in the South China Sea. Moreover, China is flexing its political influence and military muscles far beyond Asia, including the conduct of naval patrols off the Horn of Africa and the establishment of a military base in Djibouti.

Russia's seizure and annexation of Crimea demonstrated a willingness to revise international borders through the use of force. Under Vladimir Putin, the Kremlin is waging high-intensity wars in eastern Ukraine and Syria and has been implicated in cyberattacks in the United States and beyond. In Asia, the relationship between Moscow and Beijing, long cordial, has become markedly closer in recent years, highlighted by the conclusion of substantial energy export deals to China following years of negotiation. And although Russia has long been an exporter of arms to China, Moscow now appears willing to sell Beijing more sophisticated weapons.

In addition to increasing great-power competition, the United States continues to face challenges from regional competitors such as North Korea and Iran. Although the demise of the Kim family dynasty in Pyongyang has been predicted off and on for more than a quarter century, the regime remains in power in its third generation and poses a growing threat to both its internal and external enemies. North Korea is busy amassing an ever-growing nuclear arsenal and developing the ability to deliver it to increasing ranges through the development of both intercontinental ballistic missiles (ICBM) and submarine-launched ballistic missiles. Pyongyang can already strike U.S. allies in Asia, and in the not-too-distant future it will possess the ability to target the continental United States. Whereas North Korea's nuclear arsenal is growing, Iran's is latent, at least for now. Tehran nonetheless continues to develop long-range ballistic missiles and is exerting influence in the greater Middle East. Finally, for the foreseeable future the United States faces the need to counter violent extremist threats such as those posed by the Islamic State of Iraq and Syria (ISIS), al Qaeda, and their fellow travelers. U.S. leaders will thus struggle to achieve strategic coherence, let alone focus.

In addition to an increasingly complex and challenging international environment, the United States faces constraints at home. Recent years have seen a growing percentage of Americans on the left and the right question U.S. international activism. Moreover, now and for the foreseeable future, the United States will have limited resources to devote to defense. That is particularly true in the short term under the provisions of the Budget Control Act of 2011 (BCA), which has already contributed to the sharpest U.S. defense drawdown since the end of the Korean War. Even after the expiration of the BCA, or should Congress vote to lift it, the United States will face sharp tradeoffs between national security and discretionary domestic spending.

U.S. Grand Strategy: Theory and Practice[2]

The Strategy of Global Primacy

Discerning U.S. grand strategy from public statements can prove challenging. The congressionally mandated national security strategies, which are prepared for both domestic and international consumption, tend to speak in general terms. Rather than identifying a limited and prioritized set of objectives, they often contain undifferentiated lists of desirable ends. Rather than discussing particular countries or groups that threaten U.S. interests, they tend to describe challenges in only the vaguest of terms.[3] Indeed, a strong case can be made that the last such document that lived up to its name was

---

[2] Parts of this section draw heavily on Thomas G. Mahnken, "The Australia-U.S. Alliance in American Strategic Policy," in *Australia's American Alliance*, ed. Peter J. Dean, Stephan Frühling, and Brendan Taylor (Melbourne: Melbourne University Press, 2016), chap. 2.

[3] See, for example, White House, *The National Security Strategy of the United States of America* (Washington, D.C., September 2002); White House, *The National Security Strategy of the United States of America* (Washington, D.C., March 2006); White House, *National Security Strategy* (Washington, D.C., May 2010); and White House, *National Security Strategy* (Washington, D.C., February 2015).

produced during the Reagan administration: a classified document that was little heralded in public but that outlined a consistent, multipronged effort to achieve U.S. objectives.[4]

If, however, one focuses on the practice of U.S. grand strategy, considerable continuity emerges.[5] Since World War II, the United States has followed a grand strategy that seeks to ensure and protect its primacy.[6] Underlying this approach is the not-unreasonable belief that maintaining a wide margin of security is the best way to ensure a world amenable to U.S. interests and ideals. Backed by considerable economic and natural resources and protected by oceans and weak neighbors, the United States throughout the Cold War enjoyed a preponderance of power over the Soviet Union, even if it did not always appear that way at the time. Moreover, following World War II, the United States built and then maintained an open, democratic, and liberal international order on the belief that a world dominated by such values held the greatest opportunity for U.S. security and prosperity.

The dissolution of the Soviet Union eliminated the United States' only superpower rival. U.S. defense planning toward the end of the George H.W. Bush administration, embodied in the drafting of the 1992 Defense Planning Guidance, sought to consolidate the gains the United States reaped with the end of the Cold War by attempting to prevent a new would-be hegemon from arising.[7] The Clinton administration similarly sought, through its national security strategy of "engagement and enlargement," to increase the ranks of the world's democracies on the theory that democracies do not wage war on one another.[8] It also embarked on the expansion of NATO, a process that would eventually bring the Atlantic alliance to the doorstep of Russia with the admission of the Baltic states in 2004. This approach can also be seen in the George W. Bush administration's 2005 National Defense Strategy, which

---

[4] "U.S. National Security Strategy," National Security Decision Directive, no. 32, May 20, 1982, https://reaganlibrary.archives.gov/archives/reference/Scanned%20NSDDS/NSDD32.pdf. See also, "U.S. Relations with the USSR," National Security Decision Directive, no. 75, January 17, 1983, https://reaganlibrary.archives.gov/archives/reference/Scanned%20NSDDS/NSDD75.pdf. On the development of these documents, and the Reagan administration's broader strategy, see Thomas G. Mahnken, "The Reagan Administration's Strategy toward the Soviet Union," in *Successful Strategies: Triumphing in War and Peace from Antiquity to the Present*, ed. Williamson Murray and Richard Hart Sinnreich (Cambridge: Cambridge University Press, 2014).

[5] On U.S. grand strategy, see Hal Brands, *What Good Is Grand Strategy?* (Ithaca: Cornell University Press, 2014).

[6] See, for example, Melvyn P. Leffler, *A Preponderance of Power: National Security, the Truman Administration, and the Cold War* (Stanford: Stanford University Press, 1992).

[7] See, for example, Eric S. Edelman, "The Strange Career of the 1992 Defense Planning Guidance," in *In Uncertain Times: American Foreign Policy after the Berlin Wall and 9/11*, ed. Melvyn P. Leffler and Jeffrey W. Legro (Ithaca: Cornell University Press, 2011), 63–77. See also Alexandra Homolar, "How to Last Alone at the Top: U.S. Strategic Planning for the Unipolar Era," *Journal of Strategic Studies* 34, no. 2 (2011): 189–217.

[8] White House, *A National Security of Engagement and Enlargement* (Washington, D.C., July 1994).

sought, among other things, "to dissuade potential adversaries from adopting threatening capabilities, methods, and ambitions, particularly by developing our own military advantages."[9]

Supporting a grand strategy of primacy has been an enduring effort to maintain favorable balances of power in key regions. During the Cold War, the United States attempted, albeit uneasily, to ensure a stable balance of power on the Eurasian landmass.[10] The reality of the Soviet Union's geostrategic position as a continental power and that of the United States as a maritime power required Washington to establish and support alliances in Western Europe (NATO) and Northeast Asia (South Korea and Japan) to contain Soviet power. It backed the forward deployment of U.S. conventional forces with the stationing of theater nuclear forces in Europe and Asia.

The proximity of the Soviet Union to U.S. allies, its conventional military might, and its development and deployment of nuclear weapons caused the United States to be highly attentive to the military balance. The United States initially sought to counterbalance Soviet conventional strength through the widespread deployment and threatened use of nuclear weapons. As the credibility of such threats increasingly came into question, and as soldiers and statesmen developed a better appreciation of the difficulty of keeping a "limited" nuclear war limited, the United States turned to advanced technology to offset the Soviet Union's numerical preponderance.[11]

A second supporting effort has involved fostering economic and political interdependence. During the Cold War, the United States promoted interdependence as a way of strengthening the West against Communist subversion and coercion. Since the end of the Cold War, this approach has been applied more broadly to include attempts to build interdependence with neutral countries and competitors. For example, the Clinton, George W. Bush, and Obama administrations worked to bring China into international institutions in the hope that they would bind Beijing to the rules-based international order and thereby change Chinese strategic behavior.

Alternatives to the Strategy of Primacy

The main grand strategic alternative to the strategy of primacy, which is popular among some academics and which has gained greater political traction in recent years, is neo-isolationism or offshore balancing.

---

[9] U.S. Department of Defense, *The National Defense Strategy of the United States of America* (Washington, D.C., March 2005), iv.

[10] Gordon S. Barrass, *The Great Cold War: A Journey through the Hall of Mirrors* (Stanford: Stanford University Press, 2009); and John Lewis Gaddis, *Strategies of Containment: A Critical Appraisal of Postwar American National Security Policy* (Oxford: Oxford University Press, 1982).

[11] Barrass, *The Great Cold War*, chap. 22–28.

This approach would seek to scale back U.S. commitments and accept a narrower definition of the role of the United States in the world than it has adhered to for the better part of a century.[12] Such a strategy would have the United States pull back from Europe, the Middle East, and the Asian littoral and rely on allies to shoulder a greater portion of the load, husbanding resources against the possible emergence of a peer competitor.

The Obama administration pursued elements of such a strategy, in that a corollary of its "pivot" or "rebalance" to Asia was a scaled-back U.S. presence in Europe and the Middle East. Similarly, much of Donald Trump's campaign rhetoric—and some of his statements since assuming office—was aimed at shifting the burden of forward defense to U.S. allies. As Trump argued in his inaugural visit to Europe in May 2017:

> I have been very, very direct with Secretary Stoltenberg and members of the Alliance in saying that NATO members must finally contribute their fair share and meet their financial obligations, for 23 of the 28 member nations are still not paying what they should be paying and what they're supposed to be paying for their defense….This is not fair to the people and taxpayers of the United States….Over the last eight years, the United States spent more on defense than all other NATO countries combined. If all NATO members had spent just 2 percent of their GDP on defense last year, we would have had another $119 billion for our collective defense and for the financing of additional NATO reserves.[13]

Just as the United States in theory possesses a range of grand strategic options to achieve its objectives, so too does it possess national military strategic alternatives. First, the United States has, at least since World War II, followed a strategy based on forward defense backed by power projection. Indeed, power projection has been a uniquely American strategy deriving from a grand strategy of primacy. Such an approach has been made possible by enduring U.S. advantages in blue water naval operations; theater and long-range air power; combined-arms ground forces; intelligence, surveillance, and reconnaissance; and global logistics. It has maximized U.S. security by meeting threats far from U.S. shores and by promoting the free flow of goods and services that has generated economic growth for the United States and countries around the globe.

---

[12] Christopher Layne, *The Peace of Illusions: American Grand Strategy from 1940 to the Present* (Ithaca: Cornell University Press, 2006); John J. Mearsheimer, "Imperial by Design," *National Interest*, January/February 2011; Barry R. Posen, *Restraint: A New Foundation for U.S. Grand Strategy* (Ithaca: Cornell University Press, 2014); and Stephen M. Walt, "The End of the American Era," *National Interest*, November/December 2011.

[13] "Remarks by President Trump at NATO Unveiling of the Article 5 and Berlin Wall Memorials—Brussels, Belgium," White House, Office of the Press Secretary, May 25, 2017, https://www.whitehouse.gov/the-press-office/2017/05/25/remarks-president-trump-nato-unveiling-article-5-and-berlin-wall.

In both peace and war, the U.S. position in Asia has rested on a set of alliances, ground and air forces deployed on allied and U.S. territory, and carrier strike groups operating in the western Pacific. The United States has deployed ground and air forces on allied territory in Japan and South Korea and on U.S. territory (Hawaii, Alaska, and Guam) to reassure allies and deter adversaries. The United States has also routinely deployed U.S. Navy carrier strike groups in the western Pacific to demonstrate U.S. presence, reassure allies and partners, and deter aggressors. Significantly, this approach mirrors the U.S. concept of operations in wartime. That is, the United States uses its most powerful naval assets, its carrier strike groups, as instruments of peacetime presence, assurance, and deterrence. During a conflict, these forward-deployed naval forces would serve as instruments of power projection. Such a posture represents a historical novelty. Traditionally, sea powers have relied on small combatants such as frigates to show the flag and coerce adversaries, while keeping their capital ships concentrated in home waters to train and prepare for a decisive fleet battle.

Second, the United States could follow, and at times has followed, a strategy of acting as a swing state or balancer. In practice, it has pursued such an approach in situations where it lacked local allies and military infrastructure and faced unpalatable choices. For example, during the 1990s the Clinton administration undertook a strategy of "dual containment" that sought to prevent Iran and Iraq from destabilizing the Persian Gulf region by isolating and delegitimizing both countries. In the words of the 1996 National Security Strategy:

> In Southwest Asia, the United States remains focused on deterring threats to regional stability, particularly from Iraq and Iran as long as those states pose a threat to U.S. interests, to other states in the region and to their own citizens. We have in place a dual containment strategy aimed at these two states and will maintain our long-standing presence, which has been centered on naval vessels in and near the Persian Gulf and prepositioned combat equipment.[14]

Third, the United States could follow a strategy emphasizing defense of the homeland and combating internal threats. This has always been an important subsidiary goal, but the growing threat to the homeland posed by nuclear-armed ICBMs as well as by terrorist groups has increased calls for emphasizing this approach.

During the early Cold War, the U.S. military put considerable resources into continental air defense, only to abandon this mission with the advent of the ICBM. Instead, for much of the Cold War and after, the United States

---

[14] White House, *A National Security Strategy of Engagement and Enlargement* (Washington, D.C., February 1996), 30.

relied, albeit uneasily, on the threat of unacceptable retaliation to protect the U.S. homeland from an attack. However, North Korea's acquisition of nuclear weapons and rapid development of ICBMs have called into question the adequacy of such an approach. In addition, the growth of cyberattack capabilities would appear to erase geographic distance as a means of defending the U.S. homeland. The September 11 terrorist attacks further demonstrated the vulnerability of the U.S. homeland to unconventional attacks.

The Aims of U.S. Strategy

The consistency of U.S. grand strategy and national military strategy reflects stability in the ends that the United States has sought. Since at least World War II, it has pursued a consistent set of objectives in Asia and beyond.[15] First and foremost, the United States has acted to defend U.S. territory against an attack. Indeed, the most basic responsibility of any government is to protect its territory and its citizens. For the United States in Asia, this includes the need to protect not only the continental United States, Hawaii, and Alaska, but also Guam and the Northern Mariana Islands. The United States is also bound by treaty to defend American Samoa, the Federated States of Micronesia, the Republic of the Marshall Islands, and the Republic of Palau.

Second, treaty obligations commit the United States to protect its allies. In Asia, these include Australia, Japan, South Korea, the Philippines, and Thailand. The United States is also obligated to help defend quasi-allies such as Taiwan. The Taiwan Relations Act requires the U.S. government both to provide arms and services of a defensive nature and to maintain U.S. military capacity to resist coercion of Taiwan by China.

These relationships form the bulwark of forward defense. They are built on both shared interests and shared values, and their strength and vitality ebb and flow with these variables. Where U.S. and allied interests coincide, and where shared values are at play, the United States and its allies have been able to operate much more effectively together than they would have been able to individually. Conversely, when interests diverge, such as over the wisdom of directly contesting China's creeping annexation of the South China Sea by conducting freedom of navigation operations, or when values diverge, as with the Thai military's intervention in politics, then alliance cohesion is jeopardized.

As noted above, since at least World War II, U.S. strategy has been predicated on meeting threats as far from the United States' shores as possible

---

[15] See, for example, Mahnken, "The Australia-U.S. Alliance in American Strategic Policy"; and Thomas G. Mahnken et. al., "Asia in the Balance: Transforming U.S. Military Strategy in Asia," American Enterprise Institute, 2012, http://www.aei.org/wp-content/uploads/2012/05/-asia-in-the-balance-transforming-us-military-strategy-in-asia_134736206767.pdf.

through the forward stationing and rotational deployment of forces to U.S. and allied territory in the western Pacific. However, whereas geographic distance has historically protected the U.S. homeland, the fact that the United States has territory and allies in the western Pacific has historically forced U.S. planners to confront the tyranny of distance. During the years separating the two world wars, army and navy planners were consumed by the need to defend the Philippines, then a U.S. territory, from a much closer Japan. Today, U.S. soldiers and statesmen must consider how best to defend Japan, South Korea, and U.S. territories in the western Pacific from coercion and aggression by North Korea and China.

The United States has traditionally defended its allies through a strategy of extended deterrence and reassurance. Part of the U.S. commitment includes the pledge to use nuclear weapons in defense of allies.[16] Historically, one way to strengthen extended nuclear deterrence was to deploy—either permanently or episodically—nuclear weapons to the territory of U.S. allies. During the Cold War, such deployments were routine. In September 1991, however, George H.W. Bush's Presidential Nuclear Initiative unilaterally withdrew all ground-launched short-range weapons deployed overseas and ceased deployment of tactical nuclear weapons on surface ships, attack submarines, and land-based naval aircraft under normal peacetime circumstances.[17] For the next two decades the United States maintained nuclear-armed Tomahawk land-attack cruise missiles for extended nuclear deterrence in Asia. In 2010, however, the Obama administration's Nuclear Posture Review called for their retirement.[18]

As the balance of power in the western Pacific has shifted, Washington has faced growing calls by allies for reassurance. In recent years, the United States has reaffirmed its extended deterrence guarantee to both Japan and South Korea.[19] Such guarantees have helped promote stability in the face of provocation and discouraged U.S. allies from taking destabilizing actions, such as acquiring nuclear weapons of their own. Complementing extended deterrence is reassurance. The United States seeks to reassure its allies regarding its security commitments through a host of measures, including

---

[16] Evan Braden Montgomery, "Extended Deterrence in the Second Nuclear Age: Geopolitics, Proliferation, and the Future of U.S. Security Commitments," Center for Strategic and Budgetary Assessments, 2016.

[17] See the documents in Jeffrey A. Larsen and Kurt J. Klingenberger, eds., *Controlling Non-strategic Nuclear Weapons: Obstacles and Opportunities* (Washington, D.C.: USAF Institute for National Security Studies, 2001).

[18] U.S. Department of Defense, *Nuclear Posture Review Report* (Washington, D.C., April 2010).

[19] Keith Payne, Thomas Scheber, and Kurt Guthe, "U.S. Extended Deterrence and Assurance for Allies in Northeast Asia," National Institute for Public Policy, March 2010, http://www.nipp.org/National%20Institute%20Press/Current%20Publications/PDF/US%20Extend-Deter-for%20print.pdf.

the deployment of U.S. forces to their territory and in the region, foreign military sales, and a variety of joint programs, such as R&D, acquisition, training, and command arrangements.

Reassurance and deterrence are distinct, though related, phenomena. Deterrence seeks to influence the mind of an adversary to convince it that the use of military force would be unproductive—that it either would be unable to achieve its objectives or would suffer disproportionate losses in return. Reassurance seeks to influence the mind of an ally to convince it that an adversary will be deterred and that the ally will be protected in the event that deterrence fails. Of the two, reassurance is often the more difficult task because it requires building and maintaining trust with allies that may have much more at stake in a particular situation than the United States.

Third, the United States has acted over decades to ensure access to the global commons in peacetime and control of them in wartime. It has done so not out of altruism but out of self-interest: the free flow of goods and information has undergirded U.S. economic growth and prosperity for decades. Freedom of navigation operations are only one means of doing so, but one that has been used repeatedly over the course of decades.[20]

Finally, the United States for the past century has sought to preserve a favorable balance of power across Eurasia. It has repeatedly used force when U.S. territory or allies were attacked and when a would-be hegemon threatened the balance of power. The United States, for example, twice intervened in Europe when Germany was on the brink of dominating the continent, and it similarly resisted Japan's attempt at hegemony in the Pacific. During the Cold War, the United States sought to prevent the Soviet Union from becoming a Eurasian hegemon. It is worth noting that even those who advocate a constrained U.S. role in the world more generally argue that the United States should prevent the emergence of a hegemon on the Eurasian continent.[21]

The U.S. Strategic Approach under Scrutiny[22]

Despite periodic questioning, in practice U.S. grand strategy and national military strategy have been remarkably consistent, with a military strategy of power projection underpinning a grand strategy of global primacy. In the

---

[20] See the Lowy Institute's interactive map of U.S. freedom of navigation operations at http://interactives. lowyinstitute.org/fonops_maps/Overview.html.

[21] See, for example, John J. Mearsheimer, *The Tragedy of Great Power Politics*, updated edition (New York: W.W. Norton, 2014).

[22] Parts of this section draw on the author's contribution to "Why American Leadership Still Matters," American Enterprise Institute, December 3, 2015, http://www.aei.org/publication/why-american-leadership-still-matters.

aftermath of World War II, the United States deployed its economic might and technological superiority in defense of liberalism in Europe, Asia, and beyond. It rebuilt the key economic and political power centers of Europe and Asia and crafted an international political and economic order in which they could thrive. As the Soviet political and military threat grew, the United States fielded forward-deployed military forces backed by power projection to shield them as well. This approach held for the duration of the nearly half-century Cold War as well as the quarter century that has passed since its end. The question that today faces the United States, its allies, and the world is whether the United States will continue to pursue a strategy of global primacy, and if not, how far it will deviate from it.

Since its entry into World War II, and in many ways before that, the United States has pursued an internationalist strategy.[23] U.S. well-being at home has been intimately connected to stability abroad. The United States has acted over decades to ensure access to the global commons in peacetime and to protect them in wartime. Defending freedom of navigation on the high seas has benefitted not only the United States but also nations the world over. The free flow of goods, services, and information resulting from the broad acceptance of these norms has facilitated global economic development, opened up markets to U.S. goods and services, and ensured that U.S. traders and businesses can compete on a level playing field.

This internationalist consensus has endured across presidential administrations of very different political stripes and has been embraced by Democrats and Republicans across a broad swath of the American political spectrum. It has been questioned in times of difficulty, such as in the aftermath of World War II and in the wake of the Vietnam War. Now once again a growing number of politicians and academics, and a substantial portion of the American people, are questioning the assumptions that underpin American internationalism.[24]

The U.S. strategy of global primacy has been based on forward defense. Since World War II, the United States has responded to threats as far from its shores as possible through ground, air, and sea forces of sufficient size and capability to meet and stop or rapidly reverse acts of aggression and diplomatic initiatives geared to reducing, managing, and countering threats. Early, active involvement has been essential to preventing crises from becoming conflicts

---

[23] See, for example, Eliot A. Cohen, "The Strategy of Innocence? The United States, 1920–1945," in *The Making of Strategy: Rulers, States, and War*, ed. Williamson Murray, MacGregor Knox, and Alvin Bernstein (Cambridge: Cambridge University Press, 1994); and Thomas G. Mahnken, "U.S. Grand Strategy, 1939–1945," in *The Cambridge History of the Second World War*, vol. 1, *Fighting the War*, ed. John Ferris and Evan Mawdsley (Cambridge: Cambridge University Press, 2015).

[24] Hal Brands, Peter Feaver, William Imboden, and Paul D. Miller, "Critical Assumptions and American Grand Strategy," Center for Strategic and Budgetary Assessments, 2017.

and for dealing with threats before they grow and spread. Moreover, the strength of U.S. military capabilities and the demonstrated will to use them have provided deterrence against aggression from potential adversaries.

In addition to its own effort, the United States has developed a network of treaties and alliances with like-minded countries to promote common interests and shared values. These allies have multiplied U.S. strength and helped maintain global and regional security.[25] Although there were some calls at the end of the Cold War that U.S. alliances had become obsolete,[26] the number of countries allied with the United States actually grew over the subsequent quarter century due to the expansion of NATO. Moreover, U.S. alliances have adapted themselves to purposes beyond those that were envisioned at their founding. NATO, an alliance founded to defend Western Europe against the Soviet Union and its allies, has engaged in out-of-area operations in Afghanistan. The U.S.-Australia alliance, similarly founded in the Cold War, was invoked by Canberra to help defend the United States after the September 11 terrorist attacks.

Alliances have thus been a central feature of U.S. military strategy for a century. The United States has fought as part of a coalition in every war since World War I, and its alliances have been a pillar of U.S. defense strategy since World War II. Allied forces add to the strength of the U.S. armed forces in both size and expertise in peace and in war. Moreover, allies such as Japan have long contributed bases to the United States, including subsidizing the cost of forward-basing U.S. forces.

Nonetheless, many (though not all) U.S. allies are in relative decline, in terms of both their economic power and their military might.[27] As a result, we are witnessing a growing chorus of voices questioning the value of the United States' allies. That chorus began in the Obama administration and has only become louder in the Trump presidency, and it threatens to weaken the asymmetric advantage offered by U.S. alliances.

The United States has also promoted and protected global public structures that have become as crucial to U.S. national security and prosperity as they are to nations around the world. These include open markets and free trade, international standards for the environment and human rights, and responses to the new domain of cyber and information technologies. Participation in international organizations has not only provided the United States with the

---

[25] For example, U.S. security commitments have increased both bilateral and global trade. See Daniel Engel, Adam R Grissom, John P. Godges, Jennifer Kavanagh, and Howard J. Shatz, *Estimating the Value of Overseas Security Commitments* (Santa Monica: RAND Corporation, 2016).

[26] John J. Mearsheimer, "Why We Will Soon Miss the Cold War," *Atlantic*, August 1990.

[27] Hal Brands, "Dealing with Allies in Decline: Alliance Management and U.S. Strategy in an Era of Global Power Shifts," Center for Strategic and Budgetary Assessments, 2017.

opportunity to shape and influence the evolution of international standards; it has also facilitated trade and reduced the likelihood that misunderstandings between great powers will lead to military conflict.

There have been two primary reasons for this. First, more than a decade of war in Iraq and Afghanistan has eroded the willingness of some Americans to support major military operations. Some doubted the wisdom of the war in Iraq, while others questioned the effectiveness of U.S. national security institutions in waging the wars once they had been launched. For some, the seeming inability of the United States to formulate and implement an effective strategy has raised larger questions about the efficacy of U.S. military intervention in general. Second, the Great Recession and the unequal distribution of the gains from the subsequent recovery have produced a mixture of anxiety and pessimism about the United States' role in the world. A growing number of Americans are asking why the United States is expending resources abroad when many continue to struggle at home. Others see the North American energy boom as an opportunity for the United States to disengage from its overseas commitments, particularly those in the Middle East.[28] This thinking was a central feature of the presidential campaigns of both Donald Trump and Bernie Sanders.

These concerns have been reflected in public opinion surveys. For example, the main finding of the Pew Research Center's 2016 survey "America's Place in the World" was that "the public views America's role in the world with considerable apprehension and concern. In fact, most Americans say it would be better if the U.S. just dealt with its own problems and let other countries deal with their own problems as best they can."[29] Moreover, these concerns are evident in the attitudes of the rising generation, which has come of age since the September 11 terrorist attacks on the United States. The same poll in 2013 found that members of the so-called millennial generation (age 18–29) were slightly more hesitant about U.S. international leadership. Younger Americans emphasized the need for the United States to select its priorities and match resources and capabilities with the mission.[30]

Such attitudes are not without precedent in U.S. history. Time and again after major conflicts, Americans have asked whether it makes sense to continue

---

[28] "The Experts: How the U.S. Oil Boom Will Change the Markets and Geopolitics," *Wall Street Journal*, March 27, 2013, https://www.wsj.com/articles/SB10001424127887324105204578382690249436084.

[29] Pew Research Center, "Public Uncertain, Divided over America's Place in the World," May 5, 2016, http://www.people-press.org/2016/05/05/public-uncertain-divided-over-americas-place-in-the-world. See also Dina Smeltz and Ivo Daalder with Craig Kafura, "Foreign Policy in the Age of Retrenchment," Chicago Council on Global Affairs, http://www.thechicagocouncil.org/publication/foreign-policy-age-retrenchment-0; and Bruce W. Jentleson, "The Prudent, Not Isolationist, Public," *Hill*, http://thehill.com/blogs/pundits-blog/international/207987-the-prudent-not-isolationist-public.

[30] Pew Research Center, "Public Sees U.S. Power Declining as Support for Global Engagement Slips: America's Place in the World 2013," December 2013.

their leadership role, and time and again, events eventually occur that remind Americans of what the world would be like without their participation. Recent times are no exception. The United States today is experiencing the most active discussion of its role in the world since the end of World War II. With it comes a debate over the most appropriate military strategy to carry out this role. More than a half year into the Trump administration, this very much remains a debate. Those in the Defense Department and some in the White House have argued for broad continuity, while others in the White House have advocated a break with the recent past and a more constrained U.S. role in the world.

The Trump administration came to power vowing to carry out an "America first" strategy, a phrase laden with isolationist overtones harking back to the years before the United States' entry into World War II.[31] However, it soon found itself, as previous administrations have found themselves, bound by the decisions and non-decisions of its predecessors on North Korea, Afghanistan, Syria, China, Russia, and Iran, among other challenges.

The big question facing the United States and the world is how much the United States will deviate from its past and current trajectory. U.S. postwar strategy has linked prosperity at home with a liberal economic and political order abroad. That relationship is now increasingly under attack. As Colin Dueck noted in his chapter in last year's edition of *Strategic Asia*, there is a historical pattern of cyclical upswings and downswings in public support for American international activism. Today, concern about the material dimension of strategy, and in particular the state of the U.S. economy at home and American competitiveness abroad, has spurred greater introspection about the United States' international role. Diminishing U.S. relative economic power and doubts about the benefits to the American people of the liberal economic order have brought back to the surface debates over the United States' role in the world. The duration and amplitude of the current cycle will have profound implications both at home and abroad.[32]

A weaker United States could be tempted to turn inward, and the rise of great powers with values antithetical to those of the United States is creating a more contested security environment. However, history counsels that such a move could imperil the international order on which U.S. prosperity depends.

---

[31] Donald J. Trump, "Inaugural Address" (Washington, D.C, January 20, 2017), https://www.whitehouse.gov/inaugural-address.

[32] Dueck, "U.S. Strategic Culture," 212.

The Return of Great-Power Competition

For the first time in over a quarter century, the United States faces the reality of great-power competition and the small though growing possibility of great-power war. This is a stark contrast to the situation that it faced during the first decade after the end of the Cold War—a period Charles Krauthammer famously dubbed the United States' "unipolar moment"[33]—as well as the decade and a half following the September 11 terrorist attacks, which was dominated by nonstate threats. The heightened great-power competition is coinciding with changes in the military-technical environment, particularly the growth and spread of precision weapons as well as the sensors and command-and-control networks needed to employ them effectively. These developments collectively call into question the viability of the military strategy that the United States has been pursuing for decades.

In Asia, the rise of China, the growth and modernization of the Chinese military, and the Chinese Communist Party's confidence and muscle-flexing raise the prospect of a conflict over Beijing's maritime claims in the East and South China Seas or across the Taiwan Strait. In Europe, Russia is challenging the post–Cold War status quo, and is doing so with military force, indicating an increased likelihood of conflict with frontline NATO states. Russia has also been militarily active outside Europe, using the war in Syria to flex its geopolitical muscles, showcase new weapons, and develop and refine innovative operational concepts. This challenge is notably different from that posed by the Soviet Union during the Cold War. Whereas the Cold War was marked by bipolar competition, today the United States, in an era of relatively constrained budgets, is engaged in a tripolar competition with two loosely and perhaps opportunistically aligned great powers.[34]

One dimension that deserves particular scrutiny is the temporal one. Russia has been increasingly active in recent years, but its position is declining due to demographic and economic trends. China, by contrast, has a growing economy (albeit one that is unlikely to continue to grow at historically high levels) and increasingly capable military forces. However, it seems impractical for the United States to ignore the challenges posed by Russia in the near term, just as it would be unwise to defer countering the challenges posed by China. Rather, the United States will need to develop separate but interlinked strategies for competing with each, individually and in concert, over the long term.

---

[33] Charles Krauthammer, "The Unipolar Moment," *Foreign Affairs*, Winter 1990/91.

[34] See, for example, Thomas G. Mahnken, ed., *Competitive Strategies for the 21st Century* (Stanford: Stanford University Press, 2012); and Thomas G. Mahnken, "Arms Races and Long-Term Competition," in *Strategy in Asia: The Past, Present, and Future of Regional Security*, ed. Thomas G. Mahnken and Dan Blumenthal (Stanford: Stanford University Press, 2014), 225–40.

Great-power war in the 21st century is likely to differ both from past great-power conflicts and from more recent counterinsurgency campaigns in a number of key respects. In particular, it will include a lethality of a sort unseen since World War II, the absence of secure rear areas, and coalition mobilization difficulties of a type that has not been seen in decades.[35] Economic and social trends likewise indicate that great-power competition and conflict in the 21st century will be distinct from historical antecedents. Advanced economies are moving from the industrial age to the information age, with implications for industrial mobilization, although new technologies such as additive manufacturing promise new possibilities. Nevertheless, relatively small orders and long manufacturing times, coupled with the prospect of attrition warfare, call into question the robustness and resilience of current industrial approaches. In addition, the information age is providing new options for mobilizing and controlling domestic populations and influencing foreign leaders and citizens.

These developments are taking place against the backdrop of three military trends that will influence the character and conduct of future wars. The first is the incorporation of precision guidance into an ever-greater variety of munitions. The second is the proliferation of reconnaissance, surveillance, and targeting sensors, including space-based systems. The third is the widespread use of information networks that enable the passing of sensor data to weapons and firing platforms, the command and control of various military systems, and the conduct of offensive and defensive cyberoperations. Whereas precision weaponry, sensors, and command-and-control systems were once an area of unilateral U.S. advantage, all are diffusing rapidly. This trend is creating an increasingly competitive military environment and will shape the face of future wars.[36]

Historically, the mastery of new ways of war has given the innovating power a considerable battlefield advantage, allowing its military to achieve quick, decisive victories. As innovations spread, however, and opponents develop countermeasures, that advantage goes away; wars tend to be attritional and protracted. If future major wars fit the historical pattern, they may be immensely destructive, as technological symmetry contributes to protraction, precision weapons achieve previously unseen levels of lethality, and cyberwarfare negates military advantage, as well as directly attacking civilian economic infrastructure. Whereas the United States was able to

---

[35] See, for example, Mark Gunzinger and Bryan Clark, "Sustaining America's Precision Strike Advantage," Center for Strategic and Budgetary Assessments, 2015; and Mark Gunzinger and Bryan Clark, "Winning the Salvo Competition: Rebalancing America's Air and Missile Defenses," Center for Strategic and Budgetary Assessments, 2016.

[36] Thomas G. Mahnken, "Weapons: The Growth and Spread of the Precision-Strike Regime," in *The Modern American Military*, ed. David M. Kennedy (Oxford: Oxford University Press, 2013), 59–78.

fight a series of quick, decisive conventional campaigns against second-tier adversaries during a period when it commanded a unilateral advantage in precision warfare, future wars are likely to be protracted and attritional.

Despite these indications, some strategists, in both the United States and adversary countries, seem to believe that the combination of precision long-range weapons and the ubiquity of and reliance on information systems could result in short, decisive, circumscribed wars that have little effect on civilian populations. These beliefs may make major war more likely. Yet the major war that they lead to may defy expectations. Given what seems to be an increasing possibility of war, it is prudent to consider the possibility of destructive, protracted major war and plan, train, and invest accordingly.

Unlike any previous major war between great powers, future major wars would take place in the shadow of nuclear weapons. That condition would certainly be familiar to Cold War–era strategists, who considered war between two powers armed with immense nuclear weapon stockpiles and doctrines that relied heavily on their use. But the nuclear terrain has shifted since then. Some powers, such as the United States, are reducing their nuclear stockpiles, particularly their tactical theater nuclear forces, and decreasing their reliance on strategic nuclear weapons; others are expanding the size of their nuclear arsenals (e.g., China) or increasing their reliance on tactical nuclear weapons (e.g., Russia).

Changing military balances in both Asia and Europe are increasingly calling into question the strategy of power projection. If left unaddressed, the erosion of these balances will, in turn, call into question U.S. primacy. The United States thus with growing urgency faces the need to redress its eroding position through technological and doctrinal innovation.

These developments are occurring at a time when the United States faces very real constraints on defense spending, both in the short term and beyond. Uncertainty over the level of future budgets as a result of limits imposed by the BCA has harmed the ability of the Defense Department to acquire the capabilities that the United States needs to safeguard its interests in an increasingly contested environment. In particular, the United States faces a growing need to develop and acquire innovative capabilities at the very time that resources available to field new capabilities are constrained. Moreover, in a period in which existing programs face budgetary pressure, there is little appetite to field additional capabilities, however promising. In an environment where acquisition dollars are increasingly scarce, the defense industry and university-affiliated research centers will need to take on a greater role in developing innovative capabilities through advanced research, development, and prototyping.

As a result of these trends, the United States (and increasingly its allies) are placing greater emphasis on high-leverage capabilities. In mid-2014, then deputy secretary of defense Bob Work began to discuss the need for the United States to undertake a "third offset strategy" to counter the growing strength of potential adversaries and retain its military advantage. In Work's view, the first instance of an offset strategy in recent U.S. history had involved the Eisenhower administration's "new look" strategy, which sought to use nuclear weapons to balance the Soviet Union's advantage in conventional forces in the early 1950s. The second instance coincided with the development of precision-guided munitions, sensors, stealth, and networking in the 1970s in response to the Warsaw Pact threat to Western Europe.[37]

According to Work, a new offset strategy is now needed because of the growth and spread of precision weaponry. Once an area of U.S. dominance, the ability to launch precision strikes, including sensors, command-and-control capabilities, and weaponry, has spread to states such as China. As a result, the United States must adapt its approaches to combat. Work explained in a 2015 speech:

> [To] maintain our warfighting edge, we're trying to address this erosion—our perceived erosion of technological superiority with the Defense Innovation Initiative and the third offset strategy. Now, as Secretary Hagel said, this new initiative is an ambitious department-wide effort to identify and invest in innovative ways to sustain and advance America's military dominance for the twenty-first century.[38]

One difference that Work noted between previous offset strategies and the current era is that U.S. advantages are likely to be less enduring than they were in the past:

> We have potential competitors who are very, very good in this business and can duplicate—not only steal our [intellectual property]—but can duplicate things very fast....The last offset strategy lasted us for four decades. It is unlikely that the next one will last that long.[39]

---

[37] The use of the term "third offset" is somewhat anachronistic, as it was in the 1970s when the term "offset strategy" was first coined during what is now the second offset. See, for example, William J. Perry, "Technology and National Security: Risks and Responsibilities" (paper delivered at the Conference on Risk and Responsibility in Contemporary Engineering and Science: French and U.S. Perspectives, Paris, April 7–8, 2003), http://stanford.edu/dept/france-stanford/Conferences/Risk/Perry.pdf.

[38] Bob Work, "The Third U.S. Offset Strategy and Its Implications for Partners and Allies" (speech, Washington, D.C., January 28, 2015), http://www.defense.gov/News/Speeches/Speech-View/Article/606641/the-third-us-offset-strategy-and-its-implications-for-partners-and-allies.

[39] Sydney J. Freedberg Jr., "Adversaries Will Copy 'Offset Strategy' Quickly: Bob Work," *Breaking Defense*, November 19, 2014.

Although it is too early to render a final judgment as to whether the initiative will survive the Trump administration and changes in the Pentagon leadership, there is reason to believe that it will. The perception that China's military modernization is jeopardizing U.S. interests in the western Pacific is both widespread and bipartisan. Similarly, there is considerable concern over Russian military modernization, at least among U.S. civilian and military leaders in the Department of Defense.[40] Moreover, the inadequacy of existing defense programs to respond to that threat is increasingly apparent. As a result, it is likely that the Trump administration will continue, and perhaps strengthen, the initiative, in spirit if not in name.

The shape of U.S. initiatives is still coming into focus as well. According to Work, the Defense Department is increasing its investment in new space capabilities; advanced sensors, communications, and munitions for power projection in contested environments; missile defense; and cyber capabilities. The department is also investing in promising new technologies, such as unmanned undersea vehicles, advanced sea mines, high-speed strike weapons, advanced aeronautics, autonomous systems, electromagnetic railguns, and high-energy lasers.[41] Some of these technologies could have a marked effect on military balances. If, for example, the United States were to field militarily effective railguns or lasers, the task of missile defense would become much easier than it has been heretofore.[42] However, many of these systems have yet to prove themselves in an operational setting and are unlikely to be deployed before the 2020s at the earliest.

Preparing for Long-Term Competition

To be effective over the long run, U.S. responses to the challenges posed by China and Russia should exploit the United States' relative strengths and those countries' weaknesses.

Russia poses a near-term challenge to the United States and U.S. allies based on its historical and ongoing investment in its nuclear forces; its focused military modernization program, including investments in ground forces, air defenses, and electronic warfare; and the Kremlin's willingness to engage in deception, active measures, and political warfare to further its objectives.

---

[40] Dan Lamothe, "Russia Is Greatest Threat to the U.S., Says Joint Chiefs Chairman Nominee Gen Joseph Dunford," *Washington Post*, July 9, 2015, https://www.washingtonpost.com/news/checkpoint/wp/2015/07/09/russia-is-greatest-threat-to-the-u-s-says-joint-chiefs-chairman-nominee-gen-joseph-dunford.

[41] Work, "The Third U.S. Offset Strategy."

[42] Mark Gunzinger with Christopher Dougherty, "Changing the Game: The Promise of Directed-Energy Weapons," Center for Strategic and Budgetary Assessments, 2012.

Russian technology and expertise also continue to bolster China, and the two countries legitimize one another as opponents of the Western liberal order.

Although Russia poses a considerable near-term threat, long-term trends are not so favorable to Moscow. The Russian demographic outlook is poor, even if not quite so bleak as the recent past. Moreover, low energy prices will continue to hamstring the Russian economy and constrain the defense budget. As a result, a long-term strategy for addressing the challenge posed by Russia must emphasize deterrence and cost imposition. It should also seek to prevent further collaboration between Beijing and Moscow and, to the extent possible, drive wedges between the two great powers.

Whereas Russia poses a considerable challenge to the United States and the West in the near term, the more consequential challenge is from China, including the possibility of further cooperation between Beijing and Moscow.[43] A long-term strategy to compete with China should have three features. First, it should yield an expanded set of U.S. options while constraining China's choices. Second, it should give the United States momentum in the competition with China, forcing Beijing to respond to U.S. actions. Third, a viable long-term strategy should impose considerable costs on China as it responds.

A U.S. response should seek to gain an asymmetric advantage in the areas of geography, alliances, technology, and doctrine. Regarding the first area, such a strategy should seek to use Asia's geography—in particular, the barrier formed by Japan, Taiwan, and the Philippines—to constrain China's access to the western Pacific in times of crisis or war. This could be accomplished by fielding sensor and engagement networks both unilaterally and in cooperation with allies along China's maritime flanks. Associated technologies would include undersea sensors, various airborne sensor systems, and land- and sea-based strike systems. Such an approach would capitalize on the combination of geography and existing U.S. and allied sensor programs, which promise to give the United States and its allies greater situational awareness of activities in the air and on or under the sea. Japan, for example, is fielding a constellation of reconnaissance satellites, expanding its air- and surface-search radar network, and modernizing its force of land-based anti-ship cruise missiles. The United States, for its part, is considering exports of unmanned aerial vehicles like the RQ-5 Global Hawk to a number of allies in the region such as Australia and South Korea. Similarly, several U.S. allies, including Japan and Australia, possess capable fleets of anti-submarine warfare aircraft. The Japan Maritime Self-Defense Force possesses four squadrons of P-3C Orion aircraft, which it is replacing

---

[43] See, for example, Andrew F. Krepinevich, *Preserving the Balance: A U.S. Eurasia Defense Strategy* (Washington, D.C.: Center for Strategic and Budgetary Assessments, 2017).

with the Kawasaki P-1, while the Royal Australian Air Force is replacing its two squadrons of AP-3Cs with the Boeing P-8 Poseidon.[44]

The United States should also deepen its interoperability with allies to bolster their capabilities and strengthen their will. It already shares information, and the case for increasing that cooperation is strong.[45] Washington should consider building on this by establishing an open-architecture intelligence, surveillance, and reconnaissance network in the western Pacific to complement current bilateral information-sharing agreements. Support for broad information sharing in the region is likely to grow in the face of Chinese encroachment. Given the increasing quality and declining cost of both commercial imagery and the sensors that produce it, such an approach will be feasible for a growing number of states.

Undersea warfare, in terms of both submarines and unmanned underwater vehicles, is another area for cooperation. The United States should consider developing innovative approaches to expand the strike capability of U.S. and allied submarines. It should also work with allies and friends against coercion to make their networks more resilient and to harden key ports and airfields against attack. The goal would be to develop a wide variety of facilities that U.S. forces could utilize in wartime. Finally, allies and friends should be provided with counter-invasion capabilities, including land-based anti-ship cruise missiles, naval mines, and precision-guided rockets and artillery systems.

In terms of technology, the United States should develop and deploy countermeasures to hostile precision strikes as well as move into the next phase of the precision-strike competition. Counters to precision strikes include hardening and dispersal of key facilities, countermeasures to precision navigation and timing, and the development of directed-energy weapons to destroy precision weapons. The United States should also exploit its dominance in the undersea domain by greatly increasing its subsurface strike capability. At the same time, it should develop autonomous systems to mitigate the vulnerabilities inherent in reconnaissance-strike systems (such as the links between sensor, decider, and shooter). Although the United States is pursuing these technologies, such efforts are constrained by both limited budgets and technological feasibility. Finally, although the United States is currently constrained by the Intermediate-Range Nuclear Forces Treaty from developing and deploying land-based ballistic and cruise missiles with

---

[44] International Institute for Strategic Studies, *The Military Balance 2015* (London: Routledge, 2015), 231, 259.

[45] See, for example, Patrick M. Cronin and Paul S. Giarra, "Robotic Skies: Intelligence, Surveillance, Reconnaissance, and the Strategic Defense of Japan," Center for a New American Security, Working Paper, December 2010.

a range of between 500 and 5,500 kilometers, no such constraint exists on sea-based systems.

The United States should also redouble efforts to deny China access to strategic technologies, both to safeguard its technological edge and also to impose costs. China has proved adept at pursuing a fast-follower strategy of acquisition, buying or stealing technology and the underlying intellectual property from both the United States and Russia. Efforts to deny China easy access to U.S. military technology and intellectual property will at the least drive up the cost in terms of the time and effort that China is forced to expend to acquire it. In other cases, such efforts may force China to seek less capable substitutes to U.S. technology. In still other cases, the United States and its allies may be able to deny China access to critical technologies.

Such efforts should include both improved information security and updated restrictions on technology transfer. Information security forms the first line of defense for U.S. technology, and far too often China has been able to steal critical information because of poor information security practices. Both government and private industry should strengthen measures to secure information. Industrial espionage on the scale conducted by China cannot and should not be isolated from the overall Sino-U.S. relationship. U.S. leaders must make it clear that the continuation of such activities, whether actively abetted or passively tolerated by the Chinese government, will have a tangible negative impact on the bilateral relationship. That may very well mean that the United States will need to take measures that will trigger Chinese retaliation. Absent such action, however, it is doubtful that the Chinese defense science and technology sector will forgo the considerable benefits that accrue to it from stealing U.S. technology.

Restrictions on technology transfer also should be updated, both to reflect the current international technology market and to maximize their effectiveness. Moreover, it is in the national interest for the U.S. government and private industry to work cooperatively to develop best practices and share threat information. To be effective, however, such measures should prioritize technologies that are likely to provide the greatest battlefield edge in the future. These include space and cyber capabilities, unmanned systems, high-speed propulsion, advanced aeronautics, autonomous systems, electromagnetic railguns, and directed-energy systems.

In terms of doctrine, the United States should exploit the weaknesses inherent in a centralized approach to warfare, including the need to gather and process large volumes of information. Chinese military doctrine displays a strong belief that strategy is a science rather than an art and maintains great confidence in its ability to predict the outcome of conflicts.[46] In order to bolster deterrence, the United States and its allies should work to reduce the confidence of Chinese leaders in their ability to control the course and outcome of a future conflict.

Such a strategy, if implemented consistently over time, holds the promise of influencing Chinese actions at the tactical, operational, and strategic levels. Tactically, it would erode the effectiveness of Chinese counter-intervention systems. Operationally, it would deny the leadership of the People's Liberation Army the type of war it has been planning for decades, forcing it to either double down on its investment in anti-access capabilities or seek a new approach. But its greatest promise is likely to be strategic: such an approach holds the potential to alter the decision-making calculus of the leadership of the Chinese Communist Party. A strategy of this type could markedly increase the cost to Beijing of pursuing a strategy of maritime expansion and potentially rechannel Chinese attention away from its maritime flanks and toward the Asian continent. It would also increase the cost of challenging international norms and hopefully give the Chinese leadership greater incentive to accept significant elements of the existing international order.

Such an approach holds the best hope of perpetuating a military strategy at least approximating one that has supported U.S. interests since the end of World War II—one based on forward-stationed forces backed by power projection. Absent such efforts, the rise of great-power competitors such as China and Russia and the spread of precision-strike capabilities will increasingly put the United States in an unfavorable position in a series of regional military balances, which could ultimately threaten its global primacy.

---

[46] Thomas G. Mahnken, *Secrecy and Stratagem: Understanding Chinese Strategic Culture* (Sydney: Lowy Institute for International Policy, 2011).

About the Contributors

Richard J. Ellings is President and Co-founder of the National Bureau of Asian Research (NBR). He is also Affiliate Professor of International Studies in the Henry M. Jackson School of International Studies at the University of Washington. Dr. Ellings is the author of *Embargoes and World Power: Lessons from American Foreign Policy* (1985); co-author of *Private Property and National Security* (1991); co-editor (with Aaron Friedberg) of *Strategic Asia 2003–04: Fragility and Crisis* (2003), *Strategic Asia 2002–03: Asian Aftershocks* (2002), and *Strategic Asia 2001–02: Power and Purpose* (2001); co-editor of *Korea's Future and the Great Powers* (with Nicholas Eberstadt, 2001) and *Southeast Asian Security in the New Millennium* (with Sheldon Simon, 1996); founding editor of the *NBR Analysis* publication series; and co-chairman of the *Asia Policy* editorial board. Previously, Dr. Ellings served as legislative assistant in the U.S. Senate, office of Senator Slade Gorton. He earned his BA in political science from the University of California–Berkley and his MA and PhD in political science from the University of Washington.

John H. Gill is an Adjunct Professor at the Near East South Asia Center for Strategic Studies in Washington, D.C. He has been following South Asia issues from the intelligence and policy perspectives since the mid-1980s in positions with the U.S. Joint Staff and U.S. Pacific Command staff, among other assignments. A former South Asia foreign area officer in the U.S. Army, he retired as a colonel in 2005 after more than 27 years of service. Professor Gill worked on South Asia issues in the Pentagon from 1998 to 2001, including during the 1999 Kargil crisis. From August 2003 to January 2004, he served in Islamabad as the liaison officer to the Pakistan Army for U.S. forces in Afghanistan. His publications on South Asia include *An Atlas of the 1971 India-Pakistan War: The Birth of Bangladesh* (2003); chapters on current Indian and Pakistani political-military affairs in *Strategic Asia 2004–05: Fragility and Crisis* (2004), *Strategic Asia 2005–06: Military Modernization in an Era of Uncertainty* (2005), and other publications; as well as various articles and reviews in periodicals such as *The Journal of Military History, Strategic Insights,* and *Asia Policy.* Professor Gill holds BAs in history and German from Middlebury College and an MA in international relations from the George Washington University, and has completed further studies at the U.S. Army Command and General Staff College.

Christopher W. Hughes is Professor of International Politics and Japanese Studies in the Department of Politics and International Studies and Pro-Vice-Chancellor at the University of Warwick, as well as Co-editor of the *Pacific Review*. Previously, he was a research associate in the Institute for Peace Science at Hiroshima University (IPSHU). From 2000 to 2001, Dr. Hughes was a visiting associate professor, and in 2006 he held the *Asahi Shimbun* Visiting Chair of Mass Media and Politics in the Faculty of Law at the University of Tokyo. He has been a research associate at the International Institute for Strategic Studies and a visiting scholar in the East Asia Institute at the Free University of Berlin. From 2009 to 2010, he was the Edwin O. Reischauer Visiting Professor of Japanese Studies in the Department of Government at Harvard University, and he is currently an Associate in Research at Harvard's Reischauer Institute of Japanese Studies. Dr. Hughes has received research scholarships from the Japanese Ministry of Education, the Japan Foundation Endowment Committee, the European Union, the British Council, and the British Academy. He is the author of several books, including *Japan's Foreign and Security Policy Under the 'Abe Doctrine': New Dynamism or New Dead End?* (2015), and holds a BA and MA from Oxford University, an MA from Rochester University, and an MA and PhD from Sheffield University.

Mark N. Katz is a Professor of Government and Politics in the Schar School of Policy and Government at George Mason University. He was recently a visiting senior fellow at the Finnish Institute of International Affairs (April–September 2017). Dr. Katz is the author of *The Third World in Soviet Military Thought* (1982), *Russia and Arabia: Soviet Foreign Policy toward the Arabian Peninsula* (1986), *Gorbachev's Military Policy in the Third World* (1989), *Revolutions and Revolutionary Waves* (1997), *Reflections on Revolutions* (1999), and *Leaving without Losing: The War on Terror after Iraq and Afghanistan* (2012). He earned a BA in international relations from the University of California–Riverside, an MA in international relations from the Johns Hopkins University School of Advanced International Studies, and a PhD in political science from the Massachusetts Institute of Technology.

Chung Min Lee is a Professor of International Relations in the Graduate School of International Studies at Yonsei University in Seoul and a Nonresident Senior Fellow at the Carnegie Endowment for International Peace. Dr. Lee served as South Korea's ambassador for national security affairs (2013–16) and as ambassador for international security affairs (2010–11). He previously served as dean of both the Graduate School of International Studies (2008–12) and the Underwood International College (2010–12) at Yonsei University and currently serves as a member of the council of the International Institute for Strategic Studies. Prior to joining Yonsei University in 1998, Dr. Lee worked at the RAND Corporation, the Sejong Institute, and the Institute for Foreign Policy Analysis. He has also been a Visiting Research Fellow at the National Institute for Defense Studies and the Graduate Research Institute for Policy Studies in Tokyo, and a Visiting Professor in the Lee Kuan Yew School of Public Policy at the National University of Singapore. Dr. Lee is the author of *Fault Lines in a Rising Asia* (2016). He holds an MALD and PhD in international security studies from the Fletcher School of Law and Diplomacy at Tufts University.

Thomas G. Mahnken is the President and Chief Executive Officer of the Center for Strategic and Budgetary Assessments and Senior Research Professor at the Johns Hopkins School of Advanced International Studies (SAIS). From 2006 to 2009, Dr. Mahnken served as Deputy Assistant Secretary of Defense for Policy Planning. He taught for nearly twenty years in the Strategy Department at the U.S. Naval War College. From 2004 to 2006, he was a Visiting Fellow at the Merrill Center at Johns Hopkins SAIS, where he also served as Acting Director of the Strategic Studies Program for the 2003–4 academic year. He served on the staff of the congressionally mandated National Defense Panel and Quadrennial Defense Review Independent Panel, on the Commission on the Intelligence Capabilities of the United States Regarding Weapons of Mass Destruction, in the Defense Department's Office of Net Assessment, and as a member of the Gulf War Air Power Survey. Dr. Mahnken's most recent books are *Strategy in Asia: The Past, Present, and Future of Regional Security* (2014) and *Competitive Strategies for the 21st Century: Theory, History, and Practice* (2012). He holds an MA and PhD in international affairs from Johns Hopkins SAIS and BA degrees in history and international relations (with highest honors) from the University of Southern California. He is a Commander in the U.S. Navy Reserve and a recipient of the Secretary of Defense Medal for Outstanding Public Service and the Department of the Navy Superior Civilian Service Medal.

Oriana Skylar Mastro is an Assistant Professor of Security Studies in the Edmund A. Walsh School of Foreign Service at Georgetown University, where her research focuses on Chinese military and security policy, Asia-Pacific security issues, war termination, and coercive diplomacy. Dr. Mastro is the author of numerous book chapters and journal articles, including "The Vulnerability of Rising Powers: The Logic Behind China's Low Military Transparency" (2016) and "Dynamic Dilemmas: China's Evolving Northeast Asia Security Strategy" (2016). She is currently working on a book that evaluates the conditions under which leaders are willing to talk to their enemies during wars. Previously she was a Stanton Nuclear Security Fellow at the Council on Foreign Relations, a fellow in the Asia-Pacific Security Program at the Center for a New American Security, and a University of Virginia Miller Center National Fellow. Highly proficient in Mandarin, Dr. Mastro has worked on China policy issues at the Carnegie Endowment for International Peace, RAND Corporation, Project 2049, and U.S. Pacific Command. She holds a BA in East Asian Studies from Stanford University and an MA and PhD in Politics from Princeton University.

Ann Marie Murphy is an Associate Professor and Director of the Center for Emerging Powers and Transnational Trends at Seton Hall University's School of Diplomacy and International Relations. She is also a Senior Research Scholar at the Weatherhead East Asian Institute at Columbia University and an Associate Fellow at the Asia Society. Her research interests include international relations and comparative politics in Southeast Asia, U.S. foreign policy toward Asia, and governance of transnational security issues. Dr. Murphy is co-author with Amy Freedman of *Nontraditional Security Challenges in Southeast Asia: The Transnational Dimension* (forthcoming 2018) and co-editor with Bridget Welsh of *Legacy of Engagement in Southeast Asia* (2008). Her articles have appeared in journals such as *Asian Security, Contemporary Southeast Asia, Orbis, Asia Policy, World Politics Review,* and *PS: Political Science & Politics.* She is currently researching and writing a book on the impact of democratization on Indonesian foreign policy. Dr. Murphy holds a BA from Lehigh University and an MIA in international affairs and PhD in political science from Columbia University.

Alison Szalwinski is an Assistant Director for Political and Security Affairs at the National Bureau of Asian Research (NBR), where she manages and contributes to the Strategic Asia Program, the Pacific Trilateralism project, and the Space, Cyberspace, and Strategic Stability project. Prior to joining NBR, Ms. Szalwinski worked at the U.S. Department of State and the Center for Strategic and International Studies (CSIS). Her research interests include regional security dynamics in Northeast Asia and U.S.-China strategic relations. She is co-editor with Ashley J. Tellis and Michael Wills of *Strategic Asia 2015–16: Foundations of National Power* and *Strategic Asia 2016–17: Understanding Strategic Cultures in the Asia-Pacific*. Ms. Szalwinski has lived and worked as an English teacher in Shenzhen, China, where she also continued her language studies in Mandarin Chinese. She holds a BA in foreign affairs and history from the University of Virginia and an MA in Asian studies from Georgetown University's Edmund A. Walsh School of Foreign Service.

Ashley J. Tellis holds the Tata Chair for Strategic Affairs and is a Senior Fellow at the Carnegie Endowment for International Peace, specializing in international security, defense, and Asian strategic issues. He is also Research Director of the Strategic Asia Program at the National Bureau of Asian Research (NBR) and co-editor of fourteen volumes in the annual series. While on assignment to the U.S. Department of State as Senior Adviser to the Undersecretary of State for Political Affairs, he was intimately involved in negotiating the civil nuclear agreement with India. Previously, he was commissioned into the Foreign Service and served as Senior Adviser to the Ambassador at the U.S. embassy in New Delhi. He also served on the National Security Council staff as Special Assistant to the President and Senior Director for Strategic Planning and Southwest Asia. Prior to his government service, Dr. Tellis was a Senior Policy Analyst at the RAND Corporation and Professor of Policy Analysis at the RAND Graduate School. He is the author of *India's Emerging Nuclear Posture* (2001) and co-author of *Interpreting China's Grand Strategy: Past, Present, and Future* (2000). He holds a PhD in Political Science from the University of Chicago.

Michael Wills is Senior Vice President of Strategy and Finance at the National Bureau of Asian Research (NBR). He coordinates all aspects of NBR's financial, business, and programmatic operations and serves as secretary to the Board of Directors. Mr. Wills also manages NBR's publications program, including the *Strategic Asia* series and the *Asia Policy* journal. His research interests include international security and the international relations of Asia, particularly China's relations with Southeast Asia. He is co-editor with Robert M. Hathaway of *New Security Challenges in Asia* (2013) and has co-edited six previous Strategic Asia volumes with Ashley J. Tellis—including *Understanding Strategic Cultures in the Asia-Pacific* (2016), *Foundations of National Power in the Asia-Pacific* (2015), *Domestic Political Change and Grand Strategy* (2007), *Trade, Interdependence, and Security* (2006), *Military Modernization in an Era* *of Uncertainty* (2005), and *Confronting Terrorism in the Pursuit of Power* (2004). He is a contributing editor to three other Strategic Asia books and several other edited volumes. Before joining NBR, Mr. Wills worked at the Cambodia Development Resource Institute in Phnom Penh and with Control Risks Group, an international political and security risk management firm, in London. He holds a BA (Honors) in Chinese studies from the University of Oxford.

About Strategic Asia

The Strategic Asia Program at the National Bureau of Asian Research (NBR) is a major ongoing research initiative that draws together top Asia studies specialists and international relations experts to assess the changing strategic environment in the Asia-Pacific. The program combines the rigor of academic analysis with the practicality of contemporary policy analyses by incorporating economic, military, political, and demographic data and by focusing on the trends, strategies, and perceptions that drive geopolitical dynamics in the region. The program's integrated set of products and activities includes:

- an annual edited volume written by leading specialists

- an executive brief tailored for public- and private-sector decision-makers and strategic planners

- briefings and presentations for government, business, and academe that are designed to foster in-depth discussions revolving around major public-policy issues

Special briefings are held for key committees of Congress and the executive branch, other government agencies, and the intelligence community. The principal audiences for the program's research findings are the U.S. policymaking and research communities, the media, the business community, and academe.

To order a book, please visit the Strategic Asia website at http://www.nbr.org/strategicasia.

Previous Strategic Asia Volumes

Now in its seventeenth year, the Strategic Asia series has addressed how Asia functions as a zone of strategic interaction and contends with a changing balance of power.

Strategic Asia 2016–17: Understanding Strategic Cultures in the Asia-Pacific explored the strategic cultures of the region's major powers and explained how they inform decision-making about the pursuit of strategic objectives and national power.

Strategic Asia 2015–16: Foundations of National Power in the Asia-Pacific examined how the region's major powers are building their national power as geopolitical competition intensifies.

Strategic Asia 2014–15: U.S. Alliances and Partnerships at the Center of Global Power analyzed the trajectories of U.S. alliance and partner relationships in the Asia-Pacific in light of the region's shifting strategic landscape.

Strategic Asia 2013–14: Asia in the Second Nuclear Age examined the role of nuclear weapons in the grand strategies of key Asian states and assessed the impact of these capabilities—both established and latent—on regional and international stability.

Strategic Asia 2012–13: China's Military Challenge assessed China's growing military capabilities and explored their impact on the Asia-Pacific region.

Strategic Asia 2011–12: Asia Responds to Its Rising Powers—China and India explored how key Asian states have responded to the rise of China and India, drawing implications for U.S. interests and leadership in the Asia-Pacific.

Strategic Asia 2010–11: Asia's Rising Power and America's Continued Purpose provided a continent-wide net assessment of the core trends and issues affecting the region by examining Asia's performance in nine key functional areas.

Strategic Asia 2009–10: Economic Meltdown and Geopolitical Stability analyzed the impact of the global economic crisis on key Asian states and explored the strategic implications for the United States.

Strategic Asia 2008–09: Challenges and Choices examined the impact of geopolitical developments on Asia's transformation over the previous eight years and assessed the major strategic choices on Asia facing the incoming U.S. administration.

Strategic Asia 2007–08: Domestic Political Change and Grand Strategy examined internal and external drivers of grand strategy on Asian foreign policymaking.

Strategic Asia 2006–07: Trade, Interdependence, and Security addressed how changing trade relationships affect the balance of power and security in the region.

Strategic Asia 2005–06: Military Modernization in an Era of Uncertainty appraised the progress of Asian military modernization programs.

Strategic Asia 2004–05: Confronting Terrorism in the Pursuit of Power explored the effect of the U.S.-led war on terrorism on the strategic transformations underway in Asia.

Strategic Asia 2003–04: Fragility and Crisis examined the fragile balance of power in Asia, drawing out the key domestic political and economic trends in Asian states supporting or undermining this tenuous equilibrium.

Strategic Asia 2002–03: Asian Aftershocks drew on the baseline established in the 2001–02 volume to analyze changes in Asian states' grand strategies and relationships in the aftermath of the September 11 terrorist attacks.

Strategic Asia 2001–02: Power and Purpose established a baseline assessment for understanding the strategies and interactions of the major states within the region.

Research and Management Team

The Strategic Asia research team consists of leading international relations and security specialists from universities and research institutions across the United States and around the world. More than 140 scholars have written for the program since 2001. A new research team is selected each year. The research team for 2017 is led by Ashley J. Tellis (Carnegie Endowment for International Peace). Aaron Friedberg (Princeton University, and Strategic Asia's founding research director) and Richard Ellings (NBR, and Strategic Asia's founding program director) serve as senior advisors.

The Strategic Asia Program has historically depended on a diverse base of funding from foundations, government, and corporations, supplemented by income from publication sales. Major support for the program in 2017 comes from the Lynde and Harry Bradley Foundation.

Attribution

Readers of Strategic Asia and visitors to the Strategic Asia website may use data, charts, graphs, and quotes from these sources without requesting permission from NBR on the condition that they cite NBR and the appropriate primary source in any published work. No report, chapter, separate study, extensive text, or any other substantial part of the Strategic Asia Program's products may be reproduced without the written permission of NBR. To request permission, please email <publications@nbr.org>.

Index